Globe Law and Business

Production Sharing Agreements

A Global Legal Handbook

Consulting Editor **Flavio GI Inocencio**

Consulting editor
Flavio GI Inocencio

Managing director
Sian O'Neill

Production Sharing Agreements: A Global Legal Handbook
is published by

Globe Law and Business Ltd
3 Mylor Close
Horsell
Woking
Surrey GU21 4DD
United Kingdom
Tel: +44 20 3745 4770
www.globelawandbusiness.com

Production Sharing Agreements: A Global Legal Handbook

ISBN 9781787426870
EPUB ISBN 9781787426887
Adobe PDF ISBN 9781787426894

Table of contents

Introduction

Flavio GI Inocencio
Helios Advisory

1. Introduction

This book analyses the production sharing agreements (PSAs) used in major oil and gas jurisdictions around the globe.

The PSA is the most widely used host government contract and has become the instrument of choice for most developing countries in their relationships with international oil companies (IOCs). It strikes a good balance between the interests of host states and the interests of IOCs, and it is quite distinct from other host government contracts such as risk service contracts, joint ventures and concessions.

As a global comparison of PSAs in different countries, this book is the first of its kind, as most other books on PSAs are monographs or collections of articles.

This book analyses the PSAs used across all regions of the globe, from Africa to Asia, the Americas and the Middle East. The countries covered range from new oil jurisdictions such as Guyana to mature jurisdictions such as Nigeria and Malaysia. The book is thus far reaching in scope and aims to give the reader an overview of the different modalities of the PSA used in 16 different countries.

The book does not purport to be a comprehensive analysis of the PSAs used around the globe, but rather to provide an exploratory analysis of the main features of the PSA in the countries covered.

In order to understand the reasons for the widespread adoption of the PSA, one must first understand the history of its adoption by the Indonesian national oil company (NOC), Permina (now Pertamina), in 1966; and to this end, the book includes a chapter on the Indonesian PSA.

Overall, the book should be a valuable resource for practitioners, academics and professionals who are interested in the different manifestations of the PSA as one of the most important host government contracts.

2. The uniqueness of the PSA

In most jurisdictions, the state is the owner of the mineral rights. As such, the state has the prerogative and the discretion to choose how these rights should be allocated. Historically, most states have used the concession system to allocate the rights in a concession area to a given company. However, different legal arrangements have emerged over time. An important factor in this regard was the emergence of resource nationalism and the New International Economic Order,[1] which led some countries to abandon the concession system in favour of risk service contracts, which tend to be more onerous for IOCs.[2]

The PSA can be defined as a contract between a state and an oil company (typically an IOC) for the exploration and development of oil and gas resources, under which the risks of exploration and development are borne by the oil company and oil production is shared between the state and the oil company through a component called 'profit oil', while costs are recovered through 'cost oil' up to a certain percentage.[3]

The PSA has advantages over concessions, joint ventures and risk service contracts. The PSA was adopted as a host government contract as it is more beneficial for host governments than classic concessions,[4] as the state retains some degree of control over the oil and gas operations while still allowing the IOC to share in the oil produced. Pure concessions do not afford the state the same degree of control; thus, many states have adopted the PSA as the optimal compromise between the extremes of the concession and the risk service contract.

It is also noteworthy that many host government contracts are now hybrid and contain model clauses from other contractual types. For example, some PSAs will include royalty clauses, which are typical of concession agreements.

The PSA also has some advantages over the risk service contract – a contract under which IOCs are paid for services rendered to the state or the national oil company (NOC), either in oil or in money. Additionally, under a PSA, the oil company can book its oil reserves in its accounts, as it owns a share of the production; this is not the case with the risk service contract, for instance.

It is also important to point out that the PSA, as a type of contract, contains certain boilerplate clauses, such as those relating to cost recovery, profit oil, minimum work obligations, the operating committee, local content, the environment, decommissioning. applicable law and dispute resolution.

---

1 A movement led by developing countries aimed at economic sovereignty, this was quite relevant in the context of natural resources. A key instrument was approved by the United Nations Assembly General Resolution on the NEIO, https://investmentpolicy.unctad.org/international-investment-agreements/treaty-files/2775/download.

2 These are quite common in the Gulf states.

3 Kirsten Bindemann, *Production Sharing Agreements: An Economic Analysis* (Oxford Institute of Energy Studies, 1999), p13; Daniel Johnston, *International Petroleum Fiscal Systems and Petroleum Sharing Contracts* (Penwell Books, 1994), p40.

4 These concessions were usually monopolies given to IOCs to entire countries; this was the case for concessions in the Middle East before the establishment of the Organization of the Petroleum Exporting Countries.

Figure 1. Structure of the production sharing agreement

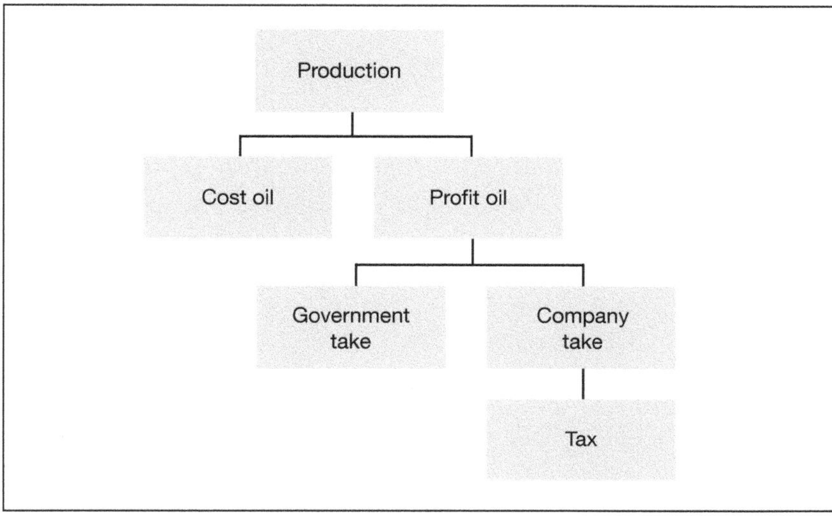

3. Comparative law

A book on the PSA essentially concerns comparative law and the comparative legal method is thus important. This is based on functionalism, and assesses both the similarities and the differences in order to arrive at a comparison.[5] In the case of the PSA, comparative law is quite important, as in most countries the applicable law of the contract will be the national law of the relevant state. This is particularly significant as countries belong to different legal families: some belong to the Roman-Germanic tradition (continental European) and are civil law countries; while others belong to the Anglo-Saxon tradition and are common law countries. Thus, the clauses of a PSA might be interpreted differently depending on the legal tradition of the relevant country. Thus, while the PSA is a type of contract with both unique and similar characteristics, the interpretation of some of its clauses will be determined by the legal tradition of the relevant country. Liability clauses are a good example: in civil law countries, these are allowed only under certain strict conditions, but they are generally accepted in common law countries.

4. The PSA and *lex petrolea*

The PSA is one of the most widely used contracts in the oil and gas industry. However, contrary to other commercial contracts, such as the joint operating agreement (JOA), one of the parties to the contract is the state, as represented

5 Konrad Zweigert and Heinz Kotz, *An Introduction to Comparative Law* (Oxford University, 1998), pp36–37. Mathias Siems, *Comparative Law* (Cambridge University Press, 2018).

by the competent authority, – whether that be an NOC, the ministry of oil or an independent regulatory agency.[6]

The PSA is part of the *'lex petrolea'*, which is part of the transnational commercial law – or *'lex mercatoria'*[7] – applicable to the oil and gas industry.[8] The sources of the *lex petrolea*, as part of transnational commercial law, include general principles of law, standard model contracts, model laws and commercial usage and practices.

Model contracts – for example, the JOAs developed by bodies such as the Association of International Petroleum Negotiators – are a key source of the *lex petrolea*. However, the PSA is a host government contract that has been individually adopted by states, and there is no generally adopted model contract which every country uses; although the PSA does have boilerplate clauses that distinguish it from other host government contracts such as concessions, joint ventures and risk service contracts.

The widespread adoption of the PSA can be attributed to its flexibility and the fact that the costs of exploration and development are borne entirely by the IOC. For instance, this is a key reason why Nigeria has adopted the PSA and has abandoned joint ventures, as the Nigerian National Petroleum Corporation could not keep up with the cash calls.[9]

In our view, the PSA – as part of the *lex petrolea* – is part of the body of rules that apply to the international petroleum industry, as it is now part of the standard practice adopted by states as the main contract that regulates the relationship between the state and the IOC. Some authors reserve the term *'lex petrolea'* for contracts that emerge from the commercial usage and practices of private parties in the industry. We would take a different opinion, however: as a widely adopted model contract, the PSA is part of the *lex petrolea* alongside with contracts between private parties[10] – even though it is an administrative or a public law contract.[11] This stems from the fact that the PSA has emerged from the practice of the international oil industry, and the *lex petrolea* – as a subset of the *lex mercatoria* – goes beyond contracts between private parties. As the PSA is

6 Flavio GI Inocencio, "Independent Regulatory Authorities in the Oil and Gas Industry", *International Energy Law Review*, Issue 4, 2018.

7 Abul FM Maniruzzaman, "The Lex Mercatoria and International Contracts: A Challenge for International Commercial Arbitration?", *American University International Law Review*, Vol 14, No 3, 1999.

8 Alex Wawryk, *Petroleum Regulation in an International Context: The Universality of Petroleum Regulation and the Concept of Lex Petrolea* in Tina Hunter (ed), *Regulation of the Upstream Petroleum Sector, A Comparative Study of Licensing and Concession Systems* (Edward Elgar Publishing, 2015), p23.

9 See the chapter on the Nigerian PSA.

10 See the discussion in Kim Talus, Scott Looper and Steven Otillar, "Lex Petrolea and the Internationalization of the Petroleum Agreements", *Journal of World Energy Law and Business*, Vol 5, n 3, 2012, pp190–193. Similarly, A Timothy Martin and J Jay Park, "Global Petroleum Industry Model Contracts Revisited: Higher, Faster, Stronger", *Journal of World Energy Law and Business*, Vol 3, n 1, 2010, pp6–8.

11 This is particularly the case in civil law countries which adopted the PSA, whereby administrative contracts are determined by the fact that one of the parties is a public entity.

12 Public law can be a source of contract law; Mary Charman, *Contract Law* (Willan Publishing, 2007), pp266 –268.

13 On legal transplants, see Mathias Siems, *Comparative Law*, (Cambridge University Press, 2018), p232.

still a voluntary agreement between the parties, and is a public law contract, it is part of the *lex petrolea*[12] and is not purely a legal transplant.[13]

5. The PSA and the petroleum regime

However, this does not mean that the PSA is completely autonomous from the legal framework of the state that adopts it. In all model PSAs, the applicable law that governs the contract is typically the law of the host state.[14] As such, PSAs must be interpreted within the wider context of the applicable legal framework; this includes the constitution, petroleum/energy laws, regulations and other norms.[15]

This legislative regulatory framework – sometimes called the 'petroleum regime'[16] – is quite relevant to the PSA, as the adopted model host government contract must be interpreted in light of the other sources of law.[17]

Figure 2. Regulatory framework/petroleum regime

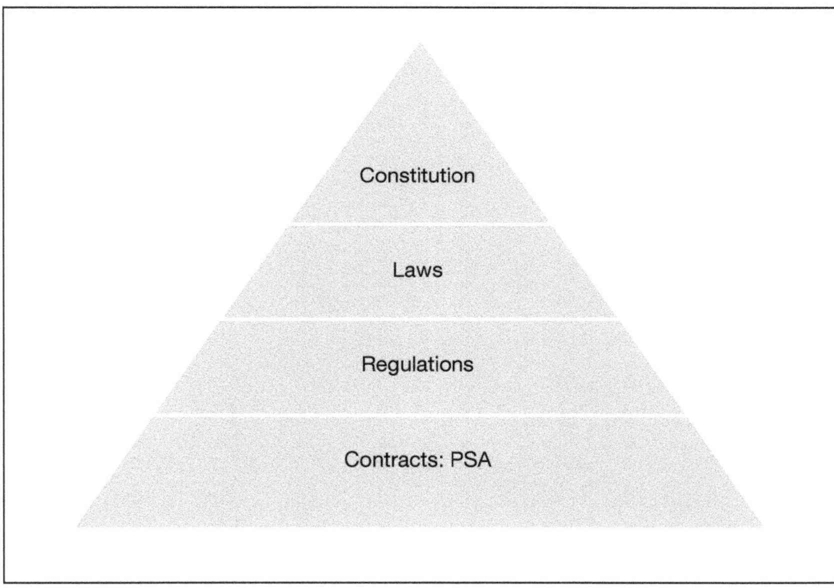

The petroleum regime starts with the constitution and the provisions on state ownership of natural resources, particularly oil and gas. Also important are the petroleum/energy laws, which establish the rules on the operation and

14 There are notable exceptions – for example, in the Kurdistan Regional Government model PSA, the law applicable to the contract is English law.

15 *Oil Contracts: How to Read and How to Understand Them*, Openoil, 2012, p24, http://openoil.net/portfolio/oil-contracts/.

16 The term 'petroleum regime' better captures the regulatory framework.

17 Particularly considering that the laws are applicable to the parties.

management of petroleum operations and the competent authority in the oil and gas industry. The petroleum regime further includes rules on the environment, local content, participation of local stakeholders, taxation and so on.[18]

Thus, in interpreting the clauses of the PSA, one must take account of the wider legislative framework applicable to the oil and gas industry. This will be directly applicable to the contract and, in the event of a dispute, an understanding of the overall petroleum regime will be vital.

6. The PSA and this book

This book does not seek to provide a comprehensive analysis of all aspects of the PSA, but rather to provide an exploratory analysis of the PSA and its key aspects in the different jurisdictions covered. As such, it is a good starting point for those interested in the different manifestations of the PSA around the globe. This is a unique book, which we hope will become essential reading for all those interested in the PSAs from a comparative perspective.

18 Flavio GI Inocencio, "Independent Regulatory Agencies in the Oil and Gas Industry", *International Energy Law Review*, Issue 4, 2018, pp138–140.

Angola

Flavio GI Inocencio
Helios Advisory

1. Introduction

Oil exploration in Angola began in 1910, but the first commercial oil discovery in Angola was not made until in 1955, in the Kwanza river basin.[1] Thus, the Angolan oil and gas industry can be considered mature. With the advent of Angolan independence in 1975, the Angolan government decided to create a national oil company (NOC) called Sonangol, which was the *de facto* regulator and was in charge of oil policies, despite the existence of the Ministry of Petroleum. Sonangol was created in 1976,[2] a year before the establishment of the Ministry of Petroleum in 1977.

Angola is the second-largest oil producing country in Africa[3] and has approximately 8 billion barrels of proven oil reserves[4] and 384 billion cubic metres of proven natural gas reserves.[5]

Angola also has plenty more potentially recoverable oil and gas reserves. This means that its potential undiscovered oil and gas resources exceed the actual proven oil and gas reserves, which makes Angola quite attractive from a geological perspective.[6]

This chapter discusses the production sharing agreement (PSA) in Angola, as the main and most widely used host model government contract adopted by Angola. The first-generation PSAs was introduced by Sonangol in 1980. The second-generation PSA was introduced in the early 1990s and remains in place today, as the most important host model contract.

For the purposes of this chapter, it is also important to note that Angola

1 Before independence, oil production reached 174,000 barrels per day in 1974; see https://anpg.co.ao/nossa-historia-2/.
2 See www.sonangol.co.ao/Portugu%C3%AAs/ASonangolEP/A%20Nossa%20Hist%C3%B3ria/Paginas/A-Nossa-Hist%C3%B3ria.aspx.
3 Angola produced an average of 1.3 million bpd in 2019, according to the Annual Statistical Bulletin of the Organisation of the Petroleum Exporting Countries (OPEC) 2020, p10 – https://asb.opec.org/.
4 According to the 2020 BP Statistical Review of World Energy (p14), Angola has 8.2 billion barrels of proven oil reserves – www.bp.com/content/dam/bp/business-sites/en/global/corporate/pdfs/energy-economics/statistical-review/bp-stats-review-2020-full-report.pdf. The Annual Statistical Bulletin of OPEC 2020 states that Angola has 7.7 billion barrels of oil of proven reserves.
5 The Annual Statistical Bulletin of OPEC 2020, p10.
6 For an overview of the Angola oil and gas sector, see the Energy Information Administration website at www.eia.gov/international/analysis/country/AGO.

inherited its legal system from Portugal, which is a civil law country. Angola has also been a member of the Organisation of the Petroleum Exporting Countries since 2009 and as such it is subject to the quota system.[7] This chapter explores the Angolan model PSA and the overall regulatory framework against the backdrop of the recent oil reforms which culminated in the creation of the new National Oil, Gas and Biofuels Agency (ANPG) as the independent regulatory authority.

2. The Angolan regulatory framework

In the oil and gas industry, the most important factor in the overall attractiveness of a country is its resource potential (geology), followed by its fiscal terms – which will define the overall 'government take' versus 'company take' – and the applicable legal framework. The PSA is part of that legal framework.

The legal framework applicable to the oil and gas industry in Angola includes the provisions of the Constitution, laws, regulations and contracts.[8] The Angolan state is the owner of natural resources, according to Article 16 of the 2010 Constitution.

The main legislative provisions applicable to the oil and gas industry are as follows:

- the Law on Petroleum Activities;[9]
- the Law on the Taxation of Petroleum Activities;[10]
- the Foreign Exchange Law Applicable to the Oil Sector;[11]
- the Customs Law Applicable to the Oil Sector;[12]
- the Rules on Competitive Bidding Applicable to the Oil Sector;[13]
- the Local Content Decree;[14]
- the Recruitment of Locals Decree;[15]
- the Rules on Tax Incentives Applicable to Angolan Companies in the Oil Sector;[16] and
- the Law Applicable to Natural Gas.[17]

Many more laws, regulations and decrees apply to the Angolan oil and gas

---

7 Flavio GI Inocencio, *A Organização dos Países Exportadores de Petróleo: O Caso de Angola* (Chiado Editora, 2015).

8 Technically these are 'statutes', as opposed to laws, as a broad concept which encompasses different sources, including case law.

9 Law 10/2004, as amended by Law 5/2019 – www.sonangol.co.ao/Style%20Library/pt-pt/Pdf/licitacoes/law_petroleumActivities_pt.pdf.

10 Law 13/2004, www.sonangol.co.ao/Style%20Library/pt-pt/Pdf/licitacoes/law_petroleumTaxation_en.pdf.

11 Law 2/2012, www.bna.ao/uploads/%7Bd9b13d19-f915-4e12-bca5-d43c970cbd4f%7D.pdf.

12 Law 11/2004, www.sonangol.co.ao/Style%20Library/pt-pt/Pdf/licitacoes/law_petroleumCustoms_pt.pdf.

13 Presidential Decree 86/2018.

14 Presidential Decree 271/2020.

15 Decree Law 17/2009.

16 Presidential Decree 3/2012. Articles 26 and 27 of the Law on Petroleum Activities.

17 Presidential Decree 7/2018.

sector. It is not the purpose of this chapter to map out all of these legal instruments, but just to mention some of the most important in the context of the analysis of the model PSA.

Article 4 of the Law on Petroleum Activities states that mining rights are attributed to the national concessionaire.[18] Article 13 imposes an obligation of association with the national concessionaire on all companies involved in exploration and production (E&P) activities.

The Angolan regulatory framework provides for the use of different types of E&P contracts. Article 14(1) of the Law on Petroleum Activities states that the national concessionaire (now the ANPG) may choose different forms of association with international oil companies (IOCs). Furthermore, Articles 14(2) and (3) determine that the national concessionaire may use incorporated joint ventures, unincorporated joint ventures, PSAs and risk service contracts.[19]

Traditionally, the Angolan state was represented in E&P contracts by Sonangol as the NOC, which was the national concessionaire. Since its formal establishment, this role is now exercised by the ANPG.[20]

Most E&P contracts use the PSA as the main host government contract. However, the national concessionaire may choose a different contract for a concession area, a risk service contract or a joint venture (incorporated or unincorporated).

Angola uses a competitive bidding process to allocate concession areas (or 'blocks').[21] These rules are set out in Presidential Decree 86/18, Article 4 of which sets out the criteria for being a partner of the national concessionaire. These include:

- the history of the company;
- legal information;
- financial capacity; and
- more specific information, such as litigation history and number of workers in the oil and gas industry.

For operators, Article 5 establishes that in conducting petroleum operations, operators must:

- have technical expertise;

---

18 Today, the ANPG.

19 Article 14, 2 reads: *"A Associação deve revestir as seguintes formas: a) Sociedade Comercial, b) Contrato de Consórcio, c) Contrato de Partilha de produção."* The term *'sociedade commercial'* may be translated as 'incorporated joint venture', although the literal translation is 'company'; however, the intention of the legislature was to establish an incorporated joint venture. The law also refers to a 'consortium agreement', which here is translated as 'unincorporated joint venture', which is a joint venture in terms of its legal nature. Here we followed the functional method set out in Konrad Zweigert and Heinz Kotz, *An Introduction to Comparative Law* (Oxford University, 1998), pp 36-37.

20 Pursuant to the changes to the Law on Petroleum Activities introduced by Law 5/2019, www.ucm.minfin.gov.ao/cs/groups/public/documents/document/aw4x/mjm3/~edisp/minfin1237053.pdf.

21 Those areas are defined by the ministry, according to Article 11 on the Law on Petroleum Activities.

- follow best practices in terms of health, safety and the environment; and
- engage in the recruitment and training of Angolans.

Article 6 contains rules on the bidding process prepared by the national concessionaire and the Ministry of Mineral Resources and Oil.

Prospecting licences are attributed by the ministry and have a duration of three years.[22] The ministry also attributes concessions through a concession decree.[23]

Angola also has a new Local Content Law, which is quite relevant to the wider regulatory framework, as it applies to the oil sector as a whole and also affects PSAs. Oil companies must hire Angolan companies and prepare a local content plan for the national concessionaire on local content.[24] Furthermore, the Angolan regulatory framework contains a provision on the tax incentives available for Angolan companies.[25]

2.1 Taxation

Taxation plays an important role, as the fiscal terms are the second most important dimension, both for investors and for states, after the country's geological potential. This directly affects the overall government take and company take – particularly in the context of the PSA, whose main feature is the sharing of oil between the IOC and the host government, represented by the NOC, a ministry or an independent regulatory agency.

In Angola, the main statute applicable to the taxation of oil and gas is the Law on the Taxation of Petroleum Activities, identified above. Under this law, three types of taxes and two types of 'contributions' may be identified:[26]

- petroleum production tax;
- petroleum income tax;
- petroleum transaction tax;
- surface area fee; and
- contribution for the training of Angolan nationals.

Petroleum production tax is not applicable to PSAs,[27] but is applicable to joint ventures and to risk service contracts at a rate of 20%.[28]

---

22 This period can be extended. Article 12 and Articles 33 to 43 of the Law on Petroleum Activities.

23 Article 44 of the Law on Petroleum Activities. The decree must contain relevant information on Articles 48 to 57.

24 Article 11 and Article 12 of Presidential Decree 271/2020. It is not the aim of this chapter to provide a detailed analysis of the new Local Content Law, but to underscore its importance in the analysis of the PSA and the wider regulatory framework applicable to the oil and gas industry. Articles 26 and 27 of the Law on Petroleum Activities also contains provisions on local content.

25 According to Presidential Decree 3/2012.

26 Article 4(1) of the Law on the Taxation of Petroleum Activities: *"a) Imposto sobre a Produção Petrolífera, b) Imposto sobre o Rendimento do Petróleo, c) Imposto de Transacção de Petróleo, d) Taxa de Superfície, e) Contribuição para Formação de Quadros Angolanos."*

27 Article 12(4) of the Law on the Taxation of Petroleum Activities.

28 *Ibid,* Article 14.

Petroleum income tax is applicable to PSAs[29] at a rate of 50% and to joint ventures and risk service contracts at a rate of 65.75%.[30] Petroleum transaction tax[31] is applicable to joint ventures and risk service contracts at a rate of 70%.[32]

The surface area fee[33] and the contribution for the training of Angolan nationals[34] are also applicable to all contracts, including PSAs. The surface area fee is a value of $300 per square kilometre.[35] Formally, these are not taxes, but they are mandatory and may be equated to taxes – particularly the contribution for the training of Angolan nationals, which in our view is a tax in terms of its legal nature, as it:

- is an involuntary levy;
- is mandatory for all 'associates' of the national concessionaire; and
- is not linked to any services that are provided.[36]

According to Article 12(2) of Decree- Law 17/09, oil companies or 'associates' must pay annually:

- $100,000 a year, for companies that hold a prospecting licence;
- $300,000 a year, for companies engaged in exploration;
- $0.15 per barrel, for companies in the production phase;
- 0.5% of the revenues, for companies engaged in the storage, transportation, distribution and commercialisation of oil products; and
- 0.5% of the value of the annual contracts, for companies or entities engaged in services.

The rates differ for natural gas and the relevant provisions are covered by a separate statute. The rate is 5% for petroleum production tax and 25% for petroleum income tax.[37] In Angola, the taxable income is for each area of development covered by the PSA 'ring fencing'.[38]

As mentioned above, after resource potential, the fiscal terms are the most important feature of a country's attractiveness to oil and gas investors. To this end, one must analyse the overall government take, which in the PSA includes both profit oil and taxes. A study conducted by the Boston Consulting Group revealed that the government take for Angola from 2009 to 2014 was an average of 65%.[39]

---

29 *Ibid,* Articles 18 and 19.
30 *Ibid,* Article 41.
31 *Ibid,* Article 44.
32 *Ibid,* Article 48.
33 *Ibid,* Article 50. It is unclear whether this a tax. We would argue that it is not a tax, but a fee, as the 'associates' of the national concessionaire still have area access.
34 Article 57 of the Law on the Taxation of Petroleum Activities.
35 *Ibid,* Article 52.
36 Thus, in our view it is a tax, not a fee as the surface area fee.
37 This decree was mentioned in Article 9 of Presidential Decree 7/2018.
38 Article 23(2)(b) of the Law on the Taxation of Petroleum Activities.
39 According to analysis of the Boston Consulting Group and Rystad Energy: Iván Martén, Philip Whittaker, Álvaro Martínez de Bourio, *Government Take in Upstream Oil and Gas: Framing a more Balanced Dialogue* (Boston Consulting Group, 2015), www.bcg.com/publications/2015/government-take-in-upstream-oil-and-gas-framing-a-more-balanced-dialogue.

3. The competent authority: the ANPG

The establishment of the ANPG marked a sea change in the Angolan oil and gas legal framework. The ANPG replaced Sonangol (as the NOC) as the competent regulatory authority for the oil and gas industry. There was a long debate on the issue of who should be the competent authority for the oil and gas industry, as Sonangol was both a commercial entity and the *de facto* regulatory body for the sector; although the Ministry of Petroleum was the formal competent authority, pursuant to the Law on Petroleum Activities. This created the potential for conflicts of interest, so as a result of the oil reforms that started in 2015, Angola decided to establish the ANPG.[40]

The ANPG was formally established by Presidential Decree 49/19. Following this decree, Article 4 of the Law on Petroleum Activities provides that its activities are subject to oversight[41] by the president as the head of the executive power, exercised by the minister of mineral resources and oil. This means that although the ANPG enjoys some degree of independence, its activities are still subject to oversight by the entity responsible for overall oil and gas policy, which is the Ministry of Mineral Resources and Oil.

The Ministry of Mineral Resources and Oil is still responsible for promoting and formulating overall oil and gas policy and local content policy.[42] The establishment of the ANPG has not affected its competences. The ANPG replaced the Angolan NOC as the national concessionaire – a role that was previously exercised by Sonangol.

4. The Angolan PSA: main provisions

The model PSA used by Angola is not unique and shares common features with other PSAs around the world. The PSA is part of the *lex petrolea*, which is part of the *lex mercatoria*[43] and can be defined as the applicable international commercial law. The PSA is part of the *lex petrolea* because it is a standard model contract developed by the industry and widely used, and as such is a source of the *lex petrolea*.[44]

---

40 Flavio GI Inocencio, "Independent Regulatory Authorities in the Oil and Gas Industry", *International Energy Law Review*, Issue 4, 2018, p 145. We proposed the creation of an independent regulatory agency in 2015: Flavio GI Inocencio (n 7), pp 100-102.

41 The legal term '*Superintendência*' can be translated as 'oversight', following the functional method used in *An Introduction to Comparative Law* (n 19).

42 Regulated by Presidential Decree 159/2020, https://mirempet.gov.ao/fotos/frontend_11/gov_documentos/estatuto_organico_mirempet_3064696326023b5ff327cf.pdf.

43 '*Lex mercatoria*' is the autonomous international (transnational) commercial law and includes several sources: general principles of law, arbitration decisions, standard model contracts, model laws, commercial usages and practices. It is created by multiple 'formulating agencies'. Gilles Cuniberti, "Three Theories of Lex Mercatoria", *Columbia Journal of Transnational Law*, Vol 52, No 1, 2014. For a more elaborate definition, see, Abul FM Maniruzzaman, "The Lex Mercatoria and International Contracts: A Challenge for International Commercial Arbitration?", *American University International Law Review*, Vol 14, No 3, 1999, p 669.

44 '*Lex petrolea*' is a subset of the '*lex mercatoria*' and incudes the different sources of law applicable to the oil and gas industry – in particular, the practices and usages of the industry. The existence of the *lex petrolea* was recognised in the famous *Kuwait v Aminoil* arbitration; Maniruzzaman (43), p 663.

The PSA must be understood within the context of the wider Angolan regulatory framework applicable to the oil and gas sector and some of the laws cited above. The PSA is a contract whereby the state[45] and the contractor group agree to explore an oil concession,[46] and the risks of exploration and development are borne by the contractor group.[47] After production, oil and/or natural gas is shared between the government in terms of 'profit oil' and costs are recovered by the contractor group in terms of 'cost oil'.[48] The state retains overall control of operations and retains ownership of the mineral rights (oil and gas).[49]

As the main E&P contract used by Angola, the model PSA contract includes certain standard provisions.[50] No royalties are applicable to the model PSA. The main tax applicable to the model PSA is petroleum income tax at a rate of 50%.

4.1 Structure of the contract

The model PSA is quite straightforward and includes several important provisions that are typical of PSAs. Article 2 of the model PSA provides that there are five annexes to the contract:

- Annex A – description of the contract area;
- Annex B – map of the contract area;
- Annex C – accounting and financial procedures;
- Annex D – corporate guarantee; and
- Annex E – financial guarantee.

Article 4 of the model PSA explicitly states that the contract does not create a new company, joint venture or consortium. This helps to clarify its legal nature: it is a PSA. The model PSA states that the contract has a duration of 25 years for the production phase.[51] The exploration phase usually lasts for three years, but this can be extended. However, the parties may choose a different duration. The parties usually designate an operator to represent the contractor group, and changes to the operator require the consent of the ministry and the nomination of the national concessionaire (Article 8).[52]

---

45 Usually represented by an NOC. In Angola, this was previously done by Sonangol and is now done by ANPG.

46 After a bidding process.

47 Article 18 of the Law on Petroleum Activities is quite clear.

48 Johnston identifies certain characteristics of the PSAs: Daniel Johnston, *International Petroleum Fiscal Systems and Petroleum Sharing Contracts* (Penwell Books, 1994), p 40.

49 Kirsten Bindemann, *Production Sharing Agreements: An Economic Analysis* (Oxford Institute of Energy Studies, 1999), p 12.

50 For a version of a model PSA contract used by the ANPG, in Portuguese, see https://webgis.anpg.co.ao/wp-content/uploads/2019/10/CPP-Template-da-ANPG_DNEG.pdf. For a version of the 2005 model contract, see https://resourcecontracts.org/contract/ocds-591adf-3213850251/view#/pdf.

51 Article 7(1) of the model PSA.

52 *Ibid*, Article 8. Article 19 of the Law on Petroleum Activities contains further provisions on the role of the operator.

4.2 Cost recovery

An important feature of the PSA is the percentage of cost recovery (cost oil) that the contractor may recover when production starts. This is set out in Article 11 of the model PSA. One example is the inclusion of 50% cost recovery in the model PSA for Block 20.[53] This means that the contractor group may recover costs up to that percentage. This is a very important provision, which allows the host government to start receiving revenues from day one of production, as the contractor group may recover only a certain percentage of production as cost. This provision must be interpreted systematically by reference to the Law on the Taxation of Petroleum Activities, and this is clearly stated in the model PSA.[54] Obviously, the national concessionaire has the option to negotiate a different percentage of cost recovery in different PSAs.

4.3 Production sharing (profit oil)

Production sharing is a key characteristic of the PSA. Article 12 of the model PSA includes provisions on production sharing between the national concessionaire and the contractor group. This sharing of oil includes all oil produced during the quarter (minus the cost oil) and takes into consideration the rate of return achieved in the preceding quarter. This calculation is done after tax. Usually, higher rates of return for the contractor increase the overall share of the national concessionaire. This type of calculation is considered a 'resource rent tax'.[55]

The rate of return is determined by the "accumulated compounded net cash flow for each Development Area", which includes:

- the sum of the contractor group's cost recovery crude oil and the share of the development area profit oil regarding the petroleum actually lifted in that quarter at the market price;
- minus petroleum income tax; and
- minus development expenditures and production expenditures.[56]

The net cash flow is calculated based on the following formula:

ACNCF (current quarter) =

(100% + DQ) x ACNCF (previous quarter) + NCF (current quarter)

100%

53 In Angola, concession areas are called blocks. This is an old contract and this contract was replaced by a risk service contract in Block 20; see: https://resourcecontracts.org/contract/ocds-591adf-0014595575/view#/pdf .

54 Article 11(1) of the model PSA.

55 Carlo Cotarelli, *Fiscal Regimes for Extractive Industries: Design and Implementation* (International Monetary Fund), p 20, www.imf.org/en/Publications/Policy-Papers/Issues/2016/12/31/Fiscal-Regimes-for-Extractive-Industries-Design-and-Implementation-PP4701.

where:
ACNCF = accumulated compounded net cash flow
NCF = net cash flow
DQ = quarterly compound rate (in percent)[57]

4.4 Minimum work obligations

The model PSA also establishes minimum work obligations for the contractor group in the exploration phase (Article 15). The model PSA provides that, following a commercial discovery, the contractor group must inform the concessionaire (Article 17). This is quite important, as the contractor group must present a general development and production plan to the concessionaire (Article 18); once the plan has been approved, the contractor group must prepare an annual work and production plan and budget (Article 19).

Also relevant is Article 22, which requires the contractor group to pay the concessionaire a bonus and contributions for social projects. This is a non-recoverable cost for the contractor and will vary according to each concession area.[58]

4.5 Commercial discovery

Commerciality is important and will determine whether oil or natural gas can be developed and explored. The contractor group must inform the national concessionaire within 30 days of whether a well is commercially viable;[59] this is followed by the digging of an appraisal well.[60] In the case of a commercial discovery, the contractor group must inform the national concessionaire in writing as to whether the discovery is commercially viable,[61] and development will proceed according to the applicable legislation and the contract. Lifting provisions are enshrined in Article 13[62] and the parties may usually dispose freely of their oil.[63]

4.6 Financial guarantees

The contractor group must provide financial guarantees for the minimum work obligations (Article 21). These are calculated according to the participating interest. This provision must be interpreted according to Annex E, which is part of the PSA contract.

---

56 Article 12(2), subparagraph (a) of the model PSA.

57 *Ibid*, Article 12(2)(c).

58 For instance, in the PSA of Block 20, on Article 22(2), it reads: "The signature bonus and the contributions for social projects and for the Sonangol Research and Technology Centre referred to in the preceding paragraph, shall not be recovered or amortized by the Contractor Group." Other PSAs contain a similar provision. Article 58 of the Law on Petroleum Activities also contains rules on the minimum work obligations.

59 Article 17(1) of the model PSA.

60 *Ibid*, Article 17(2).

61 *Ibid*, Article 17(3): "not later than six (6) Months after the completion of the second Appraisal Well, or twenty-four (24) Months after the declaration of the Commercial."

62 The operating committee needs to approve the lifting schedule. Article 20(1) of the model PSA.

4.7 Signature bonus

The model PSA provides that the contractor group must pay to the national concessionaire a signature bonus[64] and a contribution to social projects.[65] This cannot be recovered or amortised by the contractor group.[66]

4.8 Records, reports and inspections

Article 24 of the model PSA is quite instructive and highlights the importance of the national concessionaire in the management of the contract.[67] The national concessionaire is given 'regulatory' authority to verify information and data which the contractor group must provide. This is quite relevant, as the PSA structure requires the recovery of costs and unreliable information might affect both the government take and the company take.

4.9 Selling oil

Also quite significant is the obligation of the contractor group to buy the oil of the national concessionaire on request (Article 25). This means that the contractor group cannot refuse this prerogative of the ANPG, as the national concessionaire.[68] The ANPG replaced Sonangol as the national concessionaire, which means that it will represent the Angolan state in future PSAs. Existing PSAs will not be affected by this change.[69] The change is also reflected in the new model PSA.

4.10 Unitisation

The model PSA contains a provision on unitisation and states that these rules are to be found in the Law on Petroleum Activities (Article 27). The law contains detailed provisions on unitisation in Article 64. This demonstrates the importance of interpreting the PSA by reference to the wider Angolan regulatory framework. This implies that the contract cannot be interpreted without the application of the relevant laws and regulations, as under the model PSA – which is used by the national concessionaire as model for negotiation – Angolan law is the governing law of the contract.

---

63 *Ibid*, Article 13.

64 *Ibid*, Article 22(1)(a).

65 *Ibid*, Article 22(1)(b).

66 *Ibid*, Article 22(2).

67 *Ibid*, Article 24(1): "Contractor Group shall prepare and, at all times while this Contract is in force, maintain accurate and current records of its activities and operations in the Contract Area and shall keep all information of a technical, economic, accounting or any other nature, developed for the conduct of Petroleum Operations. Such records shall be organized in such a way as to allow for the prompt and complete ascertainment of costs and expenditures."

68 For instance, the model PSA contract 2005 reads: "Sonangol has the right to require Contractor Group to purchase any part of Sonangol's share of production under normal commercial terms and conditions in the international petroleum industry and at the Market Price in force at the time the Crude Oil is lifted as established in the Petroleum Activities Tax Law."

69 Article 5 of Presidential Decree 1/2020 states that this change will not affect existing contracts (including PSAs) in terms of rights or obligations.

4.11 Decommissioning

Article 28 of the model PSA contains a provision on decommissioning (entitled "Transfer and Abandonment of Assets"). This is one of the most important provisions of the model PSA and must be interpreted in accordance with Article 75 of the Law on Petroleum Activities and Presidential Decree 91/18, which regulates decommissioning in Angola. The national concessionaire and the contractor group must provide funds in an 'escrow account' to cover the decommissioning costs of abandonment, and must provide further funds if those in the escrow account prove insufficient.[70]

4.12 Natural gas

Under the model PSA, the contractor group has the right to use natural gas in the petroleum operations[71] (Article 29(1)). However, the national concessionaire has the right to any surplus of associated natural gas.[72] This provision has its roots in a historical context in which natural gas was often wasted and gas flaring was common practice. The Angolan Liquefied Natural Gas (LNG) Project[73] was established in order to monetise the associated natural gas of development areas and prevent flaring. Furthermore, Article 73 of the Law on Petroleum Activities prohibits gas flaring and establishes an obligation to recover all natural gas.

The new model PSA presented by the ANPG fully allows the contractor group to explore and develop natural gas following the new fiscal rules for natural gas.[74] It is also important to underscore the sole risk provisions[75] in the model PSA.

4.13 Operating committee

In conducting the petroleum operations, the parties under a PSA coordinate their actions through an operating committee (Article 31). Usually, the parties establish a joint operating agreement (JOA) in order to conduct the petroleum operations.[76] The operating committee is comprised of four members: two appointed by the concessionaire and the other two appointed by the contractor group (Article 31(4)).

---

70 Article 28(4) of the model PSA of the 'escrow account'. Presidential Decree 91/2018 further expands on those rules.

71 Article 29(1) of the model PSA.

72 As an example, the old model PSA reads in Article 28(2): "The available Associated Natural Gas surplus to the requirements defined in the preceding paragraph shall be made available free to Sonangol, in Angola, by Contractor Group. Sonangol shall inform the Contractor Group of its intention to utilize such Gas as soon as reasonably practical."

73 The Angolan LNG Project is a $12 billion project to monetise associated natural gas from oil blocks. It was implemented to stop gas flaring and is a partnership between Chevron, BP, Sonangol, ENI and Total; see: www.angolalng.com/.

74 Following Presidential Decree 7/2018.

75 Article 30.

76 The JOA is one of the most important agreements in the oil and gas industry. The Association of International Petroleum Negotiators has developed a model JOA which is widely used in the industry.

4.14 Ownership of assets and data

Under the model PSA, the ownership of assets belongs to the national concessionaire (Article 32). This means that all physical assets acquired by the contractor group for Angola will become the property of the national concessionaire, as long they are used for the conduct of petroleum activities.[77]

Furthermore, all information and data used in the conduct of petroleum activities also belong to the national concessionaire.[78] The relevant provision reads: "All information of a technical nature developed through the conduct of the Petroleum Operations shall be the property of Sonangol. Notwithstanding the above, and without prejudice to the provisions of the following paragraphs, Contractor Group shall have the right to use and copy, free of charge, such information for internal purposes."[79] Moreover, Article 36 of the Law on Petroleum Activities also states that the data belongs to the Angolan state.

4.15 Risk management of petroleum operations

The model PSA requires the contractor group to comply with Decree 39/01 on the risk management of petroleum operations. Health, safety and environmental rules are a keystone of the oil and gas industry, particularly after the Deepwater Horizon incident in 2010. However, these provisions also need updating and the decree also needs an overhaul to reflect best practices in the industry.

4.16 Local content: training and recruitment of Angolans

The model PSA contains an 'indigenisation' clause.[80] This forms part of the local content policy, which usually encompasses support, promotion and integration of Angolan nationals in the oil and gas industry. The Angolan regulatory framework contains rules on the indigenisation of the workforce – an initiative known as 'Angolanisation'.

Article 36(1) of the model PSA reads: "Contractor Group shall comply with Decree-Law No. 17/09, of 26 June 2009, and ancillary regulations, as well as applicable legislation regarding the recruitment, integration and training of Angolan personnel."

These provisions must be interpreted according to the specificities of Decree-Law 17/09, which contains many provisions on the recruitment and training of Angolan personnel. The decree-law provides that oil companies must sign 'contract programmes'[81] with the Ministry of Mineral Resources and Oil with plans for:

---

77 Article 32.

78 Article 33.

79 Article 33(1). The provision reads: "All information of a technical nature developed through the conduct of the Petroleum Operations shall be the property of Sonangol. Notwithstanding the above, and without prejudice to the provisions of the following paragraphs, Contractor Group shall have the right to use and copy, free of charge, such information for internal purposes."

80 Silvana Tordo, *Local Content Policies in the Oil and Gas Sector* (The World Bank, 2013), p 43.

81 Article 5 of Decree Law 17/2009.

- the labour force needed to conduct their operations;
- their occupations and numbers; and
- the recruitment and training of Angolan nationals, together with a clear calendar.[82]

The decree-law further imposes an obligation to contribute to a development fund to train Angolans in the oil sector, which is managed by the Ministry of Mineral Resources and Oil.[83]

Additionally, Article 14(4) provides that the contractor group must engage Angolan companies and obtain local goods, "as long as their services are similar in quality and availability to those available on the international market and the prices of their services, when subject to the same tax charges, are no more than ten percent (10%) higher compared to the prices charged by foreign contractors for identical services". As with other clauses of the model PSA, this must be interpreted against the background of the new Local Content Law, Presidential Decree 271/20, which requires companies to present a local content plan and a HR plan, in addition to a contract programme.[84]

4.17 Stabilisation clause

The model PSA contains a type of stabilisation clause.[85] Article 37(2) provides that in the event of changes to the Angolan regulatory framework that affect the parties' "obligations, rights and benefits" under the PSA, the parties may agree on amendments to the contract to restore those obligations, rights and benefits:

> *Without prejudice to other rights and obligations of the Parties under the Contract, in the event that any change in the provisions of any Law, decree or regulation in force in the Republic of Angola occurs subsequent to the signing of this Contract which adversely affects the obligations, rights and benefits hereunder, then the Parties shall agree on amendments to the Contract to be submitted to the competent authorities for approval, so as to restore such rights, obligations and forecasted benefits.*

This stabilisation clause is closer to an economic equilibrium clause and is not a freezing clause. The violation of this clause might lead to arbitration should a dispute arise in this regard; however, Angola has ratified several bilateral investment treaties and as such must protect certain investor rights.

The stabilisation clause requires updating and the wording should be more clearly formulated in a future revision of the model PSA. The contract should also incorporate a specific clause on the protection of investor rights arising from a treaty dispute.

---

82 *Ibid*, Article 7.
83 *Ibid*, Article 12 of Decree Law 17/2009.
84 Articles 12 to 14 of Presidential Decree 271/2020.
85 Economic equilibrium or freezing clause; AFM Maniruzzaman, "The Pursuit of Stability in International Energy Investment: A Critical Appraisal of the Emerging Trends", *Journal of World Energy Law & Business*, Vol I, No 2, 2008, p 128.

4.18 Assignment

The model PSA contains an assignment clause, allowing one of the parties to the contractor group to assign its participation interest to another party. However, this requires the consent of the Ministry of Mineral Resources and Oil.[86] The national concessionaire has the right of first refusal and may exercise this right;[87] the right may further be transferred to Sonangol as the NOC in case of non-exercise of that right by the national concessionaire,[88] and to the 'associates'[89] respectively.

4.19 Resolution of the contract

Article 39 of the model PSA contains provisions on termination of the contract. Disputes may arise in relation to these provisions, as they give the national concessionaire the right to terminate the contract under certain conditions. For instance, one of the causes of termination is if the contractor group "continuously refuses with no justification to comply with the Law";[90] this wording is quite open and requires further clarification.

4.20 Confidentiality

Article 40 of the model PSA contains a requirement to maintain the confidentiality of the contract. This provision is problematic, as greater transparency is needed in the oil and gas industry. In our view, this provision should be removed – in particular, because Angola has just decided to adhere to the Extractives Industries Transparency Initiative, and publicity and scrutiny of contracts in the oil sector are thus important in order to tackle corruption and enhance transparency.

4.21 Dispute resolution

Disputes over the interpretation of the PSA are resolved through arbitration.[91] In case of a dispute, the model PSA establishes that the Secretariat of the International Chamber of Commerce will be the administrator of the arbitration proceedings and the arbitration proceedings will be conducted by reference to the United Nations Commission on International Trade Law Arbitration Rules of 1976.[92]

Three arbitrators will be appointed: one by the national concessionaire, a second by the contractor group and a third chosen jointly by the national concessionaire and the contractor group.[93] The dispute will be resolved on the

---

86 Article 38(1) of the model PSA.
87 *Ibid*, Article 38(6).
88 *Ibid*, Article 38.
89 *Ibid*, Article 38(9).
90 *Ibid*, Article 39(1)(b).
91 *Ibid*, Article 41(1).
92 *Ibid*, Article 41(2).
93 *Ibid*, Article 41(3).

basis of Angolan law, as the applicable law of the contract. Arbitration proceedings must be conducted in Portuguese and must take place in Luanda.[94]

The model PSA also contains a waiver of sovereign immunity,[95] which allows for arbitration. Angola ratified the New York Convention of Recognition and Enforcement of Arbitral Awards in 2017. In the event of potential arbitration arising from this contract, it can now be enforced in Angola. Angola is not a member of the International Centre for Settlement of Investment Disputes and the model PSA contract is silent on investor-state dispute settlement; however, this issue may arise in the future, as Angola has ratified a few bilateral investment treaties which are now in force. This means that an oil and gas contractual dispute might give rise also to a treaty dispute that affects the minimum standard of protection under international law.

4.22 Applicable law and language

The governing law applicable to the PSA is Angolan law,[96] given that this is the main host government contract that regulates the relationship between the national concessionaire and the contractor group. The official language of the contract is Portuguese.[97] Other relevant provisions in the contract include a *force majeure* provision, which is particularly significant in light of the COVID-19 pandemic.[98]

5. Conclusion

This chapter has explored the main features of the model PSA and the overall legal framework. It is not the aim of this chapter to provide a comprehensive analysis of the model PSA, but merely an overview of its main provisions within the context of the Angolan regulatory framework. Moreover, this chapter has not covered the fiscal terms of the model PSA in detail.

The model PSA served its purpose when it was first introduced in the 1980s. However, in light of the newer model PSAs that have been introduced in other countries, it may be concluded that Angola's model PSA is now outdated.

Angola uses the PSA alongside other host government contracts, but the PSA is still the preferred choice as the main host government contract, as it strikes a good balance between the interests of the state and the interests of IOCs. That said, Angola should develop a new model PSA which reflects best practices in the industry and includes other detailed provisions on issues such as anti-corruption, environmental matters and human rights. The overall legislative

---

94 *Ibid*, Articles 41(4) and (5).
95 *Ibid*, Article 41(5).
96 *Ibid*, Article 43.
97 *Ibid*, Article 44.
98 *Ibid*, Article 42.

regulatory framework also requires updating and the incorporation of environmental, social and governance provisions.

There are other challenges for Angola, but a detailed discussion of these would go beyond the scope of this chapter. However, the most relevant include:

- declining oil production until 2030;
- the energy transition as a result of climate change and the resulting decline in global demand for oil in the energy mix; and
- the emergence of more attractive jurisdictions for IOCs and investors, with better geological potential and more beneficial fiscal terms.

Azerbaijan

Banuchichak Hilalqizi
International lawyer

1. Introduction

Azerbaijan is located in the South Caucasus region of Eurasia. It is bordered by four countries: Georgia and Russia to the north, Iran to the south and Armenia to the southwest. Azerbaijan is also bordered by Turkey to the northwest through Nakchivan. The geography of Azerbaijan is dominated by the Caspian Sea, which is the largest lake in the world. Although the Caspian Sea is an inland water body, it is classified as a sea due to the high salt content of the water. The Caspian Sea has many fertile oil fields which have been developed for centuries.

Azerbaijan's oil industry also has a long tradition. In the 13th and 14th centuries, Italian explorer Marco Polo observed that Azerbaijan oil was being transported to Eastern countries; and Ottoman explorer Evliya Chelebi noted that Azerbaijan was the main oil transportation hub between Iran, Central Asia and Turkey.[1] Azerbaijan's oil industry began to develop even before the country gained its independence.[2] In 1813, Azerbaijan began to supply oil to different countries in the Russian empire.[3] However, the development of Azerbaijan's oil industry officially began in 1846 after oil wells were established around Bibiheybet in the Absheron Peninsula.[4] Further development subsequently took place in other areas, including Balakhani, Binegedi and Priallahi. Local investors and philanthropists (eg, Hadji Zeynalabdin Taghiyev, Murtuz Mukhtarov and Shamsi Asadullayev) were also starting to participate in the oil industry. And foreign investors – including the Swedish Nobel brothers – were also taking interest and owned a number of oil tankers and oil fields in the Caspian Sea.

During World War I and World War II, all of the Soviet Union's oil was

1 Evliya Chelebi, *The Book of Travelers* (Ikdam Matba'asi, 1896).

2 Thomas Moran, "The Financial Benefits of Corporate Social Responsibility in the Azeri Oil Industry" (2015) 12 *South Carolina Journal of International Law and Business* 85.

3 *Ibid.*

4 The Ministry of Energy of the Republic of Azerbaijan, "History of Development of Oil Industry", 31 January 2020, https://minenergy.gov.az/en/neft/neft-senayesinin-inkisaf-tarixi#:~:text=The%20development%20of%20Azerbaijan's%20oil,first%20time%20in%20the%20world.&text=Their%20net%20incomes%20made%20up,15%25%20of%20the%20oil%20sold.

produced by Azerbaijan.[5] The participation of foreign investors in the oil sector also promoted the development of Azerbaijan's economy.

One of the most significant oil fields in Azerbaijan was Oil Rocks (Neft Dashlari), also known as the 'City in the Sea' or 'the Eighth Wonder of the World', which was established in 1949 in the southeast of the Absheron Peninsula. As technology developed, radiotelephone communication was established between Baku and Oil Rocks; and Mi-8 helicopters were used to transport people from Baku to Oil Rocks and vice versa. The Oil Rocks field was a milestone in the development of the oil industry in Azerbaijan, and also played host to the first operating offshore company in the world.[6] Oil Rocks is still of considerable importance to Azerbaijan's oil industry, with its 200-plus stationary platforms in the Caspian Sea.

In terms of offshore platforms, the Gunashli field began to produce oil in 1980 and accounted for nearly 57% of oil production by 1991.[7]

2. The petroleum legal regime

After Azerbaijan gained its independence in 1991, many industries began to take off, including the oil industry. In 1994, a new era began when, as an independent country, Azerbaijan signed various international contracts to attract foreign investors to its petroleum industry. More than 30 production sharing agreements (PSAs) have been signed with international oil companies (IOCs) – including from the United States, the United Kingdom, Saudi Arabia, Japan, Russia and Norway – which have brought more than $50 million in foreign investment into the country. The petroleum industry is thus the backbone of the Azerbaijani economy.

The petroleum legal regime is governed by a discretionary system. On one side, the State Oil Company of the Azerbaijan Republic (SOCAR) acts as an agent of the host government and signs petroleum contracts with international oil companies. Each PSA has its own unique and specific law, as they have all been signed with different foreign oil companies. However, the main objective of these agreements is to promote the continued development of the oil and gas industry. Conversely, almost all of the PSAs share similarities in their standard terms and clauses, including:

- the rights and obligations of the parties;
- taxation;
- the contract area;
- the costs and sharing of production; and
- the termination of agreements.

---

5 Arthur P Mizzi, "Caspian Sea Oil, Turmoil, and Caviar: Can They Provide a Basis for an Economic Union of the Caspian States?" (1996) 7 *Colorado Journal of International Environmental Law and Policy.*

6 Ema Hasanova Mehrab, "The 8th wonder of the world – 'Oil Rocks' settlement and miracle of the sea", *Azerbaijan News*, 25 December 2018, www.azerbaijannews.eu/site/the-8th-wonder-of-the-world-oil-rocks-settlement-and-miracle-in-the-sea/.

7 Mizzi (n 5).

In general, the petroleum industry in Azerbaijan is governed by both domestic law and international treaties. According to the Constitution,[8] international treaties which have been ratified by the Azerbaijani government prevail over local laws. PSAs prevail over any contradictory local laws, except the Constitution or any other act accepted by referendum.

As a major oil and gas producing country, Azerbaijan has ratified and adopted more than 40 bilateral investment treaties; and the Energy Charter Treaty has also been ratified by Azerbaijan.[9] Each PSA comes into force once it has been approved by Parliament and becomes legally effective as domestic law.

On 20 September 1994, Azerbaijan's oil industry changed dramatically when the first-ever PSA was signed, on the initiative of former Azerbaijani President Heydar Aliyev. This was called the 'contract of the century'. It was signed between SOCAR and 11 foreign oil companies. The duration of the contract was supposed to be 30 years, but in 2017 the government decided to extend the contract. The agreement concerned joint development and production sharing for the Azeri and Chirag fields, and the Deepwater portion of the Gunashli field in the Azerbaijani sector of the Caspian Sea. After ratification of the PSA, the Azerbaijan International Operating Company – comprised of 11 various IOCs from six nations – entered into an agreement with SOCAR. The relevant IOCs were Amoco, Delta, BP, Exxon, Unocal, LUKoil, Statoil, Pennzoil, McDermott, Ramco and TPAO; and they hailed from the United Kingdom, Russia, the United States, Turkey, Saudi Arabia, Bermuda, Panama and Norway.

2.1 Participating interest

According to the PSAs, the participating percentage interest of each contracting party is as follows:

- Azeri-Chirag-Gunashli (ACG):
  - SOCAR: 20%
  - Amoco: 17.01%
  - BP: 17.1267%
  - Delta: 16.8%
  - Lukoil: 10%
  - McDermott: 2.45%
  - Pennzoil: 9.8175%
  - Ramco: 2.0825%
  - Statoil: 8.5633%
  - TPAO: 1.75%
  - Unocal: 9.520%

---

8 The Constitution of the Republic of Azerbaijan, 12 November 1995.

9 1958 New York Convention on the Recognition and Enforcement of Foreign Arbitral Awards; 1965 Washington Convention on the Settlement of Investment Disputes between States and Nationals of Other States; 1961 European Convention on Foreign Commercial Arbitration.

- Shah Deniz:
  - SCA: 10%
  - BP: 25.5%
  - Elf: 10%
  - LUKoil: 10%
  - OIEC: 10%
  - Statoil: 25.5%
  - TPAO: 9%

In the remaining three PSAs – Shafag Asiman, Shallow Water Absheron Peninsula and Block D-230 – the parties each have an equal sharing interest of 50% respectively.

2.2 Grant of rights and scope

The parties are liable only for the rights which are set out in the contract – that is, rights relating to surface areas, the seabed, sub-oil and other natural resources and aquatic resources. Apart from the specified works and services, the parties cannot conduct other activities or operate in other fields under the PSAs.

2.3 Cost oil, profit oil and bonuses

Generally speaking, in most of the PSAs, oil is divided into cost recovery oil and profit oil. Cost recovery oil is divided into two categories: operational and capital expenses. Current expenses for the purchase of materials, fixed expenses and other operational expenses are included in operational expenses. Conversely, capital expenses include drilling expenses and expenses for platforms, equipment and pipeline. Before calculating the expenses, it is useful to know the price of oil, as this way it can be ascertained whether the percentage of oil will be sufficient to cover those expenses. However, in practice, the cost oil is usually adequate to cover the operating costs in full.

Furthermore, after deducting operational costs, the capital costs should be recovered from no more than 50% of the remaining total production. In essence, operational expenses and capital expenses are deducted from gross production in order to obtain profit oil. As a result, profit oil is divided between SOCAR and the contractors (IOCs). In Azerbaijan, profit oil is calculated in terms of:

- the real rate of return (adjustments resulting from inflation and other external factors); and
- the R factor (the ratio of revenue to expenses).

The division of oil expenses may vary from PSA to PSA and from country to country. However, in Azerbaijan, the extracted oil is divided between the parties before it is placed on the market.

In general, PSAs afford several benefits to countries. Apart from the profits which are derived from oil, there are also bonuses which may be considered a further source of revenue for the state, including signing bonuses, production bonuses and discovery bonuses. Bonuses are usually paid at different stages of the agreement – for example, signing bonuses at the time of signing of the PSA, production bonuses when the parties achieve a certain level of production and discovery bonuses at the point of initial discovery.

Profit oil can be obtained through various techniques, including volumetric trigger and the R factor method. As mentioned, profit oil is generally split 50/50 between the parties; however, through the volumetric trigger technique, profit oil can be divided 75% to the state and 25% to the contractor, as billions of barrels of oil are produced. However, there are also some issues associated with this method: the contractor may face some risks and delays, as its share of the profit oil is not uplifted by the time value of money. Similarly, using the R factor method, the state's share of the profit oil also increases. The R factor is calculated by dividing the contractor's accumulated income by its accumulated capital costs; and whenever accumulated income increases, this affects the state's share of oil, so it also increases accordingly.

2.4 Tax

The existing PSAs are grandfathered, but new PSAs will be taxed exclusively under the new Tax Code of Azerbaijan. The new Tax Code provides for nine main taxes in general.

According to the Tax Code and the PSA tax regime, the contractor must also pay a profit tax. The rate of this profit tax varies from 20% to 32%,[10] and is also negotiable between the parties. To pay the profit tax, the contractor must submit the financial statements and profit tax return separately, alongside the auditor's report. A profit tax return is usually paid in US dollars.

A value added tax (VAT) exemption applies to contractors, operating companies and local and foreign subcontractors – in particular, when conducting the following activities:

- supply of goods and services;
- exports of petroleum products; and
- import of works, goods and services.

A VAT exemption certificate is issued by the Ministry of Taxes, and contractors, operating companies and local and foreign subcontractors should provide documentation to the Ministry of Taxes in order to obtain eligible exemption status.

10 Deloitte, "Azerbaijan Oil and Gas Taxation Guide," 2018, www2.deloitte.com/content/dam/Deloitte/az/Documents/tax/aze/TaxBrochures2016/Azerbaijan%20Oil%20and%20Gas%20Taxation%20Guide.pdf.

In addition, foreign contractors must pay withholding tax at a rate of between 5% and 10%. This is assessed on gross revenue from works and services provided in Azerbaijan.

Moreover, according to Azerbaijani tax law, personal income tax is calculated differently for local employees and foreign employees. Local employees must pay in accordance with the Tax Code; however, foreign employees must become tax resident in order to be subject to Azerbaijani personal income tax. There are several criteria under the PSAs which foreign employees should follow. For example, foreign employees must spend more than 90 days per calendar year in Azerbaijan in order to qualify as a tax resident; this is counted from their first day as an employee in Azerbaijan. Some employees work on rotational shifts; thus, another criterion is that a foreign employee must return to his or her home country upon completion of his or her employment shift.

Furthermore, foreign employees who work under a PSA in Azerbaijan are exempt from mandatory social insurance and other types of unemployment insurance payments.

2.5 Dispute resolution

In order to avoid future disputes, the parties – especially the contractor – must check their documents regularly, as this will be essential to any future defence.[11] In general, most of the PSAs signed between SOCAR and BP are governed and interpreted in accordance with the principles of Azerbaijani law and English law.[12] Both laws may be considered as the applicable law. If a dispute arises between the parties, it should be resolved under the United Nations Commission on International Trade Law (UNICTRAL) Arbitration Rules. However, if the UNICTRAL rules fail, the arbitration tribunal should establish its own rules. The arbitration should be conducted in English. A party that seeks to arbitrate must provide the other party with 30 days' prior written notice of its intention to do so and submit a request to the secretary general of the Permanent Court of Arbitration. The arbitration tribunal has the power to award damages or costs if necessary. The tribunal's award is final and should be binding and enforceable by the parties as soon as it is issued. Each party should pay the costs of its own arbitrator and the costs of the third arbitrator in equal shares; and any costs imposed under the arbitration rules will be shared equally by the parties.[13]

---

11 Freshfields Bruckhaus Deringer, "End of PSA: Key issues to consider", November 2016, www.freshfields.com/49fb63/globalassets/services-page/disputes-litigation-and-arbitration/publication-pdfs/freshfieldsoilandgaspsaissuesreport.pdf.

12 Shahdeniz Agreement, Section 23.1.

13 Azeri Chirag Gunashli Deepwater Agreement, 20 September 1994, Appendix 6.

3. PSAs between BP and Azerbaijan

Five main PSAs have been signed between Azerbaijan and BP: ACG, Shah Deniz, Shallow Water Absheron Peninsula, Shafag-Asiman and Block D-230.

Although each PSA is different, they still contain similar clauses.

3.1 ACG

ACG was the first offshore PSA signed by Azerbaijan and established the legal framework for foreign players to invest in and develop the oil industry in the Caspian Sea region. In addition, the agreement established new oil strategies and methods alongside those of local investors. The total oil production from ACG was more than 3.6 billion barrels. The development of these fields was divided into three phases. In general, Chirag began to produce oil in 1997 and was part of the Early Oil Project at that time. The development phases were as follows:

- Phase 1 – Central Azeri;
- Phase 2 – West Azeri and East Azeri; and
- Phase 3 – Deepwater Gunashli.

However, the production start dates varied, depending on the fields – for example, the Central Azeri and West Azeri fields started production in 2005; whereas the Deepwater Gunashli field commenced production in April 2008. Subsequently, all three phases were connected through the Chirag Oil Project and the West Chirag platform also started to produce oil in January 2004.

The parties have mutual duties and responsibilities – for example, each contractor is supposed provide training to Azerbaijani citizens who are working on the project – and also enjoy other annual benefits as approved by the steering committee.

3.2 Shah Deniz

BP and contractor parties signed a PSA in the Shah Deniz field of the Caspian Sea in 1996; however, production did not commence until 2006. There was also an additional field based on this agreement – Shah Deniz 2 – which began production in 2020. According to the PSA, the exploration period is supposed to be three years from the effective day of the agreement. The obligations of contractors during the exploration period include the following:

- Shoot, process and interpret a minimum of 800 square kilometres of three-dimensional seismic data in the contract area and carry out an upper section site investigation survey in the contract area to ensure a safe and environmentally sound basis for drilling; and
- Drill at least two exploration wells in the contract area.

The contractor should also provide SOCAR with all information on operations during the drilling and other related work. The exploration work programme describes in more detail the related jobs, work methods, instructions, drilling mechanisms and so on. If a contractor fails to perform its obligations, it will be in material breach, except in *force majeure* circumstances. In addition, according to the PSA, if the contractor wishes to conduct additional exploration work, SOCAR must be informed in writing in advance and the contractor can undertake additional exploration work only once SOCAR has granted its approval. SOCAR has the right to refuse this request; in either case, it must issue its decision within 90 days of receiving the request in writing from the contractor. At the end of the exploration and additional exploration periods, the contractor must provide SOCAR with written notice of the discovery and its commerciality, setting out all relevant information relating to the discovery (eg, location plan, geological maps and interpretations, seismic and other geophysical data, drilling reports). The development and production period can continue for up to 30 years following submission of the notice of discovery and its commerciality, and may be extended for a further five years with SOCAR's approval.[14]

3.3 Shafag Asiman

Another offshore PSA was signed between BP and SOCAR on 7 October 2010. Like other PSAs, this agreement is based on the Azerbaijani petroleum legal regime – that is, the Constitution, the Constitutional Act of State Independence and the Sub-surface Law. According to these laws, the ownership of petroleum existing in its natural state in underground or sub-surface strata in Azerbaijan is vested in the Republic of Azerbaijan; and based upon the below referenced authorisations, the authority to control and manage that petroleum is vested in SOCAR. A key difference between the Safag Asiman PSA and other PSAs with BP is the exploration period, which under this agreement is four years. Under this PSA, the contractor is also entitled to request the early commencement of petroleum production before termination of the exploration period and additional exploration periods. In this case, the contractor must obtain SOCAR's approval by submitting its development proposal. SOCAR has 60 days in which to decide whether to accept or decline the request.

3.4 Shallow Water Absheron Peninsula

The fourth PSA between BP and SOCAR, relating to the Shallow Water Absheron Peninsula, was signed on 22 December 2014. There is a common interest in both the Shafag Asiman and the Shallow Water Absheron Peninsula PSAs: the works relating to drilling plans should now continue under the two PSA and the

---

14 Agreement on the Exploration, Development and Production Sharing for the Shah Deniz Prospective Area in the Azerbaijan Sector of the Caspian Sea, 1996.

seismic programmes have been completed under these PSAs. The participation interest under this PSA is the same as that under the Shafag Asiman PSA: the parties each have an equal sharing interest of 50% respectively.

According to the PSA, the exploration period is divided into two categories: the initial exploration period and the main exploration period. The former commences on the effective date of the agreement and expires immediately following a period of 30 months from the effective date or the date of the notice of prospectivity, whichever is earlier. During the initial exploration period and the main exploration period, and before SOCAR's approval of the first development programme, BP (or an affiliate of BP) acts as an operating company and prepares for operations in accordance with the terms and conditions of the agreement. One clause states that the operating company can be incorporated outside of Azerbaijan; however, it must adhere to domestic law and be registered under the current law of Azerbaijan in order to do business in the country. The operating company also has some responsibilities, including management, coordination, implementation and conduct on behalf of the contractor. All terms relating to the operating company are the same for all PSAs signed between Azerbaijan and BP.

3.5 Block D-230

Their successful cooperation encouraged BP and SOCAR to agree a new PSA in May 2016. The PSA on Block D-230 was signed on 26 April 2018 in London, in the presence of Azerbaijan President Ilham Aliyev and UK Prime Minister Theresa May, as well as SOCAR President Rovnag Abdullayev and BP Group Chief Executive Bob Dudley. The main aim of the new PSA was to support new and ongoing relations between the parties, and promote further Caspian exploration opportunities in support of long-term production in Azerbaijan. The oil production periods are the same as those in the previous PSAs (initial exploration period; main exploration period; and development and production period). Block D230 lies some 135 kilometres northeast of Baku, in the Caspian Sea. It covers an area of 3,200 square kilometres and has not previously been explored. It has water depths of 400–600 metres and anticipated reservoir depths of approximately 3,000 metres.

4. Common features of PSAs

All of the PSAs discussed in this chapter have the same aim. Conversely, they all have their own specific terms and conditions alongside their similarities. In terms of taxation and costs, each PSA has its own tax regime, which is managed between the Ministry of Taxes and the contractor in accordance with the relevant domestic laws.[15] However, all contractors and sub-contractors are

15 Alum Bati, "Oil and Gas Taxation in Azerbaijan" (2004) 2(3) *Oil, Gas & Energy Law*.

subject to tax under the PSAs, relevant domestic law, tax protocols and social insurance and employment funds law.[16] Each PSA also provides for individual bonuses, which are divided into different categories (eg, the signature bonus, the development programme approval bonus and the production bonus). The approval times and the quantum of the bonus vary, as they are calculated individually for each PSA. In addition, after the Shah Deniz PSA was signed, other PSAs have required an acreage fee,[17] which varies depending on the agreement; the average acreage fee is approximately $1,200 to $2,000 per square kilometre.

The taxation also differs depending on the employees: Azerbaijani citizens are subject to domestic tax laws, while foreign employees are not. In addition, all contractors and subcontractors are exempt from VAT with credit, including on the import and export of all goods and services, as well as the export of oil and gas. Under most PSAs, contractors are exempt from mining tax; the general provision under the Tax Code imposes tax at a rate of 26% on crude oil production and at 20% on natural gas production.

In terms of environmental protection and safety, it is the responsibility of contractors to adhere to standards in this regard, which are set jointly by SOCAR and the Ministry of Ecology and Natural Resources.[18] Moreover, each PSA includes specific safety and protection measures, and highlights the importance of regular checking and monitoring in this sphere. The signatories to the PSA should also prepare:

- an environmental work programme that is sufficient to ensure safe operations;
- an environment plan; and
- an oil spill contingency plan.

Employee health and safety is another crucial factor, especially as regards employees who work in offshore fields, and this issue must be addressed alongside the environmental work programme. As a part of the development plan, the environmental work programme should also be approved by SOCAR.

IOCs should provide training to Azerbaijani employees who work under the PSA. This training can also take place outside the country, in which case all travel and training costs must be covered by the foreign company. This affords social and economic benefits for the host country, as national employees can expand their knowledge, which could help to advance the development of the Azerbaijani oil industry.

16 Namik Atamov, "Production Sharing Agreements (PSAs) in Azerbaijan and Taxation of Foreign Employees, KPMG Azerbaijan", KPMG (2000), www.us.kpmg.com/microsite/tax/ies/2000_Flash_Alerts/fa00-59.pdf4.

17 Shah Deniz PSA, Article 28 (Bonus Payments and Acreage Fee).

18 Shafag-Asiman PSA, Article 26.1 (Environmental Protection and Safety).

5. Conclusion

Having successfully cooperated with major IOCs for more than 25 years, the Azerbaijani government was willing to extend this cooperation in the hope of facilitating further achievements and advancements on both sides. This cooperation has played a key role in furthering the development of the Azerbaijani oil and energy industry, and the economy in general; and the attraction of major IOCs to the country has boosted the country's profile on the international stage.[19] In recent years, SOCAR's share of revenues has increased, as most of the cost recovery payments have already been made to investors. This is why the parties decided to extend the duration of the ACG agreement, which was initially signed for 30 years; the new contract will be valid until 2049 and should be more profitable for Azerbaijan than its predecessor.[20] In addition, Azerbaijan's location is very convenient for the transfer of production to other countries and makes it an attractive destination for investment. Contractual transparency also encourages foreign investors to enter Azerbaijan, as all PSAs are publicly accessible; nothing is hidden from the public. Meanwhile, IOCs have benefited from the considerable profits they have earned from their activities in Azerbaijan. This could thus be considered a win-win situation for both sides.

19 Moran (n 2).

20 Ingilab Ahmadov, "Ten questions about extension of massive Azerbaijan oil deal", National Resource Governance Institute, 20 October 2017, https://resourcegovernance.org/blog/ten-questions-about-extension-massive-azerbaijan-oil-deal.

Brazil

Paulo Henrique Reis de Oliveira
KINCAID | Mendes Vianna Advogados
Barbara Mourão Sachett
São Paulo University
Júlia Schütz Veiga
NOVA School of Law

1. Introduction

With more than 7,000 kilometres of coastline, Brazil is a key player in the international oil industry. In 2018 the country occupied 10th place in the global oil production rankings produced by the National Agency for Petroleum, Natural Gas and Biofuels (ANP).[1] It is thus an attractive destination for national and international investors.

Despite the current emphasis on investment in renewable energy, oil still plays a key role in international trade. The discovery of the *Pré-Sal* area[2] was a crucial and timely development for Brazil that will ensure the continued growth of the country's oil industry. These new oil fields are among the most important discoveries in the world in recent decades and have led to the development of new technologies by Petrobras, the Brazilian national oil company – especially technologies for deep-sea mining. Brazil thus now enjoys a strategic position in the international oil context.

With regard to these new oil fields – located in the *Pré-Sal* polygon – Brazil has decided that the best way to manage these resources is through the introduction of a production sharing regime. This type of agreement was pioneered by Indonesia in 1966[3] and today is one of the most common types of oil contracts.

This chapter examines the Brazilian production sharing agreement (PSA) and its legal aspects. Section 2 outlines preliminary considerations regarding the Brazilian oil industry and its main stakeholders. Section 3 provides a brief

1 ANP, *2018 Statistical Yearbook.*

2 According to Petrobras, the *Pré-Sal* is a sequence of sedimentary rocks formed over 100 million years ago, in the geographic space created by the separation of the ancient Gondwana continent. Between the two continents (America and Africa), great depressions were formed which gave rise to great lakes. The oil generating rocks of the pre-salt region were deposited here over millions of years. As the rivers of the continents that separated ran down to the lower regions, large volumes of organic matter were deposited there. When the continents drifted apart, the organic materials accumulated in the newly created gap, which was covered by the waters of the Atlantic Ocean. A layer of salt began to form there, which is now 2,000 metres thick. This salt layer was deposited on the accumulated organic matter, preserving it for millions of years, until thermochemical processes transformed the organic layer into hydrocarbons (oil and natural gas).

3 K Bindemann, *Production-Sharing Agreements: An Economic Analysis* (Oxford Institute for Energy Studies, 1999), p1.

explanation of the different forms of oil contracts used in Brazil, together with their pros and cons. Section 4 explains how the PSA operates under Brazilian law. Section 5 discusses the legislation that governs the Brazilian oil industry. Section 6 deals with dispute resolution and legal certainty, and highlights the complexities in this regard; and section 7 sets out some final remarks.

2. Historic overview: from monopoly to PSA

For most of Brazil's history, the federal government maintained a monopoly over all petroleum reservoirs,[4] with the noteworthy exception of retail distribution. In 1938, the National Petroleum Council was established (Decree-Law 395/38), and with it the first economic policy directed to oil trade. In 1953, Petrobras – the national company that runs the oil sector – was established (Articles 1 and 2 of Federal Law 2,004/53).

The 1975 oil crisis saw the first relaxation of the federal government's monopoly, when risk contracts (risk clause service contracts) were introduced. However, these ended with the enactment of the Federal Constitution in 1988: Article 177 maintained the federal government's monopoly and made no provision for risk contracts. But this changed in 1995, when Article 177 was modified by Constitutional Amendment 9/95 to open up the sector to private investment. Since then, private companies have been engaged to conduct activities that were previously reserved exclusively to Petrobras.

In 1997, the Oil Law (9,478/97) also entered into force, which marked a sea change in the oil sector in Brazil and the start of a fruitful period for the state. The political stability in Brazil facilitated a restructuring of the energy sector, which also attracted the attentions of foreign investors. The ANP[5] – the body that regulates the oil market – was also established under Presidential Decree 2,455/98. The decree also defined the various roles and positions within the hierarchical structure of the ANP, and transferred to it the control and management of all data relating to oil exploration and production in Brazil. In the last 10 years, the autonomy of the ANP has become more constrained, but the agency still plays a crucial role in regulating the oil industry. The limitation of its autonomy resulted

---

4 "The concept of monopoly consists in either the exclusivity in the domain, the exploration or the utilization of a particular good, service or activity" (our translation), ALM Silva, *Introdução ao Direito Econômico* (Forense, 2002), p191.

5 The ANP is the federal body responsible for regulating the oil and natural gas and biofuels industries in Brazil. Linked to the Ministry of Mines and Energy, it is a special federal agency that executes national policy for the sector, with a focus on guaranteeing fuel supply and defending consumer interests. The ANP regulates more than 110,000 companies active in everything from prospecting for oil and natural gas in Brazil's sedimentary basins to procedures to ensuring the quality of fuels sold to end consumers; the ANP continually monitors the compliance of these companies with established rules. The ANP also undertakes geological and geophysical studies of Brazilian oil and gas reserves; saves and organises the data collected in these studies; suggests to the government the areas to be auctioned; promotes bidding rounds and signs concession contracts on behalf of the federal government; authorises companies to build, operate and expand refineries and facilities for the processing and storage of natural gas and liquid products; and handles assignments to act in the administrative phases of the import and export process for oil, oil products and biofuels.

from the establishment of the National Energy Policy Council (CNPE).[6] This advisory body of the presidency formulates policies and guidelines to achieve goals relating to the rational use and management of energy resources. Since the enactment of CNPE Resolution 08/03, which established policies on oil production and set guidelines for conducting bids of exploration blocks, all bidding rounds promoted by the ANP have required the CNPE's approval.

Brazil has also conducted in-depth research of its continental shelf, collecting an abundance of data on Brazilian soil and subsoil. For example, Petrobras and the Brazilian Navy mapped the Brazilian coastline, colleting extensive bathymetric and seismic data. The aim was to submit a proposal for the extension of the Brazilian continental shelf to the Commission of Limits of the Continental Shelf. It was within this context that the *Pré-Sal* area was discovered. These areas (with low geological risk) pointed to a need for a better contractual regime to preserve national interests.

Thus, a new regime for the *Pré-Sal* area was established by Law 12,351/10, known as the '*Pré-Sal* Law'. This law also created a new national oil company, *Pré-Sal* Petróleo SA (PPSA), which is authorised to perform oil exploration and production without public bidding for up to five billion barrels. Under this new regulatory framework, all proposals must now be submitted to the president for approval. The CNPE remains responsible for establishing government oil policy; the Ministry of Mines and Energy (MME) also plays a key role under the *Pré-Sal* Law. Article 8 indicates that PSAs will be executed by the federal government through the MME, and the president has the final decision.

3. Exploration and production methods

There are three types of arrangements under which exploration and production take place in Brazil:

- concessions;
- PSAs; and
- onerous assignment.

The concession contract is a simple contract, based on a clear set of rules. To cover the costs and risks of exploring and producing oil and the payments made to the government during the contract, the hydrocarbons are transferred to the concessionaire for a specified period. While this type of arrangement has furthered the development of the Brazilian oil industry, it allows for little flexibility in setting royalties. The onerous assignment is a *sui generis* contract and is unique to Brazil.[7] This process made possible the capitalisation of Petrobras through the unexplored *Pré-Sal* area.

6 The CNPE is the former National Petroleum Council, created in 1938.
7 MR de Sá Ribeiro, *Energy Law and Regulation in Brazil* (Springer Publisher, 2018) p16.

The Brazilian PSA is more complex than many of its counterparts in other jurisdictions. The main difference between the concession and the PSA concerns the ownership of mining (ie, the state's ability to interfere in technical and economic decisions regarding the exploration and production process). The main criticisms of the PSA are as follows:

- It allows for only a single operation to be conducted, which limits the *Pré-Sal* and reduces competitiveness;
- PPSA has excessive power over the PSA (eg, the president of the consortium has half the votes and veto power); and
- Political instability can also prove problematic.

Complexities arise due to the interplay between the two types of contracts. Just as the integration of the legal regimes governing the water column and the soil and subsoil under the United Nations Convention on the Law of the Sea (eg, a sectoral approach versus an ecosystem approach) proved problematic, difficulties also arise in this scenario. The definition of the *Pré-sal* area (a polygon delineated by geographic coordinates) completely ignores the geological nature of the maritime area. This regime has also been adopted for other strategic areas, which necessitates interaction between more than one type of contract (ie, some oil fields that are not part of the *Pré-Sal* area fall within this regime). Thus, unitisation is required in cases involving transboundary fields, and this process can be tricky. The unitisation agreements aim to facilitate the preservation and development of a hydrocarbon deposit identified as a single unit, in order to guarantee its efficient production and avoid waste.[8] A joint operating agreement was established to manage the unitisation process.

So far, six production sharing rounds have been held, from 2013 to 2019. The changes introduced by the PSA resulted in a record in terms of signature bonuses and profit oil in the bids made from 2017 to 2019. However, the weak results of the sixth round indicate the need for a review of the rules, especially given the ongoing COVID-19 pandemic. The country also faces new competition from its neighbours, as Uruguay and Guyana have discovered new oil fields.

Key concepts in the PSA compound the government take, which are analysed further below. The main government participations are:

- the signature bonus;
- royalties;
- special participation;[9] and
- payments due to retention of the area (or to the owner of the land).

---

8 V Becker-Weinberg, *Joint Development of Hydrocarbon Deposits in the Law of the Sea* (Springer Publisher, 2014).

9 The special participation is not included in the PSA. It constitutes financial compensation in addition to the royalties levied on the net revenue of fields with large production volumes and high profitability, and is collected quarterly. The special participation is based on a progressive rate that is levied on the net revenue of the quarterly production of each field.

Royalties are a key source of government take. Under the concession contract, royalties can vary between 5% and 10%, according to the quotation of the reference price; whereas under the PSA, the rate can range up to 15%. The signature bonus constitutes the payment made by the company or consortium that wins the public bidding and is set by the ANP.

Brazil has one of the most relevant environmental law regimes in the world, although this is scattered across different laws. The following bodies have the power to act against potential or actual environmental hazards:

- the ANP, within its remit of promoting the preservation of the environment;
- the National Board of the Environment;
- the Ministry of Environment; and
- the Brazilian Institute of Environment and Renewable Natural Resources.

4. PSAs under Brazilian law

Historically, the federal government had a monopoly on the exploration of oil. However, in 1995, the Constitution was revised; and further legislative changes were introduced in 1997, in the form of the Oil Law. The first bidding under this regime took place in 1999.

While elsewhere in the world, contracts between governments and private companies began to be utilised in the 19th century and became more common in the 20th century, in Brazil it was not until the late 20th century that these types of contracts emerged. They are thus a relatively recent phenomenon in the Brazilian oil industry, having been used for just over two decades now. This is too short a period to have established a tradition in Brazilian contractual practice, so the drafting of these contracts is still evolving.

PSAs are the most recent type of arrangement, as these were only introduced to the national legal system following the discovery of the *Pré-Sal* area. The legislation that applies to PSAs was introduced in 2010, with the objective of ensuring greater control by the federal government over the *Pré-Sal* area.

In Brazil, PSAs are used for the exploration of oil, natural gas and other fluid hydrocarbons. They are defined by law as contracts under which the contractor carries out exploration, evaluation, development and production activities at its own risk. If these activities result in a commercial discovery, the contractor acquires the right to remove the appropriation of the cost in oil from the volume destined for the payment of royalties, and to share in the surplus oil. The oil received by the contractor is also taxed.

In general, therefore, the key principles of Brazilian PSAs do not differ significantly from their international counterparts, especially since the introduction of Law 13,365/16. According to the original wording of Law 12,351/10, Petrobras was the operator of all blocks and could not have a stake of less than 30% in the contracted consortium. Thus, a non-state company that sought to conduct exploration activities in Brazil under a PSA had to enter into a consortium contract with two state-owned companies: Petrobras and PPSA.

An obligation regime was thus imposed on Petrobras: the company had to have a participation of least 30% in all blocks regulated. This undertaking was particularly challenging for Petrobras: it could not analyse the economic viability of, and commercial interest in, certain areas, as the law simply required its participation regardless. Under this model, Petrobras was subject to complex and decentralised administrative activity. In parallel, the exploration of the *Pré-Sal* area was limited by the capabilities of Petrobras.

Given the difficulties presented by this regime, Law 13,365/16 amended the wording of Law 12,351/10 to remove the requirement on the mandatory participation of Petrobras; instead, Petrobras now has a right of first refusal. And even this right is now under discussion: if Bill 3,178/19 is approved, the state company will no longer have preference. This will give Petrobras greater autonomy over its investments and should make the country more attractive to foreign investors.

In all scenarios, the obligation to establish a consortium with PPSA remains, which distinguishes Brazilian PSAs from their international counterparts. Many commentators suggest that this reduces the role of private oil companies to that of a mere investor, which makes the undertaking less interesting.

4.1 Which companies can sign PSAs in Brazil?

The ANP governs the *Pré-Sal* bidding procedure, in accordance with Resolution 24/13. The process is very transparent, with opportunities for the public to participate in hearings prior to publication of the notice. So far, six rounds have been held. The seventh and eighth bidding rounds for the *Pré-Sal* area are under preparation. The notices are published in English and Portuguese; as are the contracts to be signed.

Both national and foreign legal companies engaged in commercial activity may participate. Investment funds, which do not have their own operating capacity, can participate only through consortia. Companies must inform their controlling partner, as well as the board of directors, in addition to presenting their constitutive acts and organisation charts.

The law of the country in which the bidder is constituted cannot provide grounds for maintaining the confidentiality of any of the requested information. However, tax and labour regularisation are necessary. It is also necessary to present an offer guarantee in the form of a letter of credit or guarantee insurance. Proof of technical capacity is additionally required. Foreign companies that participate in the bid must commit to establishing a company under Brazilian law with its headquarters and administration in Brazil, or to appointing a controlled company under Brazilian law, if they win the bid. Only a Brazilian company can sign the contract.

Once the bidders have submitted all necessary documentation and paid the fees, their bids will be evaluated by the ANP, which will classify them under one of the following categories, based on their technical and financial capabilities:

- Operator A: Can operate blocks in ultra-deep, deep and shallow waters, and on land;
- Operator B: Can operate in shallow waters and on land; and
- Non-operators: Can operate only in a consortium.

The contract is not a standard contract; it is a contractual instrument written by the ANP and presented when the notice is published. To participate in the bidding round, the bidders must agree to the terms of the contract, which is governed by Law 12,351/10.

5. Brazilian laws governing PSAs

In 1995, Constitutional Amendment 9 ended the federal government's monopoly on exploration and production activities, which had applied since the entry into force of the 1988 Federal Constitution.

Paragraph 1 of Article 177 of the Federal Constitution,[10] as amended by Amendment 9, allows private companies to carry out activities that were previously reserved exclusively to Petrobras. Thus, third parties can now be granted exploration and production rights over oil and natural gas deposits throughout the national territory.

The law referred to in the text of Constitutional Amendment 9 is the Oil Law, which was introduced in 1997 and has subsequently been amended over the years.

With the entry into force of the Oil Law, the right to conduct exploration and production activities was granted under the concession regime through contracts signed between third parties and the ANP, as a representative of the federal government.

Following the discovery of the Brazilian *Pré-Sal* area from 2005 to 2007, the government proposed a new regime for the grant of rights to conduct exploration and production activities in strategic areas; instead of the concession regime, it would develop a PSA regime. Since then, the *Pré-Sal* polygon has been the only strategic area demarcated by the federal government.

Law 9,478/97 was amended by Law 12,351/10, which established the PSA regime. According to this law, only Petróleo Brasileiro SA could act as an operator in the *Pré-Sal* polygon. In 2016, Law 9,478/97 was amended by Law 13,365/16, which replaced the mandatory participation and exclusivity requirements to which Petrobras was subject with a right of preference.

---

10 Article 177, paragraph 1: "The Union may contract with a state-owned company or a private enterprise to perform the activities provided for in Items I to IV of Article, with due regard for the conditions set forth by law" (our translation).

The Oil Law:

- governs the exploration and production of oil, natural gas and other fluid hydrocarbons in the *Pré-Sal* area and in strategic areas; and
- provides for the establishment of the Social Fund, and determines its structure and sources of funding.

According to Article 2 of the Oil Law, the PSA regime governs the exploration and production of oil, natural gas and other fluid hydrocarbons. Under this regime, the contractor carries out, at its own risk and expense, exploration, evaluation, development and production activities; and in the event of a commercial discovery, it acquires the right to appropriate the cost of oil, the volume of production corresponding to the royalties due, as well as a portion of the excess oil, in the proportion and under the conditions and terms established in the PSA. The oil cost is that portion of the production of oil, natural gas and other fluid hydrocarbons which is chargeable only in the event of a commercial discovery, corresponding to the costs and investments made by the contractor in carrying out the exploration, evaluation, development, production and deactivation activities, subject to the limits, terms and conditions established in the contract.

A bid for contracting under the PSA regime must comply with the provisions of the Oil Law, the rules issued by the ANP and the respective notice. The bidding notice must be accompanied by the basic draft of the respective contract.

Rights to conduct exploration and production activities under the PSA are granted through the execution of a production sharing contract between the federal government, represented by the MME, and the contracted third parties.

According to Article 27 of the Oil Law, the production sharing contract covers two phases:

- exploration, which includes the assessment of any eventual discovery of oil or natural gas to determine its commerciality; and
- production, which includes development activities.

According to Article 32 of the Oil Law, the production sharing contract may be terminated:

- upon the expiration of its term;
- by agreement between the parties;
- for the reasons set out in the contract;
- if the exploration phase ends without any commercial discovery, as defined in the contract;
- by exercise of the contractor's right of withdrawal during the exploration phase, provided that the minimum exploratory programme has been fulfilled or the amount corresponding to the unfulfilled portion is paid, as specified in the contract; or

- due to refusal to sign the production individualisation agreement, upon the ANP's decision.

Article 33 provides that an individualisation procedure for the production of oil, natural gas and other fluid hydrocarbons must be established where it is determined that the deposit extends beyond the block granted or contracted under the PSA regime. The contractor must inform the ANP that the deposit will be subject to a production individualisation agreement.

According to Article 34 of the oil law, the ANP will regulate the procedures and guidelines for the preparation of the production individualisation agreement, which must set out:

- the participation of each party in the individual deposit, as well as the hypotheses and criteria for its review;
- the development plan for the area that is subject to individual production; and
- dispute settlement mechanisms.

The ANP will monitor the negotiations between interested parties on the terms of the production individualisation agreement.

According to Article 37 of the Oil Law, where the deposits in the *Pré-Sal* area and strategic areas extend into areas that have not been granted or shared, the federal government – represented by the public company referred to in Article 8, paragraph 1 and based on the assessments carried out by the ANP – will conclude a production individualisation agreement with interested parties. The terms and conditions of this agreement will bind the future contractor under the PSA regime.

The production individualisation agreement will be subject to the prior approval of the ANP, which must be issued within 60 days of receipt of the proposed agreement.

The development and production of the deposit will be suspended until the production individualisation agreement has been approved, except in authorised cases under conditions defined by the ANP.

Article 42 of the Oil Law relates to government revenues under the PSA regime, and states that the PSA regime involves royalties and subscription bonuses as government revenues. The royalties must be paid monthly by the contractor in Brazilian reals, and apply to the production of oil, natural gas and other fluid hydrocarbons, calculated from the date of commencement of commercial production. The criteria for calculating the value of royalties will be established in an act of the federal executive authority, based on:

- the market price of oil, natural gas and other fluid hydrocarbons;
- the product specifications; and
- the location of the field.

According to Article 45 of the Oil Law, oil, natural gas and other fluid hydrocarbons destined for the federal government will be traded in accordance with the rules of private law, according to the marketing policy referred to in Items VI and VII of Article 9.

Article 47 provides for the establishment of the Social Fund, which is linked to the Brazilian presidency, and which promotes social and regional development by funding programmes and projects aimed at combating poverty and enhancing social development in the following areas:

- education;
- culture;
- sport;
- public health;
- science and technology;
- the environment; and
- mitigation and adaptation to climate change.

According to Article 48 of the Oil Law, the aims of the Social Fund are as follows:

- to facilitate constitute long-term public savings based on the revenues earned by the federal government;
- to serve as a source of funds for social and regional development, in the manner set out in Article 47; and
- to mitigate income and price fluctuations in the national economy resulting from variations in the income generated by exploration and production activities.

Article 49 provides that Social Fund resources comprise the following:

- that portion of the subscription bonus allocated to the Social Fund by the PSA;
- that portion of royalties which falls under the responsibility of the federal government, apart from that destined for specific government organs, as established in the PSA;
- revenues from the sale of oil, natural gas and other fluid hydrocarbons, as defined by law;
- royalties and special participation in the *Pré-Sal* area, as contracted under the concession regime for the direct administration of the federal government, subject to the provisions of Article 49, paragraphs 1 and 2;
- the return on financial investments, in cash and cash equivalents; and
- other resources allocated to the Social Fund by law.

6. Dispute resolution and legal certainty

The oil industry demands a very high degree of legal certainty in order to make exploration and production activities feasible. In addition to the significant investments involved, exploration is a long-term activity compared to other activities that attract foreign investment.

The applicable legislation must be objective, easy to understand and uniformly interpreted. The absence of legal certainty increases the cost of operations, deters foreign investors and reduces the value and permanence of investments.

Legal certainty is even more important in the context of PSAs, as the risk essentially falls on the contractor. This requires greater security in relation to everything from the public notice to the exercise of contractual clauses.

While Brazil has not adopted a standardised PSA, the Brazilian courts have sometimes experienced difficulties in the interpretation of standard contracts and the application of international precedents; however, these challenges have largely been overcome.

Undoubtedly, the main issue when disputes arise in relation to exploration of the *Pré-Sal* area is that either the Federal Court of Rio de Janeiro or the Arbitral Court may have jurisdiction, depending on the point in the relationship at which the dispute arises and the specific contractual clause to which it relates.

In the bidding phase, the competent court is the Federal Court of Rio de Janeiro. Thus, that court is competent to resolve disputes concerning:

- the corporate purpose;
- the constitution of a company that is governed by Brazilian law; and
- any other matter provided for in the public notice and in the bidding phase.

The Federal Court of Rio de Janeiro also has jurisdiction over the natural gas pledge contract.

The insurance required in the public notice involves a complex structure for the resolution of disputes. The general conditions of the Superintendence of Private Insurance provide for arbitration; but the specific conditions formulated by the ANP provide for the jurisdiction of the Federal Court of Rio de Janeiro. The public notice itself provides that specific conditions will prevail.

In Brazil, arbitration is fully applicable to available equity rights, including in disputes involving the public administration.

Law 12.351/2010, which regulates PSAs, provides for the resolution of disputes through arbitration. In this sense, the contracts formulated by the ANP, with or without the participation of Petrobras, include an arbitration clause.

The arbitration clauses in these contracts is open: that is, they do not specify a particular arbitral institution. However, they do include rules on the choice of arbitral chamber.

If the parties do not choose the arbitral institution by mutual agreement, it will be up to the ANP to choose between:

- the International Court of Arbitration;
- the London Court of International Arbitration; or
- the Permanent Court of Arbitration.

If the ANP does not make this choice, the contractor can select any of these institutions.

The choice of arbitration institution is thus relatively free, subject to the other contractual rules. However, the International Centre for Settlement of Investment Disputes has no jurisdiction in Brazil.

The arbitral tribunal will comprise three arbitrators, based in Rio de Janeiro, and Portuguese will be the official language of the proceedings. The proceedings must be public, although confidential information will be protected.

Urgent measures must be requested from the Federal Court, and arbitration must be instituted within 30 days of implementation of the precautionary measures.

The Federal Court of Rio de Janeiro has jurisdiction over contractual disputes that do not concern available equity rights.

As a result of this regime, a contractor must be comfortable with the prospect of both the state jurisdiction and arbitration. Furthermore, given that the arbitral institution may be freely chosen, it is not possible to know in advance of a dispute which arbitration rules will apply, as the rules vary by institution. The choice of arbitration as a dispute resolution mechanism is appropriate, given the specificity of oil and gas disputes and the equality afforded to the parties in arbitration. In addition, the procedure is less adversarial than litigation in the Federal Court.

However, in the context of PSAs, avoiding disputes in the first place is more important than resolving them. The Brazilian legal system has a series of rules that apply not only to the contract, but also to exploration and production activities, such as tax, environmental and labour rules.

Thus, the involvement Brazilian lawyers at all stages of the process – from study of the initial public notice to exercise of the contract – is essential. Compliance and preventive assistance are vital to maximise legal certainty.

7. Final remarks

There are some challenges associated with the PSA regime. While six bidding rounds have been held thus far, the results of the last round, held in 2019, were weak. Only one consortium – Petrobras with a Chinese company – entered a bid and thus won the most valuable block in the round at a relatively low price. This could be due to the current political instability in Brazil; or – as some commentators have pointed out – the Brazilian PSA regime may not be seen as affordable and competitive.

However, since 2017, the federal government and its regulatory body have been taking steps to improve the oil sector. The goal is to make the bidding rounds more attractive, in order to attract the interests of foreign investors and companies, while preserving the country's rights of sovereignty and its natural resources – guaranteed by the United Nations Convention on the Law of the Sea (Article 77) – for future generations. Oil production in Brazil has been continually increasing for decades, from 1.2 million barrels per day (b/d) in 2000 to three million b/d in 2020, according to Platts Analytics, which further predicts that production will increase by an additional one million b/d by 2040.

There have been recent discoveries in Latin America of deposits which are easier to exploit. Pre-salt exploration is very costly – hence the need for PSAs, which subject contractors to greater risk in their operations, in addition to the fluctuating oil price.

However, the future looks promising. Government officials at different levels and in different areas have conducted studies and made efforts to increase competitiveness. Legal certainty is increasing and arbitration is becoming more popular. Related services – notably maritime support – have been developed and modernised to serve an industry that is expected to grow further in the coming years.

Colombia

Julian Cardenas
University of Houston Law Center

1. Introduction

Today, Colombia is the third-largest oil producer in Latin America, just behind Brazil and Mexico; it displaced Venezuela from the top three following the collapse of Venezuelan oil production.

In January 2020, Colombia was producing 900,000 barrels of oil per day (b/d), fuelled by rising investments which at the time were projected to reach nearly $5 billion. This subsequently declined to 742,000 b/d due to the contraction in global demand caused by the COVID-19 global pandemic. By December 2020, however, production had recovered, reaching a yearly average of 800,000 b/d for 2020. However, Colombia faces key challenges in retaining investments and restoring production to the levels of 2012 and 2015, when it hit production records of one million b/d.

In 2021, hydrocarbons reserves stood at 1.77 million of barrels of oil equivalent, which provides a timeframe of 6.2 years of local production at current consumption levels. In addition, natural gas reserves stood at 3.1 trillion cubic feet, providing 9.8 years of local consumption. Thus, further investments are needed to address this decline in oil reserves, which could eventually turn Colombia into a net oil importer.

The need for further investment in oil and gas exploration has prompted the National Hydrocarbons Agency (ANH) to launch an assignment process through bid rounds as well as through a permanent process of assignment of areas. In this regard, the authorities must keep, for disposal to all interested parties, complete and updated information on all related regulations and projects, in order to increase investment opportunities through an open-door policy. Colombian investment needs have driven multiple policies and debates among key stakeholders, led by government agencies, the private sector and academia. The purpose of these discussions is to enhance the country's attractiveness to private and foreign investors.

The legal regime that governs oil investment in Colombia is based on the interconnectivity between Colombian law, exploration and production (E&P) contracts, international treaty law, global oil and gas industry practices, international arbitration law and jurisprudence. This is particularly true in the case of investments made by foreign investors, which can structure their investments through a transnational legal regime. A different situation may apply to local investors, whose investments are framed under Colombian law and the jurisdiction of national courts or domestic arbitration.

One of the issues that have captured the attention of local authorities is the continual improvement of E&P model contracts which have evolved over the years. In particular, the ANH has worked on multiple reviews of the ANH Exploration & Production Model Contract in order to adapt to changing market scenarios and the country's evolving E&P needs.

Unlike in Brazil, Mexico, Ecuador and Guyana, in Colombia, production sharing agreements (PSAs) have not been used as a standard form of contract. Before 2003, the Colombian E&P market was dominated by Ecopetrol, the Colombian national oil company, which entered into joint venture contracts called 'association contracts' that governed its partnerships with national and foreign investors. The ANH was established in 2003, amid a public debate on the appropriateness of association contracts to increase investments in the oil and gas sector. At the time, different PSA models were reviewed, as well as concession agreement forms; the latter option prevailed and was finally adopted by the ANH. As stated by ANH President Armando Zamora:

> *two possible contracts were considered to replace the association contract were discussed in a seminar in Cartagena in November 2003, the production sharing contract and the modern concession contract, and after consultations with the industry and the economic and administrative analyzes, it was concluded that the structure of the modern concession contract was more convenient given the circumstances of the Country and given the circumstances at the time.*[1]

However, principles from standard PSAs can be found in the previous association contracts, as well as in the current modern concession contracts, such as production sharing provisions under which, in certain circumstances, Ecopetrol or the ANH is entitled to oil production delivered in kind.

This chapter seeks to analyse the common principles of PSAs that are reflected in Colombian E&P contracts, as well as the contractual improvements proposed by the ANH to attract further investments in the oil sector.

2. PSA provisions in ANH E&P contracts

Colombian law does not require the adoption of a single kind of model contract, which gives the ANH flexibility to structure different formulae for participation and remuneration. The ANH works on the design of E&P model contracts, which are specifically designed to respond to investment needs. Examples include:

---

1 Testimony of ANH President Armando Zamora (2003-2011 and 2020 to present) in the arbitration case *Petrominerales Colombia v ANH*, Award, 2017.

- the contract for technical evaluation (seismic contract);[2]
- the E&P contract for onshore;
- the E&P contract for offshore; and
- more recently, the special contract for investigation projects (CEPI), for the development of non-conventional hydrocarbons.

Under these contracts, investors can operate, explore for and exploit hydrocarbons independently and at their own risk and cost, in compliance with Colombian regulations and good oil and gas industry practices.[3]

Under the E&P model contracts, the contractor owns the hydrocarbons produced, after deducting:

- a series of tiered royalties from 8% to 25%;
- the ANH participation in the production; and
- additional surface rights and taxes.

The contractor's remuneration can be agreed in a variety of forms, including rights, rates, a single or percentage periodic sum, or even a participation in the exploitation of the granted area. Thus, both contracting parties – the ANH and the contractor – receive a participation in the production results of E&P contracts.[4] The Colombian government's take is based on the benefits from the petroleum production through royalties, income tax, windfall taxes, production and revenue bonuses; while the contractor's take comprises reimbursement of operational costs, development costs and exploration costs and production profits.

According to the most recent model contract, where the ANH considers this appropriate, the contractor must make available to the ANH at the delivery point the percentage of hydrocarbon production established in the law that corresponds to royalties. This royalty collection can be done either in kind or in money, as determined by the ANH. If the ANH opts to receive royalties in kind, it will agree with the contractor on the terms and procedure for the storage and commercialisation of the production share. These terms can include the contractor's compensation for costs and a reasonable margin agreed by the parties. Oil production must be sold at the highest market price possible, while taking account of local supply market needs.

21.3 Participation in Production (X%)

21.3.1 In accordance with Article 84 of Agreement 2 of 2017 and Annex C, Number C.3 of this contract.

2 Technical evaluation contracts are short-term contracts for seismic studies and technical evaluation carried out by investors at their own risk, including seismic interpretation and the drilling of exploration wells, for a period of two years, which can be extended by the ANH.

3 Article 13 of ANH E&P Model Contract of 2021.

4 *Ibid*, Article 22.

22. Royalties

THE CONTRACTOR shall make available to the ANH, at the Delivery Point, the percentage of Hydrocarbon production established in the law corresponding to royalties. The collection of royalties will be done in kind or in money, as determined by the ANH.

22.1. Collection in kind: When the collection of Royalties is made in kind, THE CONTRACTOR will deliver to the ANH the corresponding amount of Hydrocarbons, for which the Parties will agree on the procedure for scheduling deliveries and other necessary aspects.

In any case, the ANH will have one (1) Month to withdraw said amount. Once this term has expired without the ANH having withdrawn the volume corresponding to the royalties, and if there is the availability of storage in the facilities of THE CONTRACTOR, the latter undertakes to store the Hydrocarbons for up to three (3) consecutive Months. In this case, the ANH will recognize a storage fee that, for each case, will be agreed upon between the Parties. If there is no agreement, this rate will be defined by the Ministry of Mines and Energy, or by the entity that regulates the transportation of Hydrocarbons in the country. At the end of this last period, THE CONTRACTOR may commercialize such volume, in accordance with numeral 22.3 and has the duty to deliver the product to the ANH.

CLAUSE 12 – ROYALTIES

12.1. Collection: *THE CONTRACTOR shall make available the percentage of the Hydrocarbon production set forth in the appropriate royalties law to the ANH in the Point of Delivery. Collection of royalties shall be made in cash or in kind, as per the competent authorities so establishes.*

12.2. Payment of participating interests: *ANH shall pay to entities provided by law the participating interests of royalties, as appropriate, and it shall be the only responsible for such payment.*

12.3. Collection in kind: *When the collection of royalties is made in kind THE CONTRACTOR shall submit to ANH the appropriate amount of Hydrocarbons, for which purpose the Parties shall agree the procedure for scheduling the deliveries and other needed issues. In all event, ANH shall have one (1) month to withdraw such amount. Once said term is due and ANH has not withdrawn the volume corresponding to royalties, and if there is storage availability at THE CONTRACTOR's facilities, he shall be bound to store said Hydrocarbons for up to three (3) consecutive months and ANH shall pay the storing fees which shall be* *agreed between Parties for each event. At the end of last term THE CONTRACTOR shall trade said volume pursuant to following section.*

16.4. Participation interests in production during extension of Exploitation Period: *In all extension events of Exploitation Period of the Exploitation Area, THE CONTRACTOR shall recognize and pay to ANH as the participation rights in production, an amount equivalent to ten percent (10%) of the production value of light Liquid Hydrocarbons at the Delivery Point, or five percent (5%) in the event of non-related Natural Gas or of Heavy Liquid Hydrocarbons, obtained by THE CONTRACTOR as of the expiration date of the initial term of the Exploitation Period and valued at the Delivery Point, after deducting the percentage corresponding to royalties. On said participation no economical rights mentioned in sections 16.1.2. and 16.2. shall be caused. During extension of Exploitation Period the rights for use of subsoil and for high prices mentioned in sections 16.1.2 and 16.2, respectively, shall only be caused on THE CONTRACTOR's volume after having deducted the participation right mentioned herein.*[5]

Failure to comply with the royalty terms and payments may be considered a breach of contract and a reason for unilateral termination of the contract by the ANH according to the terms of the contract.

A sliding scale of royalties from 5% to 25% will apply according to production levels.

3. High oil price right and contract extensions

The high oil price right was introduced as a mechanism to improve the government take where changing market conditions may result in a profit windfall. It was also a response to calls from investors for the replacement of the previous production allocation provisions, which involved the implementation of the R factor. In previous association contracts, after the contractor had deducted the percentages covering the royalty, the remaining hydrocarbons produced in each commercial field constituted the property of the parties in the proportion of 50% for Ecopetrol and 50% for the contractor, until the accumulated production of each commercial field reached 60 million barrels of liquid hydrocarbons, and applying the R factor as follows:

R factor – production sharing after royalties

0.0 to 1.0	*50*	*50*
1.0 to 2.0	*50/R*	*100-50/R*
2.0 or more	*25*	*75*

5 ANH Hydrocarbon Exploration and Production Contract – Luna Llena, 2005, www.sec.gov/Archives/edgar/data/313478/000119312506041151/dex1010.htm.

However, this formula reduced the number of barrels that investors could book in their financial statements. Thus, in 2003 the new ANH was requested to modify this clause in a way that allowed investors to pay in cash, so that they were better able to book reserves:[6] by including these in their financial statements, such companies could benefit from advantages such as enhanced company value and greater access to funding, among other things.

The ANH studied this request and duly structured the government take in a way in which its royalties would be captured by cash payments, while reserving its rights when payments in kind are requested.

These include its rights to participate and increase the government take at times of high oil prices through the exercise of the high oil price right, which will be triggered if the accumulated production of the exploitation area, including the volume of royalties, exceeds five million barrels of liquid hydrocarbons. If the West Texas Intermediate (WTI) price is higher than the price determined in the contract (the trigger is 30% over $27 per barrel for light crude oil and over $40 per barrel for heavy crude oil), the contracting party must pay, at an agreed delivery point, a participation for the production net of royalties. This additional royalty can be paid in cash or in kind, at the ANH's option.

In 2017 the high oil price right was analysed by the tribunal in *PetroMinerales v ANH*. The ANH attempted to apply the clause to the accumulated global oil production of a contractual area, but this was rejected by the tribunal on the grounds that the right is calculated based on the accumulated oil production of exploitation areas (subdivisions of a contractual area) where:

- there is an oil discovery;
- there is a declaration of the commerciality of a field;
- there is an exploitation area, since the right is predicated on each exploitation area;
- the accumulated production of the respective exploitation area, including the volume of royalties, exceeds five million barrels of liquid hydrocarbons; and
- the price of WTI crude exceeds the base trigger price.[7]

These conditions must be met cumulatively in order to trigger the obligation to pay the ANH the high oil price right. The tribunal clarified that the terms 'contractual area', 'exploration area' and 'commercial field' are different, and apply to different phases of the project. It thus confirmed that the productions of exploitation areas and commercial fields are calculated individually, and

---

6 Testimony of Tomás de la Calle in the arbitration case *Petrominerales Colombia v ANH*, Award, 2017.
7 *Petrominerales Colombia v ANH*, Award, 2017.

cannot be added together to determine the high oil price right in favour of the ANH. In this case, which concerned PetroMinerales' contractual area of CORCEL, only two of eight exploitation areas were subject to the high oil price right; the right did not apply to the other six.[8]

4. Contract production extensions

The ANH can approve production extensions that will result in greater economic benefits for the state. Thus, contract production extensions will afford additional economic rights to the ANH in the form of an additional participation share. The extension could also include the development of fields, new exploitation projects and the use of new technologies.

In the case of the extension of the production period, the economic rights for the use of the subsoil and the high oil price right are applied to the volume of production owned by the contractor only once the production participation rights have been discounted or subtracted (X%), and additional participation in production has been calculated.[9]

5. Programmes for the benefit of local communities

Programmes for the benefit of communities (PBCs) consist of activities and/or social projects defined by the contractor within the framework of its contractual obligations, in response to the needs of the populations located in the area of interest of the PBC, during exploration, evaluation, development and production activities.

The investment in the development of PBCs must be at least equivalent to 1% of the total value during each of the different phases of the contract. The contractor may allocate a maximum of 10% of the PBC for administrative expenses; the remaining 90% must be allocated to the development of the PBC.

6. Abandonment fund

Until final completion of the project, the contractor must schedule and undertake, in a timely, effective and efficient manner, each abandonment activity as a consequence of exploration or production activities in accordance with Colombian law, contractual provisions, the abandonment programme and the good practices of the petroleum industry.

In order to fulfil this obligation, the contractor must establish an abandonment fund to cover the execution of the abandonment programme, in order to restore the area according to Colombian regulations and the terms of the contract.

---

8 *Ibid.*

9 ANH E&P Model Contract 2021.

7. International arbitration

For years, the ANH insisted on the jurisdiction of the local courts or on domestic arbitration under the rules of arbitration of the Chamber of Commerce of Bogota for international business and foreign investors. This was accepted by oil and gas companies at the time, which thus agreed to submit their investments to national courts[10] or to domestic arbitration;[11] however, some also structured their investments in a way that allowed them to resort to international investment arbitration through the protection of an international investment treaty. However, international arbitration treaty claims do not always extend jurisdiction to contract claims, so in recent years international companies have insisted on the inclusion of international arbitration clauses in contracts.

It took a lengthy dialogue between government agencies and industry actors – including professional associations and academics – to introduce a standard international arbitration provision in the ANH E&P contract aligned with international arbitration practices.[12] This change was also facilitated by Presidential Directive 4 of President Iván Duque of 18 May 2018,[13] which provided clarification, in relation to Article 62 of the Arbitration Law (1563/2021), that international arbitration is possible where one of the following criteria is met:

- The parties to an arbitration agreement are domiciled in different states at the time the arbitration agreement is entered into;
- A substantial part of the obligations of the commercial relationship are performed outside the state in which the parties are domiciled; or
- The dispute affects the interests of international trade.

These criteria can easily be met, as complex and sophisticated legal transnational transactions are common practice in the Colombian oil and gas sector.

Arbitration Clause

*[*** At the time of entering into the Contract, the Parties will determine if one or more of the assumptions indicated in article 62 of Law 1563 of 2012 are met and, consequently, they will determine whether the arbitration is international or*

---

10 See ANH E&P model contracts before 2018.

11 See ANH E&P model contracts after 2018.

12 Different institutions such as the *Asociación Colombiana de Petróleo* participated in discussions, forums and events in order to promote international arbitration for E&P contracts with foreign corporations. This was also promoted by events of the *Centro Minero Energético de la Universidad Externado*, as well by international companies investing in Colombia. See also Julian Cardenas, "'Lex Petrolea Offshore', a presentation at the Agencia Nacional de Hidrocarburos (ANH) de Colombia, Bogotá, April 2017", *ANH Newsletter*, April 2017. The presentation explained the transnational elements of E&P operations and its connection with the practice of international arbitration as a neutral and independent system of dispute resolution adapted for transnational oil and gas investments.

13 Presidential Directive 4, *Diario Oficial* 50.597, 18 May 2018.

*national. Depending on said determination, they will adopt in its entirety one of the following clauses: If the determination is that the arbitration is international, it should proceed according to the Presidential Directive No. 4 of May 18, 2018. ***]*

Arbitration clause of international arbitration

23.2.1. Unless otherwise provided in this Contract, all disputes relating to this Contract, or arising from or related to it, including the economic consequences of administrative acts issued in the exercise of exceptional powers, will be resolved by a court of arbitration (the "Tribunal") through international arbitration, in accordance with the following rules:
23.2.1.1. The Tribunal will be subject to the latest published version of the International Chamber of Commerce Arbitration Rules (the "ICC Rules") and will be administered by the ICC.
23.2.1.2. The Tribunal will be composed of three (3) arbitrators appointed in accordance with the ICC Rules.
23.2.1.3. The referees must meet the following qualities:
23.2.1.3.1. They may have any nationality;
23.2.1.3.2. They must be lawyers duly authorized to exercise law in any jurisdiction;
23.2.1.3.3. They must have experience in the resolution of conflicts through arbitration and in the matter that raises the controversy;
23.2.1.3.4. They must act diligently and in good faith in the conduct of arbitration proceedings.
23.2.1.4. The Court will decide in law.
23.2.1.5. The language to be used in the arbitration proceedings, in the parties' briefs, in the hearings and in any award, decision or communication issued by the Tribunal will be Spanish, with the possibility of obtaining simultaneous translation into another language at the cost of the party that requires such service.
23.2.1.6. All face-to-face hearings must be held in Bogotá D.C., Colombia.
23.2.1.7. The seat of the arbitration will be Bogotá D.C., unless the Parties, by mutual agreement, choose a different seat, prior to the arbitration.
23.2.1.8. The law on the merits of the controversy will be the law of the Republic of Colombia.
23.2.1.9. The Court will decide on the confidentiality of the arbitration process or any other matter related to arbitration, taking into account what the applicable law establishes in this regard.

This clause not only provides access to international arbitration under the rules of the International Chamber of Commerce (ICC), but also gives the parties the option to select an arbitration seat outside Colombia. This is important as foreign investors can assess whether the 1958 New York Convention on the Recognition and Enforcement of Foreign Arbitral Awards applies to the arbitration, and whether it is appropriate that an annulment procedure against a potential arbitration award issued in Bogota would fall under the jurisdiction of the Colombian courts. Thus, the option to select a seat abroad is an incentive to oil and gas companies, which may choose a different seat to avoid the Colombian courts having jurisdiction over an annulment procedure against an arbitration award.

An additional element of internationalisation of the E&P contract is the incorporation by reference of Article 21 of the 2021 ICC Arbitration Rules,[14] which affords wide discretion to an arbitration tribunal to apply not only the substantive law agreed by the parties – in this case, Colombia law – but also the rules of law which it determines to be appropriate, as well as the provisions of the contract and relevant trade customs, with reference to generally accepted international oil and gas industry practices.[15]

8. Autonomy clause and good oil industry practices

The operator is exclusively responsible for planning, preparing for, performing and controlling the oil and gas activities. It has full and direct technical and management autonomy, according to Colombian law, and must strictly observe the good practices of the oil industry.[16] To this end, Ministry of Mines and Energy Resolution 40185/2020 includes an appendix of references to the good practices of the international oil industry. However, this is intended merely as a reference, and will not excuse the operator from its obligation to implement the appropriate generally accepted oil industry practices. Should the operator decide to modify the technology that it has agreed to implement or to alter any of its components, it must inform the ANH of the reasons, justifications and effects of this modification, and obtain the agency's approval for it.[17]

Hence, the operator remains accountable for the identification, selection and implementation of good oil industry practices to achieve the maximum economic benefit and reserve recovery, minimising losses and environmental damages.[18]

9. Investment treaty protection

Like most oil-producing countries, Colombia has a network of international

---

14 See the arbitration clause in the ANH E&P Model Contract 2021.

15 ICC Arbitration Rules, Article 21. Julian Cardenas, *Lex Petrolea Offshore* (Transnational Petroleum Law Institute, 2012), www.lexpetrolea.org. Also, John Bowman, "LEX PETROLEA: Sources and Successes of International Petroleum Law", King & Spalding, 13 February 2015, www.kslaw.com/blog-posts/lex-petrolea-sources-successes-international-petroleum-law.

16 ANH E&P Contract – Non-conventional hydrocarbons 2021, Article 11.

17 *Ibid*, Article 33.

18 ANH E&P Model Contract of 2021, Article 13.

trade and investment treaties that afford additional protection to foreign investors that invest in the hydrocarbons sector.[19] The country is also member of the 1965 Washington Convention, which affords access to investment arbitration at the International Centre for Settlement of Investment Disputes (ICSID).[20]

Since 2016, foreign investors have initiated 14 claims against the Colombian state in the mining, telecommunications, banking and oil and gas sectors.[21] Investors have used bilateral investment treaties (BITs) and international trade agreements that include investment protection provisions to file claims against the state for violation of international obligations under these treaties, including claims relating to indirect expropriation, violation of fair and equitable treatment and breach of legitimate expectations.

A landmark case for Colombia involved mining country Glencore. In 2019, an ICSID tribunal found that Colombia had frustrated the legitimate expectations of the Swiss mining company and its investment in Colombia in breach of the non-impairment and fair and equitable clauses of the Colombia-Switzerland BIT due to the imposition of arbitrary fiscal controls by local authorities. The tribunal ordered Colombia to pay Glencore over $19 million in compensation plus interest, roughly half of its legal costs and the full arbitration costs.[22]

10. Fines for breach of contract

If the contractor partially fails to comply with its obligations under the contract, the ANH may impose fines of up to twice the value of the non-compliant activity.

If the value of activities cannot be calculated, a fine of $50,000 will be imposed for the first breach, $100,000 for the second breach and so on, with the value of the fine doubling up to the value of the guarantee, at which point the ANH may unilaterally terminate the contract without having to resort to the default procedure. Fines will be imposed on the contractor in the following situations:

- unjustified suspension of operations;
- failure to deliver the technical information required by the ANH in accordance with the provisions of the contract;
- failure to provide any information required by the ANH;

19 United Nations Conference on Trade and Development – Colombian International Trade and Investment Treaties, https://investmentpolicy.unctad.org/international-investment-agreements/countries/45/colombia.

20 Presidential Directive 4. *Diario Oficial* 50.597, 18 May 2018, also makes reference to the practice of investment arbitration and distinguishes between commercial arbitration (contractual arbitration) and investment arbitration (treaty arbitration).

21 ICSID case database, https://icsid.worldbank.org/cases/case-database.

22 *Glencore v Colombia*, ICSID Arbitration Award, 2019.

- the provision of information to the ANH that contains manifest errors or omissions;
- failure to deliver the exploitation plan to the ANH within the timeframe specified in the contract;
- failure to pay the economic rights due to the ANH within the specified timeframe;
- failure to maintain the insurance required under Colombian law or by the good practices of the petroleum industry, whether by the operator, its subcontractors and/or the designated operator; or
- any other circumstance or facts that, at the discretion of the ANH, do not comply with its obligations under the contract or under current Colombian legislation.[23]

The ANH keeps a record and publishes details of the fines imposed on oil and gas contractors; this information is publicly accessible on its website.

11. Pilot projects under CEPI contracts for non-conventional hydrocarbons

Colombia is currently debating whether to allow the development of non-conventional hydrocarbons. The implementation of hydraulic fracturing ('fracking') is a socially and politically controversial topic, not least due to the environmental implications.[24] Pilot projects are being run in order to minimise the risks associated with hydrocarbon activity and improve the provision of information to the public, to prevent scientific matters from being politicised in a way that could significantly affect and compromise Colombia's energy security.

Colombia requires investment in non-conventional hydrocarbons in order to increase its oil and gas reserves. To this end, a number of pilot projects have been approved under CEPI contracts in order to tap the potential afforded by Colombia's non-conventional resources in the short term, while offshore developments remain far off on the horizon.[25]

The ANH has awarded CEPI contracts for the development of non-conventional hydrocarbons to Ecopetrol, Exxon and Drummond.[26] The

---

23 ANH Presentation on Fines and Sanctions, www.anh.gov.co/hidrocarburos/Paginas/Multas-y-Sanciones.aspx.

24 Maria Isabel Ortiz, "*Prueba Clave que llegó al Consejo de Estado Abre Debate*", *Diario El Tiempo*, March 2020, www.eltiempo.com/justicia/investigacion/informe-de-fracking-de-universidad-nacional-y-debate-en-el-consejo-de-estado-478284.

25 While for onshore projects the exploration phase has a duration of six years and the production phase has a duration of 24 years, the exploration phase for offshore projects has a duration of nine years, or three years for areas where reserves has been discovered but not developed. This puts the timeframe for new offshore projects at a decade at minimum. Once a commercial discovery is declared, the production period has a duration of 30 years according to Clauses 4.2. and 5.2 of the ANH Offshore E&P Model Contract.

contracts aim to test fracking technology and international industry practices in order to confirm the environmental and economic feasibility of this technique in Colombia. Upon being awarded a CEPI contract, the contractor must apply for an environmental licence before commencing operations.

The pilot projects are conceived as temporary scientific and technical experiments aimed at:

- collecting social, environmental, technical and operational information on non-conventional reservoirs, which require the use of multi-stage fracking with horizontal drilling for their extraction;
- enhancing institutional knowledge;
- encouraging citizens' participation and promoting greater transparency and access to information; and
- evaluating the potential impact of non-conventional hydrocarbon resources and techniques.

If the studies confirm the feasibility of non-conventional hydrocarbon exploitation, the contractor may exercise the area nomination right set out in the CEPI contract and governed by ANH Agreements 6/2020 and 4/2021 in order to have the area of interest assigned, and sign a contract or additional contract for the exploration and production of hydrocarbons in non-conventional reservoirs.

To exercise the area nomination right, the contractor must meet the following conditions:

- It has undertaken the necessary investigatory and operational activities to determine the dimensions of the field in accordance with Colombian regulations;[27] and
- It can prove that its activities will comply with the applicable legal regime for the development of non-conventional reservoirs.

Contractors that successfully overcome the technological, environmental, social and political challenges of using fracking techniques will have the right to develop these resources once an E&P contract has been signed for the contracted area.

The oil industry is awaiting a final decision from the State Council – the country's highest administrative court – on the validity of Decree 3005 and Resolution 90341, which set out the regime that will govern the future implementation of fracking and horizontal drilling techniques.

---

26 ANH website, www.anh.gov.co.

27 Resolution 40185/2020 of the Ministry of Mines and Energy.

Ecuador

Carlos Manosalvas Silva
Manosalvas & Partners Abogados

1. The history of oil exploitation in Ecuador

The word 'oil' has various connotations: from prosperity, employment and opulence to violence, power struggles and environmental destruction. Perhaps the best definition of 'oil' is 'black gold' – a commodity which enriches and allows for business and trade all around the world.

Oil and its by-products have been used throughout Latin America for centuries. For example, the Inca empire – which also extended to modern-day Ecuador – used it to coat the bottoms of their boats, for medicinal purposes and in shamanic rituals.

Oil exploration and exploitation began in Ecuador in 1859, when asphalt was first discovered in Loreto, in the province of Orellana in the Amazon region of the country. However, it was not until the early 1900s that exploration and exploitation began in the Santa Elena peninsula, located in the province of Santa Elena in the coastal region of Ecuador. Several oil companies benefited from oil concessions or leases in this region.

According to sociologist Henry Llánes Ampudia Suarez,[1] Anglo Ecuadorian was one of the companies that exploited Ecuador's hydrocarbon fields until they were depleted over a period of 50 years. This oil was considered the best in the world by some, as it had an American Petroleum Institute gravity of 40. The profit percentage agreed with Anglo Ecuadorian was 99% for the company and 1% for the Ecuadorian state. Both Carolina Oil Co and Cautivo Petrolera Ecuatoriana also benefited from hydrocarbon exploitation in the Santa Elena peninsula. This area is now a desert, which many researchers attribute to the environmental impact of oil exploitation; although a detailed technical investigation would be necessary to verify this.

In 1911 the Mining Code was enacted, establishing oil as state property. This was a major development, as it meant that all exploitation activities now had to be authorised by the Ecuadorian state.

In 1964, during the *de facto* government of the military junta, the Texaco-

1 Llanes Suárez Henry, *Contratos Petroleros. Inequidad en el reparto de la producción* (Second edition, 2008), p21

Gulf consortium was granted a concession for around one million hectares in the Amazon region for a period of 10 years, extendable for further 10-year periods; the concession ultimately allowed for 40 years of oil exploration and exploitation.

It was not until 1967 that new oil reserves were discovered in the Amazon region by the Texaco-Gulf consortium. This is when the exploitation of oil in the Amazon region began.

From the 1960s onwards, the exploitation of oil was promoted by the military or *de facto* government of General Guillermo Rodríguez Lara, which endeavoured to encourage production. However, with the passing of time, as normally happens, changes in government led to changes in policies – and even the law – in this field.

In the 1970s, Ecuador's oil policy changed drastically and new guidelines were established – to such an extent that in 1972, oil began to be managed as a natural resource of the state without the intervention of foreign companies. In 1972, the Corporación Estatal Petrolera Ecuatoriana (Ecuadorian State Petroleum Corporation) (CEPE) was also established to undertake several activities, including the construction of the Esmeraldas state refinery, located in the province of Esmeraldas in the coastal region of Ecuador. CEPE also acquired shares in the Texaco-Gulf consortium to become the majority shareholder; and, most importantly, it was tasked with overseeing the exploration, transportation, storage, industrialisation, refining and commercialisation of oil and its by-products in Ecuador. That same year, Ecuador also became a member of the Organization of the Petroleum Exporting Countries (OPEC).

In the 1980s, different types of contracts were created which reflected different policies and points of view, as will be discussed later in this chapter. Crucially, they did not provide for Ecuador to receive royalties and were thus harmful to the national economy. However, by the 1990s, Petroecuador (the institution that replaced CEPE) had completely recovered, and the development of the oil sector really took off.

During the 1990s, different governments adopted different policies on the oil sector. From 1992 to 1996, the government of President Sixto Duran Ballén introduced new regulations which allowed for the possibility of privatisation. Previously, this was precluded by constitutional and legal regulations. The new regulations triggered a sea change in Ecuador: they captured more wealth under a neoliberal policy; facilitated the revision of oil contracts; aimed to encourage foreign investment; extended the term of both exploration and exploitation contracts; and allowed for the creation of so-called 'participation' contracts and 'marginal oil field' contracts. As a result of this excess of contracts and wealth, several officials – including senior figures in government – ended up embroiled in political trials for irregular actions. In an unfortunate mistake, the Ballén government also orchestrated Ecuador's withdrawal from OPEC.

The government of President Abdalá Bucaram lasted only six months, from 1996 to 1997, but introduced some important changes nonetheless. Bucaram modified the service provision contract for participation in Block 16 without consulting on or analysing how the conditions of that contract could be improved, which was unhelpful for the Ecuadorian economy.

From 1997 to 1998, the interim government of President Fabián Alarcón entered into profit sharing contracts to transfer various fields to oil companies, as required by law.

From 1998 to 2000, the government of President Jamil Mahuad Witt switched from service provision contracts to participation contracts in some blocks. It also entered into contracts for marginal oil fields with foreign companies.

From 2000 onwards, the Hydrocarbons Act was reformed by the government of Gustavo Novoa and there were further switches from service provision contracts to participation contracts in some blocks. Strategic alliance agreements were prioritised, with the aim of allowing them to be signed directly rather than through a bidding process.

A key development occurred in 2009, when – after 21 years of being a state-owned company – Petroecuador was transformed into a public company; it thus became a single company, rather than merely a holding company as previously. The new Constitution, enacted in 2008, set a clear objective to guarantee state participation in all hydrocarbon-related activity, so that the losses and abuses that had occurred in other decades would never be repeated.

Today, depending on the situation, oil contracts are awarded in different forms, but service provision contracts are generally favoured over participation contracts.

2. Forms of oil contracts in Ecuador

A number of different types of oil contracts have been established in accordance with the provisions of the Hydrocarbons Act.

Throughout its history, Ecuador has entered into the following main types of contractual arrangements in the oil sector:

- service provision contracts;
- participation contracts;
- operational alliances;
- specific service contracts;
- contracts for additional exploration and exploitation of marginal oil fields;
- strategic alliances;
- exploration of unified and shared fields; and
- the establishment of mixed economy companies.

From the 1930s to the 1970s, concession contracts were signed by the various governments in power. From the 1970s to the 1980s, partnership contracts were primarily used. From the 1980s to the 1990s and in the early 21st century, service provision contracts with non-reimbursable costs were primarily used. From the 1990s to 2010, participation contracts were signed. The current law provides for the use of service provision contracts, with a fee; while efforts are being made to modify existing participation contracts in accordance with Executive Decree 449 and supported by Article 2 of the Hydrocarbons Act.[2]

This approach is based on Article 312 of the Constitution,[3] which recognises hydrocarbons as part of the strategic sector and thus the right of the state to regulate, administer, control and manage them. Such control is exercised through Empresa Pública de Hidrocarburos del Ecuador (the Public Hydrocarbons Company of Ecuador). Essentially:

- all contracts must be entered into a manner that benefits the state;
- the state can form alliances with other states, and thus establish mixed companies, in order to increase its participation; and
- the state can enter into contracts for the exploration and exploitation of hydrocarbons – an activity previously carried out by Petroecuador – as a counterparty to the private companies in the contracts.

The different contract models used in Ecuador are discussed further below.

2.1 Concession contracts

Concession contracts were the first form of oil contracts entered into in Ecuador. They are based on territory: the contractor has an exclusive right to exploitation in the territory for which the concession was granted. This type of contract was damaging for Ecuador in all senses, as the state profited only through taxes and royalties, or where the state held some equity interest in the company; they did not compensate the state for the exploitation profit that the concessionaires enjoyed, thus jeopardising the state's interests in the future. These types of contracts were entered into due to the government's inexperience at the time.

2.2 Partnership contracts

The Hydrocarbons Act defines a 'partnership contract' as a contract under

---

2 Article 2 of the Hydrocarbons Act reads:

> *the State shall explore and exploit the deposits indicated in the previous article directly through the Public Hydrocarbon Companies. Exceptionally, it may delegate the exercise of these activities to national or foreign companies with proven experience and technical and economic capacity, for which purpose the Secretariat of Hydrocarbons may enter into partnership contracts, participation contracts, service provision contracts for the exploration and exploitation of hydrocarbons, or other contractual forms of delegation in force in Ecuadorian legislation. Mixed economy companies may also be formed with national and foreign companies of recognised competence legally established in the country.*

3 Constitution of the Republic, *Official Gazette* 449 dated 20 October 2008.

which the state, through the Secretariat of Hydrocarbons, grants rights over areas, fields, hydrocarbons or other patrimonial rights; and under which the partner company commits to make the investments agreed by the contracting parties.

The Hydrocarbons Act also states that if areas are abandoned or fully returned due to unproductivity, the Secretariat of Hydrocarbons will not owe the associated company anything and the contractual partnership will be terminated. Importantly, in these types of contracts, the parties must agree on the extent to which each will participate in the results of production. This definition is established in Articles 13 to 15 of the Hydrocarbons Act.

2.3 Participation contracts

Participation (or association) contracts are based on Decree 449/2018. The state is integral to this type of contract, as one of the parties thereto; the counterparties are national and foreign companies legally incorporated in Ecuador. Dr Monserrath Barreno[4] describes the characteristics of this type of contract as follows:

> *a) that the State shall have a share in the contracts no less than 12.5% of the total audited production, b) the Contractor assumes on its own account and risk all the investments, costs and operating expenses required for the exploitation, development and production of the contract area, c) the State will participate in the benefits from the use of these resources, in an amount that will not be less than the benefits of the contractor that exploits them, d) State benefits: accumulated income established in article 11 of the Executive Decree and e) as benefits of the Contractor there is accumulated net current annual cash income associated with the contract.*

Under this type of contract, the contractor assumes all costs (ie, capital and operating costs) at its own risk.

2.4 Profit sharing contract

In 1998, the interim government of President Fabián Alarcón introduced so-called 'profit sharing contracts'.

Production or profit sharing contracts are found in the Hydrocarbons Act. This type of contract was established specifically to attract international investors to Ecuador's oil and gas sector. Eight blocks in the Amazon region were included in the Intercampos licensing round, in order to encourage investors to opt for contracts other than service contracts. These contracts have a 20-year duration over 2,500 hectares.

---

4 Dr Monserrath Barreno, partner of Quevedo & Ponce Abogados Ecuador: "The oil contracts in Ecuador will be carried out under the form of participation"; Quevedo & Ponce Abogados, 17 August 2018, www.quevedo-ponce.com/los-contratos-petroleros-en-ecuador-se-realizaran-bajo-la-modalidad-de-participacion/.

Article 18A of the Hydrocarbons Act states that shared management contracts are those signed by the Ecuadorian state, through Petroecuador, with public or private national or foreign companies or consortiums of companies, with the aim of:

- increasing and optimising the production of hydrocarbons;
- maximising the recovery of their reserves; and
- conducting exploration and exploitation activities in the area covered by the contract.

According to the regulations, the selected company or consortium will undertake all investments and technology transfers at its own risk. These operations must be carried out by Petroecuador through its subsidiary Petroproducción and/or the selected company or consortium.

The essential point in these contracts is that in no case will the state's share of incremental production[5] be less than 40%. Each tender is different, and thus a higher participation percentage may also apply, depending on the characteristics of the field and the evaluation factors.

Ecuador's hydrocarbon regulations provide that, with respect to profit sharing contracts, if the operations are to be carried out by the selected company or consortium, they must be carried out with input from the necessary personnel from Petroproducción, an affiliate of Petroecuador, and the facilities of the respective field. This requirement will apply for the duration of the corresponding operating agreement. Private companies must cover all costs, amortisations, depreciations, employers' obligations, labour participations and other obligations as are determined in each contract, as well as their tax obligations in accordance with the law.

A special feature of profit sharing contracts is that partners are selected by public tender, which is announced by issuing a call to tender through newspapers or the press. Contractors will be selected in light of their financial economic capacity and their experience, in addition to the offers that are submitted. To this end, a technical report will be prepared through the relevant state body, which will be sent to a tender committee so that it can award the contract to the winning bidder.

If the contractor discovers reserves once the profit sharing contract has been signed, this discovery cannot be added to the contract and a new one must be signed.

Profit sharing contracts must include clauses on the following points:

- the identities of the contracting parties;

---

5 Incremental production is understood as that which is above the base production curve defined by Petroecuador, which should consider the historical average annual rate and the future projection that current proven reserves allow.

- the term of the contract;
- the participation of the state, which must be at least 40% of the incremental production, as stipulated in the Hydrocarbons Act;
- technical reports and all documents that served as the basis of the contractual stage, and;
- guarantees from the consortium.

The only example of a profit sharing contract that the author has found to date relates to the Palo Azul field contract, and was signed on 2 August 2002 between Petroproducción, Ecuadortlc SA, Cayman International Exploration Company and Petro Manabi SA.[6]

2.5 Contracts for the exploitation of marginal oil fields

Fields that have low-quality crude are defined as 'marginal' – that is, fields with low economic capacity or where the exploitation techniques would be very expensive.

Based on this definition, contracts for the exploitation of marginal oil fields are those in which the state grants the contactor the right to explore and exploit such marginal fields. From this point, a crude baseline is established which is the exclusive property of the state, and the costs that the contractor invests in the operation are recognised; however, if the volume of production exceeds the baseline, both the state and the contractor can distribute this surplus in accordance with the signed contract and the established percentages.

These contracts were signed in particular by the governments of Jamil Mahuad and Alfredo Palacios, in relation to fields such as Bermejo, Pindo, and Tiguino.

2.6 Contracts for specific works or services

Contracts for specific works or services are governed by the Hydrocarbons Act. They are defined as contracts under which a legal entity agrees to execute specific works or services on behalf of CEPE (or the relevant state authority at the time), providing the necessary technology, capital and equipment or machinery to fulfil the obligations assumed in exchange for a fee or monetary compensation, the amount and form of payment of which will be agreed upon by the parties in accordance with the law.

So-called 'alliance contracts' derive from this type of contract, as well as from unified exploration agreements.

---

6 Exploitation was established in Block 18, located 180 kilometres from Quito, in the Amazon region. This region initially had reserves of 100 million barrels; but due to exploitation, this decreased over time. This field was declared a shared field in 2000. In 2002, the shares of the different companies were transferred to Brazilian state-owned company Petrobras. In 2005, the shares were transferred to Japanese company Teikoku. Several legal actions were taken against Ecuador by the companies that invested and signed the relevant contract concerning the Palo Azul field. These companies filed a lawsuit internationally claiming that they had been harmed. Today, the Palo Azul field is entirely state owned.

2.7 Service provision contracts

Service provision contracts for the exploration and/or exploitation of hydrocarbons are contracts under which previously and duly qualified legal entities, whether national or foreign, enter into a partnership with the corresponding state authority – in this case, the Secretariat of Hydrocarbons – and devote their own economic resources to the exploration and/or exploitation of hydrocarbons in the areas designated for such purpose, investing the necessary capital and using the necessary equipment, machinery and technology for the performance of the contracted services.

If hydrocarbons that are potentially commercially exploitable are located or discovered in the relevant area, the law states that the contractor will be entitled to the payment of a fee per barrel of net oil produced and delivered to the state at an inspection point. This fee – which constitutes the contractor's gross income – will be contractually determined, taking into account an estimate of the amortisation of investments, costs and expenses, and a reasonable profit that reflects the risk incurred.

Under service provision contracts, the Ecuadorian state will set aside 25% of the gross income from production corresponding to the area covered by the contract as a sovereignty margin. Transport and marketing costs incurred by the state will be covered by the remaining amount. Once these deductions have been made, the fee for the services provided will be paid.

The contractor will have a preferential option to purchase the production from the area covered by the contract at a price that will in no case be less than the reference price defined in Article 71 of the Hydrocarbons Act;[7] however, it provides that it will be awarded to the company that offers the best price and the best conditions.

Under service provision contracts, in case of payment in kind, the price of the hydrocarbons will be determined based on the latest average monthly price of external sales of hydrocarbons of equivalent quality carried out by Petroecuador. An additional fee may be paid to privilege production from additional activities undertaken by the contractor, in order to promote the

---

7 Article 71 of the Ecuadorian Hydrocarbons Act reads:

Royalties, income tax, state shares and, in general, taxes dependent on the sale price of hydrocarbons in the foreign market, shall be regulated by the effective sale or reference prices, according to the prevailing circumstances. The amount equivalent to the royalties payable to PETROECUADOR and the shares of state entities dependent on the sale prices of hydrocarbons on the external market shall be regulated by the effective FOB sale prices of such hydrocarbons. Those corresponding to the companies shall be regulated in accordance with the provisions of the previous subsection. The reference price of the hydrocarbons shall be the weighted average price of the most recent month of external sales of hydrocarbons made by PETROECUADOR, of equivalent quality. In the case of natural gas, it shall be considered the reference price of replaceable energy sources. The reference prices may be discussed with the producing companies in order to analyse and revise them whenever new conditions affecting the above factors make it necessary or justified. The royalties to be paid by the companies and PETROECUADOR respectively, for own consumption and losses of hydrocarbons in their normal operations, shall be regulated by the sales prices in the domestic market of the country.

discovery of new reserves or the implementation of new techniques for improved recovery of existing reserves.

The contractor must guarantee the implementation of the investments agreed in the respective development plan or five-year plan. A definition of the commercial viability of the fields will be included in the contract terms and conditions.

2.8 Operational agreements

Doctors Teodoro Bustamante and Oscar Zapata explain when operational agreements are used and describe them as follows:

> *although this is not a modality specifically established by law, it is a frequent practice. In fact, 27% of the oil extracted by private companies in Ecuador comes from this type of arrangement. There have been questions about a possible abuse of this modality, in the sense that the law foresees that this formula is used only for common fields and in some cases, it would have been used for non-common fields.*[8]

Table 1. Oil contracts in Ecuador that are currently in force[9]

Block	Operating company	Type of contract	Date signed	Valid until	Observations
Bermejo	Tecpecuador	Marginal field	1 July 1999	20 July 2019	
Charapa	Bellwether	Marginal field	19 November 1999	16 December 2019	
Palanda	Petrosud	Marginal field	1 July 1999	30 July 2019	
Pindo	Petrosud	Marginal field	1 July 1999	30 July 2019	
Tiguino	Petrobell	Marginal field	10 December 1999	7 January 2020	
01	Canada Grande	Participation	26 December 1996	23 April 2012	

continued on next page

8 Teodoro Bustamante and Oscar Zapata, *Characteristics of Oil Contracts in Ecuador*, https://biblio.flacsoandes.edu.ec/catalog/resGet.php?resId=13245.

9 Based on data from Petroecuador and Petroproducción, www.eppetroecuador.ec.

Block	Operating company	Type of contract	Date signed	Valid until	Observations
03	EDC Ecuador	Participation	2 July 1996	2 October 2006	
07	Perenco	Participation	23 March 2000	16 August 2010	
11	CNPC (Amazon)	Participation	18 January 1995	16 November 2021	
14	Petrooriental SA	Participation	21 May 1999	21 July 2012	
16	Repsol-YPF	Participation	27 December 1996	31 January 2012	
17	Petrooriental SA	Participation	23 March 2000	29 December 2018	
18	EcuadorTLC	Participation	19 December 1995	17 October 2022	
21	Perenco	Participation	20 March 1995	8 June 2021	
23	CGC	Participation	27 July 1996		*Force majeure*
24	Burlington	Participation	27 April 1998		*Force majeure*
28	TRIPETROL	Participation	8 March 1995		Termination proceeding
Tarapoa	Andes Petroleum Ecuador Limited	Participation	25 July 1995	1 August 2015	
10	AGIP Oil Ecuador	Service provision	16 June 1988	13 March 2017	

3. Conclusion

Ecuador has had two major periods of oil exploitation: one in the coastal region of the Santa Elena peninsula in the first half of the 20th century; and the other in the Amazon region, which continues to this day.

The different contractual forms used have varied over the years, depending on the governments in power and the policies they implemented. With the establishment of CEPE, the government assumed responsibility for the different phases of the production process – exploration, exploitation, transport and commercialisation – which was a crucial development for the Ecuadorian state.

The main contractual arrangements that Ecuador has used in the past include:

- service provision contracts;
- participation contracts;
- operational alliances;
- specific service contracts;
- profit sharing contracts;
- contracts for additional exploration and exploitation of marginal oil fields;
- strategic alliances;
- exploration of unified and shared fields; and
- establishment of mixed economy companies.

Under a profit sharing contract, the contractor makes investments and technology transfers on its own account, and thus increases oil revenues, maximises the recovery of reserves and conducts exploration activities areas of operation of 2,500 hectares over a 20-year period. There are few such contracts in existence; and the only example that the author has been able to identify is the contract for the Palo Azul field. If Ecuador had known how to use this contractual form to its advantage, it would have enjoyed many benefits therefrom; but there has been a general lack of precision in the contractual clauses.

There is significant room for improvement in the analysis and consultancy on the oil sector – above all, at the contractual level – to protect the interests of the state while also ensuring that national and international companies feel at ease and benefit from legal certainty and security. It is also important to implement a policy that provides for the arbitration of any conflicts arising from the different forms of oil contracts, including in international venues. Although the Constitution (2008) recognises arbitration, this is limited and allowed only in certain areas, as it affords jurisdiction only to a single arbitration centre; moreover, it does not recognise the existence of bilateral investment treaties that provide for the use of different centres, such as the International Centre for Settlement of Investment Disputes.

The principles of bilaterality and contractual will must prevail, unconditionally and with the aim of ensuring legal security in oil contracting.

As an oil producing country, Ecuador must develop effective policies not only in the hydrocarbon field, but also in the environmental field, as in the past environmental damage from such activities has been not been remedied as it should have been. The courts' lack of experience of such cases resulted in negative rulings or sentences for the plaintiffs. There is a pressing need for environmental education and special clauses should thus be incorporated in the various contracts that investors sign with Ecuador. There would thus be no misunderstandings or restrictions, and the risk of new international lawsuits would be minimised.

Ghana

Adam Abukari
Coventry University

1. Background

For many years, natural resources have played a vital role in the economic development of many developing countries. However, for many reasons, Ghana's mining and extraction industry (traditionally dominated by gold mining) has had a chequered history and disappointing outcomes.

First, the general legal and regulatory environment is largely complex and is skewed against a sustainable collective sovereign interest. There are often gaps in legislation; the definition of the nature and structure of fiscal terms is poor; and it is difficult for Ghanaians to derive maximum benefits from their resource wealth.

Second, contracting processes and transactions have been characterised by limited transparency and public oversight.

Third, environmental concerns arising from the disruptive activities of natural resource extraction have been given little consideration.

Fourth, management of natural resource revenues has been ineffective and the impact of the country's resource wealth has been minimal, in terms of the availability against relevant uses to which those resources are put. For example, when oil was first produced in significant commercial quantities in December 2010, there was no proper petroleum revenue management legislation in place to regulate the revenues from petroleum wealth. It was not until 2011 that the Petroleum Revenue Management Act (815/2011) was passed to regulate the management of revenues from the oil and gas industry. Although the law includes provisions aimed at ensuring transparency and accountability, in practice it has not prevented political actors from diverting some of the revenues to questionable uses. On many occasions, the Public Interest and Accountability Committee (PIAC)[1] has had reason to question the lack of timely accountability from the government of Ghana, in terms of the reporting and application of revenues.[2]

1 The PIAC is an independent statutory institution which is responsible for promoting "transparency and accountability" in managing revenues drawn from petroleum resources. See www.piacghana.org/portal/.

2 See PIAC, "PIAC Wants Fin. Ministry to Account for use of Oil Funds", www.piacghana.org/portal/12/13/457/piac-wants-fin-ministry-to-account-for-use-of-oil-funds.

Fifth, there have been ongoing policy issues, particularly with respect to clarity and stability. For example, when oil production began in 2010,[3] there was no solid national policy on the development of petroleum resources. It was not until later that such a policy was formulated; and this policy is still burdened with uncertainties, due in part to political differences and the lack of a clear, unified national policy direction on the development of oil and gas resources.

Sixth, poor institutional capacity and coordination within the resource exploitation framework have long undermined Ghana's ability to effectively harness its resource wealth for sustainable prosperity. For years, natural resource exploitation in Ghana has largely been to the benefit of a few companies and elites, rather than the sustainable development of the public.

When oil and gas were finally discovered[4] in commercial quantities[5] in June 2007 – after several decades[6] of exploration activities, low-scale discoveries and exploitation – the hope was that lessons would be learned from the past bad experiences of petroleum contracting and mining of gold, diamonds and other minerals. It was also hoped that global best practices would be adopted in the oil industry to ensure that oil wealth generated sustainable prosperity for the citizens of Ghana. Indeed, with the discovery of oil and gas and the start of production in the last quarter of 2010, the Ghanaian public hoped that their economic circumstances would change for the better.

The Petroleum Exploration and Production Law 1984 provided for the use of production sharing agreements (PSAs) in the petroleum industry. This law was operational when the foundational agreements between the Ghanaian government/Ghana National Petroleum Corporation (GNPC) (the national oil

---

3 Before oil production began in earnest in December 2010, the commercial partners in the consortium carried out about three and a half years of hard work. They incurred a capital investment of more than $4.1 billion. The Jubilee Field partners originally had the following shares: Tullow Oil plc 34.7%; Kosmos Energy 23.49%; Anadarko Petroleum Corp 23.49%; the Ghana National Petroleum Corporation 13.75%; Sabre Oil and Gas 2.81%; and EO Group 1.75%. The shares of Tullow rose to 36.45% when Tullow acquired EO Group's shares in 2011. See PIAC, "Annual Report on revenue management for 2011", www.piacghana.org/portal/files/downloads/piac_reports/piac_2011_annual_report.pdf.

4 The independent petroleum companies that worked, in collaboration with the GNPC, to discover the commercial high-grade oil (about a 312-foot net column) in the Mahogany 1 well in the West Cape Three Points Licence were Kosmos Energy (a block operator), Anadarko (a technical operator), Tullow Oil and EO Group. See Petroleum Commission, Ghana, "Exploration History", www.petrocom.gov.gh/exploration-history/.

5 The Jubilee Field (the main oil field) has had a reported 800 million to 1.8 billion barrels of proven reserves or recoverable oil with a potential to have an estimated three billion barrels of oil. The Jubilee Field is located at the Deepwater Tano and West Cape Three Points blocks, about 60 kilometres offshore Ghana and 130 kilometres west-southwest of Takoradi. After the Jubilee Field, 23 other discoveries of petroleum in the areas of Deepwater Tano and West Cape Three Points were made, most in commercially viable quantities. These discoveries include Odum, Ebony, Tweneboa, Sankofa, Dzata, Owo, Teak-1, Paradise-1, Banda-1, Gye Nyame, etc. Fields such as Tweneboa-Enyenra-Ntomme and Sankofa with significant potential have since subsequently come onstream. Many other active exploration activities are ongoing in the waters of Ghana. In the Keta basin, a reasonable exploration is being carried out. See Petroleum Commission, Ghana, "Exploration History", www.petrocom.gov.gh/ exploration-history/.

6 As far back as 1896 when exploration started in onshore Tano basin in the Western Region. See Petroleum Commission, Ghana, "Exploration History'" www.petrocom.gov.gh/exploration-history/.

company (NOC))[7] and private companies such as Kosmas Energy, Anadarko, Tullow Oil, EO Group[8] (a Ghanaian company), Hess Corporation and Tullow Oil were concluded, granting rights to explore and produce petroleum in Ghana's deep waters.[9] However, these agreements adopted a hybridised form that made use of royalty/concession-type payments along with the main features of the PSA.[10]

Although governments that have just discovered petroleum often find it difficult to manage expectations, sound contractual arrangements and management structures can provide strong leverage for such governments to meet those expectations. It was therefore imperative that Ghana establish the appropriate legal, institutional and manpower infrastructure to ensure that its oil and gas industry is prudently managed, in contrast to what happened and is still happening in the mining sector.

In August 2016, when the new Petroleum (Exploration and Production) Act (919/2016) repealed its predecessor, the contractual terms thereunder also favoured a hybridised form of petroleum agreement. This act has since become the primary legal instrument that regulates the exploration and production of petroleum in Ghana's upstream sector.[11]

While Ghana has thus far made efforts to adopt best practices in harnessing its petroleum wealth, questions remain regarding the nature of the petroleum agreements used to achieve the benefits desired by the Ghanaian public. This chapter seeks to explore the nature of the PSA in Ghana's petroleum legal framework in light of international best practices.

2. Scope and structure of the PSA

The PSA is essentially a contractual arrangement between the host government and oil and gas exploration and production (E&P) companies, under which E&P companies are mandated by the host government to manage E&P activities on its behalf. All accompanying costs and risks are borne by the E&P companies, with no expectation to be compensated by the host government should any losses occur. The contractual arrangement typically stipulates further that a pre-agreed formula for profit and oil sharing between the parties will apply in case of the discovery of petroleum and realisation of profits.[12]

---

7 Ghana National Petroleum Corporation Act, 1983 (PNDCL 64).

8 This group spearheaded the mobilisation of partners in the arrangement.

9 The Jubilee Field (main production field) has a water depth from 1,000 metres to 1,700 metres.

10 See Richmond Osei-Hwere, "Can a Developing Country Like Ghana Control its Oil and Gas Resources Through Production Sharing Agreements?" (2010) 4 *Oil, Gas & Energy Law*, www.ogel.org/article.asp?key=3062.

11 George Ndi, "Act 919 of 2016 and its contribution to governance of the upstream petroleum industry in Ghana" (2018) 36(1) *Journal of Energy & Natural Resources Law* 5.

12 Bernard Taverne, "Production Sharing Agreements in Principle and in Practice" in Martyn R David (ed) *Upstream Oil and Gas Agreement* (Sweet & Maxwell 1996) 43; Tengku Nathan Machmud, *The Indonesian Production Sharing Contract: An Investor's Perspective* (Kluwer Law International 2000); Bernard Taverne, *Petroleum Industry Governments: A Global Study of the Involvement of Industry and Government in the Production and Use of Petroleum* (2nd edn, International Energy & Resources Law & Policy, Kluwer Law International 2008).

Usually, in countries with an NOC, the host government is represented by the NOC, which takes a participating share. According to Act 919/2016, 15% is the minimum participating carried interest enjoyed by the GNPC as the NOC. This minimum initial participating interest attracts no risks and costs. However, any additional interest which the NOC acquires does attract costs and risks, which the E&P companies equally bear.[13]

Depending on the petroleum regime in the jurisdiction in question, royalty oil can be enjoyed by the host government. This dimension is external to the traditional PSA. In this way, the PSA can be described as a hybridised form. Act 919/2016 presents a structure that integrates features of concessions and petroleum agreements such as service and joint venture agreements. Before the enactment of Act 919/2016 and the discovery of commercially viable petroleum, Ghana utilised a more typical PSA.

3. Main features of the PSA

The PSA has different configurations, depending on the features adopted by the host government and the other parties. However, the key features of the PSA, according to Blinn *et al*,[14] are as follows:

- The host government (represented by the NOC) enters into an agreement with an E&P company (usually a foreign company or a local company partnership thereof).
- The E&P company acts as a contractor or operator.
- The contractor conducts E&P operations, bearing the risks and costs partially or fully.
- The host government and the E&P company share the petroleum produced based on a pre-agreed ratio of the quantity of petroleum produced.
- The E&P company has the right to take a pre-agreed share of the amount of petroleum that is produced – this can be part of or represent the carried interest of the NOC. Royalty oil may also be taken by the host government.
- The host government is entitled to a pre-agreed share of the petroleum that is produced in order to recover any costs incurred (if the NOC takes an interest beyond the initial participating or carried interest).
- The E&P company is entitled to a pre-agreed share of the petroleum that is produced in order to recover any costs incurred. This cost is otherwise referred to as cost recovery for the E&P company.
- The host government may also be entitled to collect certain taxes, such as corporate income tax, from the E&P company.

---

13 Section 10(14)a of the Petroleum (Exploration and Production), 2016 [Act 919].

14 Keith W Blinn *et al*, *International Petroleum Exploration and Exploitation Agreements: Legal, Economic and Policy Aspects* (2nd edn, Barrows Company Inc 2009).

- The parties are both entitled to a share of any profit oil realised.
- A surface rent in the initial exploration phase may also be taken by the host government.
- Signature bonuses may also be granted under the PSA.
- Depending on the contractual arrangement, the equipment and installations used in the E&P will be owned by the host government at a certain point in the E&P lifecycle or at the decommissioning[15] stage.[16]

Figure 1 illustrates the key features of a typical PSA.[17]

Figure 1. PSA model

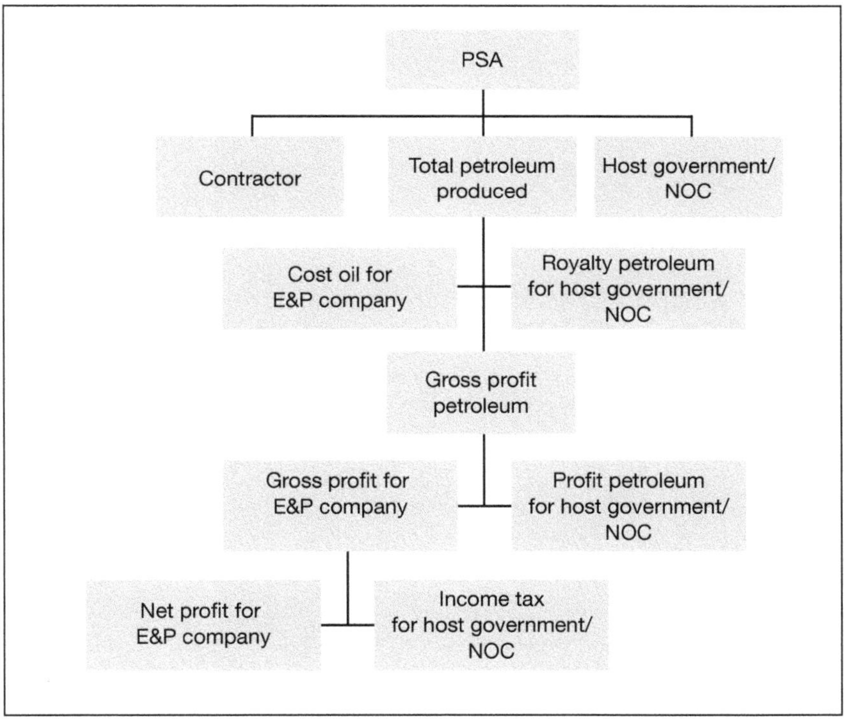

These features comprise the structure of the typical modern PSA and are aligned with the petroleum fiscal regime in Ghana. A number of different revenue streams may be negotiated for or provided for by law in advance by the

15 See Section 43 of Act 919.

16 See Z Gao (ed), *International Petroleum Contracts: Current Trends and New Directions* (1st edn, Kluwer Law International 1994).

17 Kirsten Bindemann, *Production-Sharing Agreements: An Economic Analysis* (Oxford Institute for Energy Studies 1999); Blinn *et al* (n 14); Taverne (n 12).

host government. However, individual petroleum agreements may have some specific tailored provisions that differ from the above provisions or from Ghana's Model Petroleum Agreement (MPA).[18] The key fiscal features of the PSA under Ghana's MPA are:

- GNPC's initial interest (carried);
- royalty;
- GNPC's additional interest (paying);
- corporate income tax; and
- surface rent in the initial exploration phase.

These features have been captured by Act 919/2016.

Act 919/2016 is regarded as a consolidating statute because it has been built on "a substantial corpus juris of legislative enactments which together make up the legal framework" that regulates the upstream petroleum sector. In particular, it builds on the Petroleum Exploration and Production Law and the Ghana MPA.[19] Efforts are underway in Parliament to amend Act 919/2016 to make Ghana's petroleum industry more favourable to investors, while also ensuring that the citizens of Ghana benefit significantly from the exploitation of the country's natural resources.

Ghana has adopted international best practices through its participation in the standards of Extractive Industry Transparency International and the Natural Resource Governance Institute (NRGI), which seek to ensure transparency, accountability and respect for the rule of law in the exploitation of petroleum resources. Ghana scores particularly highly among sub-Saharan African countries in the NRGI's resource governance index scores. The particulars of the Ghana's PSA under Act 919/2016 are further illustrated in Table 1.

A PSA is thus an agreement under which:

- an E&P company is engaged by the host government as a contractor;
- the host government allows the petroleum company to recover E&P costs annually or periodically;
- the host government recovers any costs incurred;
- other entitlements for the host government to cater to the interests of its citizens are granted; and
- the E&P company is granted an entitlement to receive a share of the petroleum that is produced to cover the exploration risks and costs once commercially viable quantities of petroleum have been discovered.[20]

PSAs have flexible terms that change to suit specific sharing arrangements

18 GNPC, "Model Petroleum Agreement of Ghana" (17 August 2000).
19 Ndi (n 11).
20 Gao (n 16).

Table 1. Key features of Ghana's petroleum PSA under Act 919/2016

PSA components	Share	Nature of available choice
Initial minimum participating carried interest	15%	Mandatory
Additional participating interest	Based on the petroleum agreement	Optional
Corporate income tax and capital gains tax	Based on the prevailing tax regime set out in the Petroleum Revenue Management Act (815/2011) and/or other relevant legislation	Mandatory
Royalty	Based on the petroleum agreement	Mandatory
Bonus	Based on the petroleum agreement	Mandatory
Annual fee per acreage	Based on the prescription of the relevant sector minister or the petroleum agreement	Mandatory
Additional oil entitlement	Based on the after-tax, inflation-adjusted rate of return that the contract achieved with respect to each field of petroleum produced	Mandatory

that replicate the provisions of, or fall within, the tax and royalty regimes. An additional advantage of the PSA is that it presents an opportunity to vary the fiscal/economic terms in a given contractual area without having to amend the fiscal legislation. It also gives the host government the opportunity to keep or dispose of its petroleum share (in particular, the additional participating paid interest in the case of Ghana). PSAs also have a ring-fencing feature which may optionally be used, depending on whether the host government wishes to prioritise maximum development or early revenue. It is not mandatory for the host government to provide budget funds to finance costs until it decides to take a paid participating interest. Thus, the initial participating carried interest for the host government does not attract costs.

In effect, the uniqueness of the PSAs is related to the fact that the circumstances and tendencies/interests of the parties, as well as the mutuality of such interests, are highly valued in most of the contractual terms. The stability of the contractual arrangements, as mutually agreed, thus cements the relations between the parties.[21]

The challenge is that a host government that has no significant capacity in terms of negotiation and willpower may end up being disadvantaged. The same applies to E&P companies, whose investments can be better protected only if they are able to engage effectively with the host government. At both ends of the spectrum, the cardinal principle of mutual relevance is that the E&P company must be seen to be interested in making reasonable (not extraordinary) profits; while the host government must be seen to be maximising the interests of its citizens for the benefit of society as a whole.[22]

4. The role of the competent authority in the contract

When commercial petroleum reserves were discovered in Ghana, the GNPC was initially tasked with overseeing upstream oil and gas regulation and management and serving as the NOC, exploring and representing the country's interests in contractual arrangements. In 2011 the Petroleum Commission Act (821/2011) was promulgated, which established the Petroleum Commission of Ghana (PCG) to oversee the management and regulation of the "utilisation of petroleum resources and, coordinate policies" in the upstream oil and gas sector.[23] All licensing, regulation and management activities, including investor relations, are now carried out by the PCG. The PCG is responsible for promoting, regulating and managing "the efficient conduct of upstream petroleum operations and all allied activities and the utilization of petroleum resources on a sustainable basis for the overall benefit of the citizens of Ghana".[24]

Meanwhile, the GNPC is responsible for leading "the sustainable exploration, development, production and disposal of the petroleum resources of Ghana, by leveraging the right mix of domestic and foreign investments in partnership with the people of Ghana".[25] To this end, the GNPC is particularly mandated to

21 *Ibid.*
22 *Ibid.*
23 Petroleum Commission, Ghana, "Organizational Brief", www.petrocom.gov.gh/organizational-brief/.
24 *Ibid.*
25 GNPC, "About us – overview", www.gnpcghana.com/overview.html.

"undertake the exploration, development, production and disposal of petroleum", among other things. The tasks of the GNPC thus include:

- promoting "the exploration and the orderly and planned development of the petroleum resources of Ghana";
- ensuring that Ghana derives "the greatest possible benefits from the development of its petroleum resources";
- ensuring "the effective transfer to Ghana of appropriate technology relating to petroleum operations";
- ensuring that citizens of Ghana are trained and that "national capabilities in all aspects of petroleum operations" are developed; and
- ensuring that "petroleum operations are conducted in such a manner as to prevent adverse effects on the environment, resources and people of Ghana".[26]

These objectives closely resemble much of what NOCs can pursue in global practice.

Both the GNPC and the PCG are supervised by the Ministry of Energy. The ministry is responsible for providing policy direction and overseeing high-end negotiations and contractual arrangements in the oil and gas industry. The ministry's vision is for Ghana "to become an energy economy with reliable supply of high-quality energy services for the Ghanaian economy and for export".[27] The name of the ministry has changed every now and then over the years, and the power/electricity and petroleum components have been separated and are now governed by separate ministries. However, at any material point in time, the relevant ministry responsible for E&P activities has supervised the regulatory framework and the actors involved in the sector.

The challenge, however, is that without proper coordination and collaboration, there may be misalignment or a conflict of functions between the GNPC and the PCG. At the same time, the Ghana Gas Company (which manages the processing and disposal of the gas component of the petroleum resources in Ghana) also plays a critical role in harnessing the country's petroleum wealth. Meanwhile, the Energy Commission is responsible for regulating the transmission chain. In the upstream/midstream sector, the GNPC, the PCG and the Ghana Gas Company, along with the Ministry of Energy, are the most prominent players that engage with investors and other stakeholders. As the GNPC has had decades of experience of licensing and regulation, it is imperative that the other relevant agencies closely liaise with it in order to ensure their proper functioning.

For its part, the GNPC must focus on making itself more competitive and

---

26 *Ibid.*
27 Ministry of Energy, "Welcome to the Ministry of Energy", www.energymin.gov.gh/about.

commercially vibrant, in line with Precept 5 of the Natural Resource Charter, which provides that the NOC should not only be competitive and commercially focused, but also "avoid conducting regulatory functions or other activities". The decoupling of the regulatory functions from the GNPC was thus a major step forward. Corruption is a serious bane to the efficient functioning of the petroleum industry and must be checked at every stage of the transaction chain between the national agencies on one hand and investors and other interested parties on the other.

5. Analysis of the main clauses of the contract

Most of the petroleum contracts (at least for 18 contract areas) entered into between the government of Ghana/GNPC and E&P companies have been published on the online petroleum register (www.ghanapetroleumregister.com/contract-areas). These have similar terms, except for some minor variations, as they were all drafted on the basis of Ghana's MPA. The following contract areas provide specific details of PSA-related contractual terms:

- Deepwater Tano;
- West Cape Three Points;
- Offshore Cape Three Points;
- Deepwater Tano/Cape Three Points;
- Cape Three Points Block 4;
- Central Tano Block;
- Deepwater Cape Three Points West Offshore;
- East Cape Three Points;
- East Keta Block;
- Expanded Shallow Water Tano Block;
- West Cape Three Points Block 2;
- Offshore South-West Tano Block;
- Onshore/Offshore Keta Delta Block;
- South Deepwater Tano;
- South West Saltpond;
- Shallow Water Cape Three Points;
- Offshore Cape Three Points South; and
- Deepwater Cape Three Point.[28]

For example, in the Deep Tana contract area, the agreement between Tullow Ghana (as operator) and the other contracting parties includes the terms set out in Table 2.

28 Petroleum Commission, Ghana, "Contract Areas", www.ghanapetroleumregister.com/contract-areas.
29 Petroleum Commission, Ghana, "Deepwater Tano", www.ghanapetroleumregister.com/deepwater-tano.

Table 2. Deep Tano contract area key fiscal terms[29]

Contracting parties	Interest in block	Comments
Tullow Ghana Limited	35.48%	Majority stake and operator
Anadarko Petroleum Corporation	24%	Second-highest stake
Kosmos Energy Ghana HC	24%	Second-highest stake
Ghana National Petroleum Corporation (NOC)	14%	Third-highest stake (not up to the 15% minimum initial participating carried interest in Act 919/206).
PetroSA Ghana Limited	2.52%	Lowest participating stake
5% royalty of the gross production of crude oil. The royalty for any crude oil with an American Petroleum Institute gravity of less than 18 degrees is 4%.		
The royalty for natural gas is 3% of the annual gross production of natural gas.		
35% income tax in accordance with the provisions of the Income Tax Law, and petroleum income tax.		
5% withholding tax from the aggregate amount due to any subcontractor (other than the state or any entity that is wholly owned or controlled by the state).		
Surface rental varies between $30 and $100 per square kilometre, depending on the phase of operation.		
The assets possessed by these parties are the Jubilee Field, the Tweneboa-Enyenra-Ntomme Fields and the Wawa Discovery Area. There may have been subsequent takeovers or realignments, which are not reflected here. These assets are in the development and production.		
Effective date: 10 March 2006[30]		

30 *Ibid.*

6. Relationship of the PSA with the petroleum law/regulatory framework

In conjunction with Act 919/2016, the following laws provide the legal framework under which the hybridised PSA is operationalised in Ghana:

- the Petroleum Commission Act (821/2011);
- the Petroleum Income Tax Act 1987;
- the Petroleum Revenue Management Act (815/2011);
- the Petroleum (Local Content and Local Participation) Regulations 2013 (LI 2204);
- the Petroleum (Exploration and Production) (Data Management) Regulations 2017 (LI 2257);
- the Petroleum (Exploration and Production) (Measurement Regulations), 2016 (LI 2246);
- the Petroleum Commission (Fees and Charges) Regulations, 2015 (LI 2221);
- the Petroleum (Exploration and Production) (Health, Safety and Environment) Regulations, 2017 (LI 2258);
- the Petroleum (Exploration and Production) (General) Regulations), 2018 (LI 2359);[31] and
- the 1992 Constitution.

These legal instruments address various issues, including:

- NOC operations;
- corporate income tax;
- local content;
- E&P measurement;
- data management;
- environmental management;
- revenue management; and
- E&P legalities in the upstream sector.

The provisions of the 1992 Constitution that address natural resource ownership and exploitation are set out in Chapter 21, Articles 257 to 269. The provisions of Act 919/2016 have further been expanded by standalone legislation and regulations to ensure that there is certainty, clarity and stability in contractual terms, in particular as regards both fixed matters and those requiring negotiation. While Ghana's environmental protection regime may be strong in theory, its application in practice is less so. The local content provisions are similarly strong in theory, but the skill sets required in this niche industry remain limited in Ghana. While the GNPC has built up significant local expertise over the years,

31 Petroleum Commission Ghana, "Upstream Petroleum Legislations" (Petroleum Register), www.ghanapetroleumregister.com/laws.

and more and more people are being trained and financed by the PCG and the GNPC, as well as by the Ghana Education Trust Fund, certain expertise is still lacking, especially within the regulatory architecture and in certain fields of science and engineering. Addressing this gap is the only way to actualise the local content provisions. Another critical feature of the regime is the E&P measurement regulatory framework, which ensures that the right standards are used to measure the petroleum that is pumped up from the wells. If this is monitored carefully, the opportunity for deliberate oil underreporting can be curtailed, to ensure that the oil that is shared between parties in the PSA is exactly what has been produced.

7. Conclusion

Ghana – a West African country with significant petroleum potential – currently uses a hybrid PSA model which shares some features with concession and joint venture arrangements. Ghana, as the host state, deliberately selects contractual terms which make it possible for the NOC (GNPC) to have a working participating stake in projects, bearing some costs and risks and sharing in the cost oil and profit oil. The host government also collects royalties and taxes such as corporate income tax and capital gains tax. However, the NOC/host government can choose not to incur any costs while still having an entitlement to the initial minimum participating carried interest (currently 15%) and other public interest or trust entitlements, such as surface rentals.

While this model may look sophisticated, it would appear that significant returns for both citizens and investors could be realised if capabilities on both sides were enhanced and fair play was secured for both participating parties and their shareholders (in the case of investors and E&P companies) and citizens (in the case of the host government/NOC). To this end, the parties should mutually examine their specific circumstances and ensure that a resilient contractual arrangement that maximises control and ownership of petroleum resources is adopted and operationalised with integrity and a collective sense of purpose.

It thus appears possible to maintain the hybridised PSA and make the best use of it for all contracting parties. However, this contractual model can also be used in sub-optimal ways. Other contractual models – such as direct concessions and service agreements – may likewise be used either optimally or sub-optimally. It is crucial to ensure that a particular model is used only where the parties have the capabilities to ensure that there is reasonable benefit from the investment for the E&P company and maximum economic benefit for the host government/NOC. Ghana should continue to adopt international standards and best practices, and continue refining its legal, regulatory and investment framework to attract more foreign investment.

The Ghana petroleum industry is a great investment destination. However, investors must submit to best practices and support government authorities in countering corruption and mismanagement whenever and wherever possible.

Guyana

Alicia Elias-Roberts
University of the West Indies

This chapter examines the 2016 production sharing agreement (PSA) between the government of Guyana and ExxonMobil (through its subsidiary Esso Exploration and Production Guyana Limited) and their partners.[1] It analyses the main clauses in the Guyana-ExxonMobil PSA – namely, the fiscal provisions on cost oil and profit oil split, as well as the provisions on stabilisation, local content and decommissioning. The chapter also discusses the role of the competent authorities in the Guyana-ExxonMobil PSA – that is, the Department of Energy, the Ministry of Natural Resources and the Guyana Geology and Mines Commission (GGMC). The relationship between the Guyana-ExxonMobil PSA and the petroleum laws of Guyana is also discussed.

1. Main fiscal provisions of the Guyana-ExxonMobil PSA

Oil discoveries in Guyana's offshore areas have positioned the country as an emerging frontier oil and gas producer.[2] It is estimated that ExxonMobil has discovered approximately 10 billion barrels of oil equivalent of recoverable oil in the Stabroek Block, a deep water exploration block about 120 miles offshore.[3]

Guyana's fiscal system and the general legal framework governing the oil and gas sector are outdated and are currently undergoing legislative reform.[4] The 2016 Guyana-ExxonMobil PSA included very generous terms on royalty, cost recovery, taxation and profit sharing for the international oil companies (IOCs). Arguably, these generous terms were offered to attract investment. Under Article 15.5 of the Guyana-ExxonMobil PSA, the contractor agrees to pay

1 Petroleum Agreement between the Government of Guyana and Esso Exploration and Production Guyana Limited, CNOOC Nexen Petroleum Guyana Limited and Hess Guyana Exploration Limited (2016).

2 Clifford Krauss, "With a Major Oil Discovery, Guyana is Poised to Become a Top Producer", *The New York Times* (13 January 2017), www.nytimes.com/2017/01/13/business/energy-environment/major-oil-find-guyana-exxon-mobile-hess.html.

3 Keith Myers, Westwood Global Energy Group, "Latest Guyana discovery opens the way to a new 10 billion barrel oil province and transformation for one of South America's smallest countries", *Westwood Insight* (5 September 2018) www.westwoodenergy.com/news/westwood-insight/latest-guyana-discovery-opens-the-way/.

4 Editor, "US, local law firms hired to revamp, develop legislation for oil sector", *News Room* (11 February 2020) https://newsroom.gy/2020/02/11/us-local-law-firms-hired-to-revamp-develop-legislation-for-oil-sector/.

the government a royalty of 2% (increased from 1%). Article 11 on cost recovery and production sharing provides that Guyana will receive 50% of the share of profits after deducting up to a maximum of 75% of recoverable costs from monthly revenues. The agreement also provides that any excess recoverable costs are to be carried over to the following month. The agreement further provides that the government of Guyana will pay the taxes of the contractor out of the government's share, and that this will be considered income of the contractor. This means that the government will give a tax receipt to ExxonMobil and its partners in their names, which states that they have paid their taxes. When the prospects of finding oil in commercial quantities in Guyana were uncertain, generous terms were used to attract investors. However, these can now be limited, and the government has stated its intention to develop a new fiscal framework and new petroleum legislation. The International Monetary Fund (IMF) and several other international bodies have advised the government to draft a model PSA with the minimum fiscal terms or package to be accepted for future contracts.

2. Other main clauses of the PSA: stabilisation, local content and decommissioning

2.1 Stabilisation

There is nothing under the laws of Guyana that speaks to the nature that stabilisation provisions should take in PSAs. However, the model articles in a PSA available through the GGMC website refer to "Stability of Agreement", which seeks to protect "the investment potential for the contractor against unforeseen major economic upheaval".[5] The current model PSA in Guyana is focused on protecting and attracting investments, and freezes the existing laws and regulations applicable to the contract at the time of signing. However, there is no economic equilibrium provision aimed at maintaining the status quo and ensuring that in the event of windfall profits, the government gets a fair share.

The 2016 Guyana-ExxonMobil PSA provides for the stability of the agreement. The contract covers the Stabroek Block, which is 26,800 square kilometres in size. ExxonMobil affiliate Esso Exploration and Production Guyana Limited is operator and holds a 45% interest in the Stabroek Block. Hess Guyana Exploration Ltd holds a 30% interest; and CNOOC Petroleum Guyana Limited – a wholly owned subsidiary of CNOOC Limited – holds a 25% interest.[6] The 2016 Guyana-ExxonMobil PSA was negotiated between the government of Guyana and the oil companies. The government did not conduct any

5 Guyana Geology and Mines Commission, *Articles in Guyana's Petroleum Agreement*, www.ggmc.gov.gy/services/all/articles-guyanas-petroleum-agreement.

6 ExxonMobil Corporate, *Guyana Project Overview*, https://corporate.exxonmobil.com/Locations/Guyana/Guyana-project-overview.

competitive bidding before entering into this agreement with ExxonMobil and its partners. The government explained that one reason for this decision was because the country's petroleum sector was as yet undeveloped, so it felt it was appropriate to conduct a one-off negotiation for the Guyana-ExxonMobil PSA. The applicable law under the agreement is the law of Guyana. Article 27 provides that: "This agreement shall be governed by, interpreted and construed in accordance with the laws of the Cooperative Republic of Guyana and consistent with such rules of international law as may be applicable or appropriate, including the generally accepted customs and usages of the international petroleum industry."[7]

The Guyana-ExxonMobil PSA provides for a freezing stabilization clause. Article 32 states: "Except as may be expressly provided herein, the Government shall not amend, modify, rescind, terminate, declare invalid or unenforceable, require renegotiation of, compel replacement or substitution, or otherwise seek to avoid, alter, or limit this Agreement without the prior written consent of the Contractor."[8]

The government of Guyana has the sovereign power and right to change its laws. So if the government exercises this right, what is the impact of the above clauses? It could be argued that the freezing stabilisation clause means that the government has contractually denied itself the right to change laws that could affect the Guyana-ExxonMobil PSA. If this answer is correct, then in the strict sense, this means that although new laws may be passed, such as tax laws, they will not apply to the Guyana-ExxonMobil PSA, as that contract will operate under its own separate legal regime. On the other hand, some take the view that the freezing stabilisation clause limits the state's sovereignty and is illegal and unenforceable.

The Guyana-ExxonMobil PSA further provides as follows:

32.2 After the signing of this Agreement and in conformance with Article 15, the Government shall not increase the economic burdens of the Contractor under this Agreement by applying to this Agreement or the operations conducted thereunder any increase of or any new petroleum related fiscal obligation, including but not limited to, any new taxes whatsoever, any new royalty, duties, fees, charges, value-added tax (VAT) or other imposts.

32.3 If at any time after the signing of this Agreement there is a change in the laws of Guyana whether through the amendment of existing laws (including the hydrocarbons law, the customs code or tax code) or the enactment of new laws or a change having the force of law in the interpretation, implementation or application thereof (whether the change is specific to the Agreement, the Contractor or of a general application) and such change has a materially adverse effect on the

7 *Ibid*, Article 27.
8 *Ibid*, Article 32.1.

> *economic benefits, including those resulting from the fiscal regime provided by this Agreement, accruing to the Contractor hereunder during the term of this Agreement, the Government shall promptly take any and all affirmative actions to restore the lost or impaired economic benefits to the Contractor, so that Contractor receives the same economic benefit under the Agreement that it would have received prior to the change in law or its interpretation, application or implementation...*[9]

Article 32.2 seems to be in line with a freezing clause and Article 32.3 seems to resemble an economic equilibrium clause. Interestingly, the same agreement provides for a freezing clause and an economic equilibrium position. This simply confirms the fact that the parties were eager to protect the investor's position and arguably were aware of current challenges regarding the freezing clause; otherwise, they would not have included a freezing clause and an economic equilibrium provision at the same time. These two provisions clearly should not co-exist in the same agreement, unless one should prevail over the other – or at least work in a subsidiary form to the extent that one is not legally enforceable.

Interestingly, unlike an economic equilibrium clause, which protects the interests of both parties, the above clause mentions only the interests of the contractor. This contract is not in line with modern trends. Guyana as a sovereign state has the right to exercise its legislative power and the right to enact, modify or cancel any law at its own discretion. It may be argued that by deciding to invest, the investor assumes the business risk associated with a change of laws that may possibly or even likely be detrimental to its investment, notwithstanding this stabilisation clause. A prudent investor knows that laws will evolve over time. Apart from the freezing provisions in the Guyana-ExxonMobil PSA, a 2017 IMF Assessment Report[10] indicated that the contract has the lowest average effective tax rate (AETR) of all the fiscal regimes evaluated.[11] This observation strengthens the argument that the fiscal terms offered in the agreement are very generous to the investor and that the contract is lopsided.

Another important aspect of the Guyana-ExxonMobil PSA is that the contract provides for International Centre for Settlement of Investment Disputes arbitration under Articles 26 and 32.4. Article 26 is entitled "Sole Expert and Arbitration".[12] These provisions might be considered a waiver of sovereignty. The issues here are whether these provisions are enforceable and

9 *Ibid*, Articles 32.2 and 32.3.

10 "Oil agreement generous to Exxon – IMF team-loopholes for abuse seen", *Staborek News*, (24 December 2017) www.stabroeknews.com/2017/12/24/news/guyana/oil-agreement-generous-to-exxon-imf-team/.

11 The revenue-generating capacity of the fiscal regime is evaluated by estimating the AETR or 'government take'. The AETR is calculated as the ratio of government revenue to the project's pre-tax net cash flows over the life of the project using a discount rate.

12 *Ibid*, Article 26.

the proper interpretation of Article 32.4 of the Guyana-ExxonMobil PSA under Guyanese law, the governing law of the contract. Unfortunately, Articles 32.4 and 26 further demonstrate that the Guyana-ExxonMobil PSA is lopsided and arguably favours the protection of the investor's interest. Repeated mention is made in the PSA of protecting the contractor's economic benefits, while no mention is made of protecting the interests of the state. Ironically, while the contract makes mention of "generally accepted customs and usages of the international petroleum industry",[13] and states that the contractor and subcontractors must operate in such a manner as is "customary in the international petroleum industry in accordance with good oil field practices",[14] it can be argued that the very core of the contract does not adhere to general international petroleum industry practices.

The Guyana-ExxonMobil PSA has been severely criticised by various media commentators in Guyana. Not only is it argued that the contract should be renegotiated, and that the stabilisation clause is in violation of the sovereignty of the state; but the Transparency Institute of Guyana Inc has also argued that the Guyana-ExxonMobil PSA is illegal at its very root and irretrievably flawed.[15] While there have been calls for the government to renegotiate the PSA, the newly formed Department of Energy has made it abundantly clear on several occasions that it will not be seeking to renegotiate the contract.[16] In addition, Sir Paul Collier, a renowned University of Oxford professor of economics and public policy, cautioned the government against pulling back from the Guyana-ExxonMobil PSA, warning that this could spell doom for Guyana's investment climate.[17] Instead, he suggested, as it has been determined that there is oil and more companies are now seeking to invest, Guyana should seek to extract better terms on future contracts while simultaneously building capacity to determine what these investors will pay in taxes. "What would be absolutely disastrous is tearing this contract up. If you tear this contract up, nobody else will come. That is the brute reality,"[18] Collier stated during a visit to Guyana. "Governments have to establish credibility over the contracts they sign and if

13 *Ibid*, Article 27.

14 *Ibid*, Article 20.2 (c).

15 "ExxonMobil contract illegal, irretrievably flawed and is either the result of grand corruption or grand incompetence" *Stabroek News*, (6 June 2019), www.stabroeknews.com/2019/06/06/news/guyana/exxonmobil-contract-illegal-irretrievably-flawed-and-is-either-the-result-of-grand-corruption-or-grand-incompetence/.

16 "Energy Dept. taking incorrect stance on important issues – Should be focused on renegotiation of oil contracts, etc. – Dr. Mangal," *Kaieteur News* (16 April 2019), www.kaieteurnewsonline.com/2019/04/16/energy-dept-taking-incorrect-stance-on-important-issues-should-be-focused-on-renegotiation-of-oil-contracts-dr-mangal/; "Don't be fearful of renegotiation...Exxon will not walk away from Guyana, no matter what – says Houston University Instructor," *Kaieteur News* (19 May 2019), www.kaieteurnewsonline.com/2019/05/19/dont-be-fearful-of-renegotiation-exxon-will-not-walk-away-from-guyana-no-matter-what-says-houston-university-instructor/.

17 "Tearing up Exxon deal would be 'disastrous' – Sir Paul Collier," *Staborek News*, (22 March 2018). www.stabroeknews.com/2018/03/22/news/guyana/tearing-up-exxon-deal-would-be-disastrous-sir-paul-collier/.

18 *Ibid.*

the first contract you sign, you tear up within a couple of years of signing it, you're dead. Credibility is vital," he added.[19]

Under the miscellaneous provisions of the Guyana-ExxonMobil PSA Article 31.2 provides that: "This Agreement shall not be amended or modified in any respect except by written agreement entered into by all the Parties which shall state the date upon which the amendment or modification shall become effective." One question here is whether this implies that there is room for renegotiation to the extent that there is mutual agreement. It is submitted that this article provides for amendment or modification of the agreement, which is separate from renegotiation, since a renegotiation clause will typically refer to a triggering event, such as a fundamental change in circumstances.

2.2 Local content

Turning to local content, this is critical to the development of Guyana's oil and gas economy. Before the announcement of the oil discovery in 2015, Guyana had laws relating to local content in the extractive industries. Several laws which allow foreign investors to engage in extractive activities, such as forestry and mining,[20] make implicit reference to local content. Like several new oil and gas producing countries, Guyana sought to develop a local content policy specifically for the petroleum sector.[21]

The Guyana Petroleum (Exploration and Production) Act (1986)[22] is outdated. Like the Mining Act, the Petroleum (Exploration and Production) Act includes general obligations concerning the employment and training of Guyanese nationals, as well as the procurement of goods and services that can be procured locally. The Petroleum (Exploration and Production) Act and the Petroleum (Exploration and Production) Regulations 1986 do not mention the term 'local content'. Section 36(1) of the act provides as follows:

> *A petroleum production licence shall not be granted to an applicant therefor unless – …*
>
> *(iv) the applicant's proposals for the employment and training of citizens of Guyana are satisfactory;*
>
> *(v) the applicant's proposals with respect to the procurement of goods and services obtainable within Guyana are satisfactory…*[23]

---

19 *Ibid.* Collier led a group of international researchers and petroleum policy advisers in meetings with cabinet ministers in Guyana to discuss the emerging oil and gas sector and give insight into prudent preparations for the revenues that will be generated from the industry.

20 See the Forest Act (Cap 67:01 Laws of Guyana), subsequently repealed by the Forest Act (6/2009); the Mining Act, (20/1989, Cap 65:01, Laws of Guyana); the Guyana Geology and Mines Commission Act (1979) (Cap 65:09, Laws of Guyana), subsequently amended by the Guyana Geology and Mines Commission (Amendment) Act (3/1987, Laws of Guyana).

21 See Government of Guyana, Ministry of the Presidency, Department of Energy, *Guyana Petroleum Sector Realising Local Content Benefits and Value Retention from Guyana's Petroleum Resources' Local Content Policy* (January 2020).

22 The Petroleum (Exploration and Production) Act (3/1986), Cap 65:10, Laws of Guyana.

23 The Petroleum Regulations (Legal Notice 5/1986) made pursuant to Section 70 of the Petroleum (Exploration and Production) Act (3/1986), Cap. 65:10, Laws of Guyana.

The Guyana-ExxonMobil PSA makes provision for local content. Article 18 provides that the contractor must require the operator to give preference to:

(a) *the purchase of Guyanese goods and materials, provided that such goods and materials are available on a timely basis of the quality and in the quantity required by the Operator at competitive prices; and*

(b) *the employment of Guyanese Sub-Contractors insofar as they are commercially competitive and satisfy the Operator's financial and technical requirements and meet the requirements of ...*

The requirement that the arrangement be 'commercially competitive' is ambiguous and does not add anything to local content implementation in Guyana. As Michael Warner[24] observed when reviewing similar local content provisions to that in the Guyana-ExxonMobil PSA, to argue that such clauses give preference to domestic suppliers is perhaps a little disingenuous, because the requirement to be 'commercially competitive' requires the domestic supplier to meet technical international performance requirements and to match its international rivals on price. As such, the domestic supplier could be awarded the contract with or without the stated 'preference' in the clause in the PSA. This demonstrates that, notwithstanding some form of local content provision in the laws or contractual agreements, the very existence of local content does not lead to improvements in the local economy.

Article 18.3 of the Guyana-ExxonMobil PSA further stipulates that the contractor must make "reasonable efforts to train Guyanese suppliers and subcontractors in the mechanics of participating in tenders and competing for contracts to be offered pursuant to the petroleum operations". Contractors should thus train Guyanese suppliers and subcontractors to participate in competitive bidding processes and strengthen their capacity to compete successfully for tenders to do work for international oil companies. However, the term 'reasonable efforts' is another ambiguous phrase. The contract also fails to explain exactly what is meant by 'the mechanics of participating in tenders and competing for contracts'. Unlike the local content laws in Nigeria and Indonesia, and the contractual provisions in the agreements from Afghanistan and Timor-Leste, the local content provisions in the Guyana-ExxonMobil PSA do not stipulate specific training requirements. However, it is submitted that the tools utilised in oil producing countries such as Indonesia and Nigeria, which require very specific quotas regarding goods and services, would be unsuitable for Guyana, because Guyana first needs to ensure that it has the capacity to supply the required goods. On the other hand, similar tools to those utilised in the Afghanistan contract, on the training and education of nationals to provide

24 Michael Warner, Chapters 1 and 2, *Local Content in Procurement: Creating Local Jobs and Competitive Domestic Industries in Supply Chains*, (Routledge, 2011) at p17.

the labour to meet the needs of the oil and gas sector, could be adopted in Guyana.

The Guyanese local content policy and future PSAs with IOCs should include succession plans for the employment of Guyanese in the industry. Such contracts could require IOCs to agree that, insofar as possible, they will employ qualified Guyanese nationals in the petroleum operations and require their contractors and subcontractors to do the same. There should also be obligations for IOCs:

- to give priority to Guyanese nationals with equivalent qualifications and experience; and
- to gradually replace a percentage (eg, 80%) of their expatriate staff with qualified Guyanese nationals within a given timeframe (eg, four years after grant of the licence).

2.3 Decommissioning

The provisions in the Guyana-ExxonMobil PSA dealing with decommissioning must further be highlighted. Decommissioning is the end stage of the lifecycle of petroleum operations and oil producing states have certain environmental responsibilities under general public international law and domestic laws. Guyana has a responsibility to balance the pursuit of oil exploration and production alongside legal environmental obligations, to ensure that the risk of negatively impacting the environment is minimised and that measures are put in place to help restore the areas at the end of the petroleum operations.

Historically, little attention was paid to the issue of decommissioning in Guyana. 'Abandonment' was the original term used in various laws, regulations and contractual provisions; and this term is still used in many legal documents today. The 1986 Petroleum Regulations are the most significant regulations that focus on decommissioning in Guyana. The Petroleum (Exploration and Production) Act does not mention the terms 'abandonment' or 'decommissioning'; while the 1986 Petroleum Regulations mention abandonment once and provide for the removal of property at the end of the production by the petroleum production licence holder under Regulation 9.

The 1986 Petroleum Regulations also provide that the holder of a licence must furnish to the minister responsible for petroleum (ie, the minister of natural resources), through the chief inspector, reports, data and other information and samples acquired in the course of the prospecting operations under the licence, within one week of completion of any drilling or geological operations, abandonment, suspension or completion design under Regulation 25(3).[25] Additionally, Regulation 6(5) provides that a licensee must furnish to the chief inspector reasonable notice of its intention to abandon any well,

25 Petroleum Regulations (n 23), Regulation 25(3)(iii)(E).

giving reasons therefor and the techniques to be used therein; and the closure or plugging of any well must be carried out only with the prior written consent of the minister responsible for petroleum and in the manner approved by the minister.[26]

Turning to the Guyana-ExxonMobil PSA, Article 20 provides that "(a)ll funds required to carry out the approved abandonment programme shall be made available by Contractor when the cost for abandonment are incurred";[27] and that "(a)ll costs included in the approved abandonment programme and budget shall be Recoverable Contract Costs as operating costs".[28] In addition to the 1986 Petroleum Regulations and the Guyana-ExxonMobil PSA, a few other laws prescribe obligations relating to abandonment and decommissioning activities in Guyana.[29]

Guyana's legislative framework requires revision to include decommissioning provisions that are satisfactory considering current best practices in the energy industry, as well as the country's domestic and international law obligations. A major gap in the laws and regulations of Guyana is that there is no requirement for a decommission fund or for moneys to be placed in an escrow account. The weakness of the legislative framework is compounded when one reviews the Guyana-ExxonMobil PSA. As pointed out above, there is no pre-funding required and no fund created under Article 20 of the PSA. This is unusual by today's oil and gas industry standards.

3. Relationship of Guyana-ExxonMobil PSA with the petroleum laws

Under the laws of Guyana, property in the mineral estate follows the common law; hence, petroleum is vested in the state and the state has the exclusive right to search for and extract such petroleum.[30] The Petroleum (Exploration and Production) Act and the 1986 Petroleum Regulations govern and regulate the exploration and exploitation of petroleum in Guyana. The act empowers the minister responsible for petroleum to grant a petroleum prospecting licence and a petroleum production licence for the prospecting of petroleum and for matters connected thereto. The act also sets out the conditions on the duration, renewal and cancellation of the licence, and other powers relevant to petroleum operations.

A petroleum prospecting licence usually last for 10 years. It consists of an initial period of four years with provisions for two further periods, at the option of the licensee. Relinquishment is mandatory and the licensee must relinquish blocks or a percentage of the licensed area at given intervals during the terms of

---

26 *Ibid*, Regulation 6(5).

27 *Ibid*, Article 20.1(d)(iii)(ff).

28 *Ibid*, Article 20.1(d)(iii)(gg).

29 See, for instance, the Environmental Protection Act, (11/1996), Laws of Guyana; see also the Environmental Protection (Amendment) Act (17/2005), Laws of Guyana.

30 Petroleum (Production) Act, Cap. 65:05, Laws of Guyana, Section 2.

the licence. These mandatory relinquishments exclude the discovery areas. With regard to the petroleum production licence, this is issued if a commercial petroleum discovery is made. This licence has an initial period of 20 years, with a single renewal period of up to 10 years which can be applied for if necessary. PSAs between the government of Guyana and oil companies for licences granted to and held by oil companies are provided for under the act. The terms and conditions of the petroleum prospecting licence are usually established through negotiations. The act envisages that a PSA not inconsistent with the act will document any such settled terms and conditions to be included in licences granted under the act. The minister responsible for petroleum is authorised by the act to conclude such agreements.

4. The role of the competent authority in the Guyana-ExxonMobil PSA

The Department of Energy, the Ministry of Natural Resources and the GGMC all play central roles under the Guyana-ExxonMobil PSA, and in the regulation of oil and gas in Guyana generally. However, the roles of these agencies are unclear, which can lead to duplication of work and other problems. There is an urgent need for the government to streamline the roles of these various agencies and strengthen their institutional capacity to regulate the burgeoning energy sector.

The minister responsible for petroleum is authorised by the act to conclude PSAs. PSAs between the government of Guyana are provided for under the act. The terms and conditions of the petroleum prospecting licence are usually established through negotiations. Section 10 of the act provides that a PSA consistent with the act will document any such settled terms and conditions to be included in licences granted under the act.[31] The discretion to change the law is expressly stated only with regard to the tax system and the minister responsible for finance may apply for an order to modify the tax laws in respect of a licence as follows: "The Minister assigned responsibility for Finance may, by order, which shall be subject to affirmative resolution of the National Assembly, direct that any or all of the written laws mentioned in subsection (2) shall not apply to, or in relation to, a licensee where the licensee has entered into a production sharing agreement with the Government of Guyana."[32]

The Guyana Geology and Mines Commission Act (1979), as amended in 1987, created the GGMC and sets out its functions and roles. The GGMC provides for the effective stewardship of all mineral resources by ensuring that the opportunities for mineral resources development (exploration and

---

31 *Ibid*, Section 10: "The Minister may enter into an agreement (not inconsistent with this Act) with any person with respect to all or any of the following matters, namely— (a) the grant to that person or to any other person (including anybody corporate to be formed), identified in the agreement, of a licence."

32 *Ibid*, Section 51(1).

extraction) increase, and promoting and supporting investment in the mining sector. The Department of Energy was newly created, but there is no law that clearly outlines its function – that is, the laws do not provide for the establishment of this department. The department was established to effectively manage the hydrocarbon resources of Guyana and optimise the benefits therefrom.[33]

5. Conclusion

Guyana is a new frontier in the petroleum industry, but the legal framework governing oil and gas exploration and production is outdated. The Guyana-ExxonMobil PSA has not filled the gap to provide protection where the law is lacking. As a result, there is a need for urgent law reform in several areas. There is a need to prescribe laws which address decommissioning, local content, stabilisation and several other areas. The laws and regulations in Guyana, as well as the model PSAs that are currently being used by the GGMC and the Department of Energy, do not contain satisfactory provisions to protect the interest of Guyana. Guyana would benefit from creating a model PSA which includes provisions aligned with best industry practices in the areas highlighted in this chapter.

33 See Government of Guyana, Ministry of the Presidency, Department of Energy's Vision and Mission Statement, https://nre.gov.gy/department-of-energy/.

Indonesia

Ali Nasir
Marlina Tambunan
Premier Oil Indonesia

1. Introduction

The Indonesian upstream oil and gas industry pre-dates the independence of Indonesia. The first oil discovery was made in North Sumatra in 1885. The subsequent expansion of oil exploration and exploitation activities led to the promulgation of the East Indies Mining Law of 1899 by the colonial government, which constituted the legal basis for certain petroleum concessionaires.

When Indonesia gained independence from the Netherlands, Article 33 of the Constitution 1945 provided that the state "controls and exploits the natural resources contained in the land and the water to the greatest benefit of the people". However, the Indonesian government did not have a clear idea of how to replace the colonial concession system, which contradicted the constitutional mandate for the petroleum industry under Article 33 of the Constitution; the concessionaires that dominated the oil industry were thus permitted to continue to operate under 'let alone' agreements.[1] No new concessions were issued until 1960, when Law 44/1960 on Oil and Natural Gas was introduced, which officially ended the colonial concession system.

Pursuant to Law 44/1960, the concept of the 'concession' was replaced with the 'authority to mine', which was vested in the state enterprise established to execute oil and gas mining activities. Law 44/1960 allowed the state enterprise to enter into a contract of work (COW) with another party as the contractor to the state enterprise in carrying out the authority to mine. However, the COW fell short of the constitutional mandate, as under the COW management of the operations remained fully in the hands of the contractor and ownership of the hydrocarbons passed to the contractor at the wellhead.

As a result, the production sharing concept was introduced as a pilot project between PN Permina and two small foreign companies that worked for PN Permina as contractors. PN Permina actually managed the operations, but the foreign companies retained operational control of the field and provided funds

1 Tengku Nathan Machmud, *The Indonesian Production Sharing Contract – An Investor's Perspective* (Kluwer Law International BV, 2000), pp45–46.

as a working interest. They were compensated in kind by lifting their share of production, and the costs were agreed mutually and recovered by the foreign companies from production. In 1966, the first-generation prototype production sharing contract (PSC) was executed between PN Permina and Independent Indonesian American Petroleum Company; it became effective in January 1967. The key principles were as follows:

- The mineral rights to oil and gas remained with the government;
- The mining rights were vested in PN Permina (based on an authority to mine); and
- The economic rights to the contractor's share passed to the contractor at the point of export.

Major changes to the concept of the PSC were made in 2001 through the issuance of Law 22/2001 on Oil and Gas and in 2017 through the issuance of Ministry of Energy and Mineral Resources Regulation 8/2017 on Gross Split PSCs, as amended from time to time. Law 22/2001 retained the arrangement whereby mineral rights, mining rights and economic rights are vested in the state as it was introduced in the original PSC. The cost recovery mechanism of PSC is also retained in Law 22/2001: the contractor recovers the costs incurred in conducting exploration and exploitation once commercial production commences and upon approval of the work programme and budget and authorisation financial expenditure by Badan Pelaksana Kegiatan Usaha Hulu Minyak dan Gas Bumi (BPMIGAS) (see section 4).

Over the years, a number of critics have drawn attention to the cost recovery regime, which the Supreme Audit Agency maintains was allegedly abused by oil and gas contractors. This led to the issuance of Regulation 8/2017, pursuant to which new PSCs must comply with a new model PSC, which dispenses with the cost recovery system that was previously a feature of all Indonesian PSCs by adopting the gross split concept. Under the gross split PSC system, contractors are expected to be more cost conscious and cost effective in allocating their budget to funding exploration and production activities. Regulation 8/2017 expressly requires that gross split PSCs, at a minimum, incorporate the following provisions:

- Ownership of the natural resources remains with the state up to the delivery point;
- The state party controls the operational management of the working area; and
- Capital and operational costs are borne entirely by the contractor.

2. Scope and structure of the PSC

The gross split PSC evolved from the production sharing concept. Therefore, most of the features of the PSC are adopted in the gross split PSC, except for the cost recovery mechanism. The following outline contains typical sections that are covered in the PSC model for cost recovery PSCs and gross split PSCs:

- scope and definitions;
- term;
- exclusion of areas;
- work programmes and expenditures;
- rights and obligations of the parties;
- recovery of operating costs and handling of production;
- valuation of petroleum;
- compensation assistance and production bonus;
- payment;
- title of equipment;
- consultation and arbitration;
- employment and training of Indonesian personnel;
- termination;
- books and accounts and audits;
- other provisions;
- participation;
- Exhibit A: description of contract area;
- Exhibit B: map of contract area;
- Exhibit C: accounting procedure; and
- Exhibit D: memorandum of participation.

3. Main features of PSCs: cost oil and profit oil

As mentioned above, there are two categories of PSCs: traditional cost recovery PSCs and gross split PSCs. The main difference between the two regimes is the abolition of the cost recovery scheme in the gross split PSC. Cost recovery or cost oil is the means by which the contractor recoups the costs of exploration, development and operations from gross revenues.

3.1 Cost recovery PSC system

Under the Indonesian PSC, the contractor's entitlement consists of cost recovery or cost oil, investment credit (if applicable) and its equity share or profit oil. The first-generation PSCs allowed for a maximum of 40% cost recovery from gross annual production; the remaining production was shared 35/65 between the contractor and PN Permina respectively. The unrecovered portion of the accumulated cost recovery account was to be recovered in subsequent years, until such time as a lesser percentage than the 40% cost recovery ceiling would suffice. The second-generation PSCs did away with the cost recovery limit. Under the second-generation PSCs, in the initial years of production, the contractor could conceivably claim 100% of production as cost recovery. Pertamina (see section 4) started to receive a share of production only when the contractor reached a point where less than 100% of production was needed for cost recovery, which normally occurred after several years of production. Therefore, the third-generation PSCs introduced a new contract feature that effectively works exactly like a cost recovery limit, called first tranche petroleum (FTP), to ensure that Pertamina and the government receive a share of production regardless of the operating cost situation. The FTP element requires that 20% of gross production be shared between the parties[2] to the PSC in favour of the government before cost recovery. The contractor's share is taxed. The remaining 80% of gross production is available for cost recovery.

Elements that make up cost recovery are normally recovered on a first in, first out basis. Any costs carried forward from prior years are recovered first. These elements normally include operating costs and investment credit. Exhibit C of the PSC on accounting procedures provides that operating costs consist of the following.

(a) ***Current year non-capital costs***

'Non-capital costs' are those operating costs that relate to the current year's operations, as well as the costs of surveys and the intangible costs of drilling exploratory and development wells.

(b) ***Current depreciation for capital costs***

'Capital costs' are expenditures for items which normally have a useful life beyond the year incurred. Depreciation of capital costs will be calculated beginning from the calendar year in which the asset is placed into service, with a full year's depreciation allowed for the initial calendar year using the declining balance depreciation method. Once the original exploration and development costs have been recovered, operating costs comprise the majority of recovered costs. The calculation of annual depreciation is based on the capital cost of each asset multiplied by the depreciation factor as follows:

- Group 1 = 50%; and
- Group 2 = 25%.

Group 1 is applicable to assets whose useful lives are five years, such as cars, trucks, buses, construction equipment, tools and office furniture. Group 2 is applicable to assets whose useful lives are 10 years, such as offshore platforms, production facilities, drilling equipment and barges.

Abandonment and site restoration costs are recovered through cost recovery prior to abandonment, and site restoration activities are carried out where they are accumulated through a sinking fund that matures at the time of abandonment and site restoration. The estimates of moneys required for the

2 Some PSCs provide only for 10% FTP to the government (non-shareable).

funding of any abandonment and site restoration programme are established in the approved plan of development (POD) for the relevant field. The costs of exploratory well abandonment and site restoration, however, are directly charged to the operating costs.

(c) ***Current year allowed recovery of prior years' unrecovered operating costs***

The Indonesian PSC allows the contractor to carry forward unrecovered costs for recovery in subsequent periods. However, sunk costs or past costs that have not been recovered can be recovered only after commercial production commences.

Since the issuance of Government Regulation (GR) 79/2010 on Cost Recovery and Provisions on Income Tax in Oil and Gas Activities, the recovery of these operating costs is subject to the negative list set out in GR 79/2010.

Under the Indonesian PSC, investment credit is granted as an incentive to the contractor which:

- is immediately recoverable before cost recovery;
- need not be depreciated like the costs that justified the credit; and
- can be carried forward.

Investment credit applies only to facilities such as platforms, pipelines and processing equipment. Investment credit reduces the ultimate profit oil split for both parties to the PSC.

The amount of gross production after deducting FTP, investment credit and cost oil is called 'profit oil'. Profit oil is split between the parties to the PSC according to the terms of the PSC. Profit oil has gone through changes from the first-generation PSC as described above. These changes were made in order to improve contract economics, which ultimately were intended to attract investment.

3.2 Gross split PSC system

Cost recovery or cost oil is not recognised in the gross split PSC system. Contractors are responsible for incurring costs necessary to carry out the petroleum operations under the PSC and these costs are not subject to cost recovery. However, Regulation 8 provides that these costs are deductible for income tax purposes, subject to the fulfilment of requirements set out in the implementing regulations of Regulation 8/2017.

Regulation 8/2017 provides that the gross production of oil and gas is to be divided between the parties to the PSC calculated using the base split percentage specified in Table 1, which is then adjusted according to a number of variables as described below.

Table 1. Base split percentages

	Contractor	Indonesian government
Oil	43%	57%
Gas	48%	52%

(a) ***Base split***

Base split is utilised as a base reference in stipulating the production sharing amount upon the approval of a POD. The base split percentage is adjusted by reference to:

- variable components; and
- progressive components when the POD is approved to determine the percentage gross split to be applied to a field.

The percentage gross split to be applied to a first POD is determined by the minister of energy and mineral resources based on a proposal from SKK Migas (see section 4). The percentage gross split to be applied to subsequent developments is determined by the chairman of SKK Migas.

(b) ***Variable components***

The base split will be adjusted by the following variable components that address specific matters affecting the costs of developing and commercialising the field:

- the field status (POD I/subsequent POD/no POD);
- the location of the field (onshore or offshore and, if offshore, the water depth);
- the vertical depth of the reservoir;
- the type (conventional or non-conventional) of reservoir;
- the availability of supporting infrastructure;
- whether the field contains heavy oil or the petroleum specification requires additional costs to be incurred due to high levels of carbon dioxide or hydrogen sulphide;
- the fulfilment of local content requirements during field development; and
- whether the field is in the primary, secondary or tertiary phase of production.

(c) ***Progressive components***

There are two progressive components which cause the percentage gross split to fluctuate:

- for oil projects, the price at which adjustments will be based on the formula set out in Regulation 8/2017; and for gas projects, the price at which additional split will be awarded for projects with a gas price of less than $7 per metric million British thermal units; and
- cumulative oil production (the contractor's production share will also be adjusted in its favour when a field begins production; and as cumulative production from the field increases, the favourable adjustment will be reduced until it ceases once cumulative production reaches 175 millions of barrels of oil equivalent).

The progressive components focus on the revenue generated from the field and adjust the gross split percentage from time to time.

The application of the above adjustment factors means that the contractor's overall gross split percentage (before tax) will fluctuate based on the following formula:

Base split (+ / -) Variable components (+ / -) Progressive components

If a commercial evaluation of a field or fields indicates that the project does not meet a 'certain economic level', the minister of energy and mineral resources has the discretion to award an additional split to the contractor. If a commercial evaluation of a field or fields indicates that the project exceeds a 'certain economic level', the minister has the discretion to award an additional split to the state party. This gives the minister flexibility to adjust the overall gross split percentage to the contractor. Regulation 8/2017 is silent on how this discretion should be applied and on what the term 'certain economic level' means in practice.

Once commercial production has commenced, adjustments of the production share may be made if the actual conditions deviate from the variable and progressive components used in setting the production share during field development. Further, adjustments to the crude oil price and gas price element of the progressive components will be made monthly based on the results of evaluations carried out by SKK Migas. The evaluation of the crude oil price will be based on the monthly calculation of the Indonesia Crude Price. The evaluation of the gas price will be based on the realisation of the weighted average gas price calculation.

The gross split PSCs do away with:

- the FTP structure, which was designed to ensure that the state receives a share of production without having to wait until all approved costs are first recovered from production; and
- investment credit allowances, as the variable components are designed to incentivise contractors to invest in frontier, deepwater and other high-risk/high-cost areas by giving them a greater share of production as compensation for the additional investment risks and costs.

4. The role of the competent authority: NOC, ministry or independent agency?

Article 33 of the 1945 Constitution suggests that only the state or a state enterprise representing the state may control production and the use of petroleum and petroleum products to promote the best interests of the people. Therefore, Pertamina[3] was established as a national oil company (NOC), holding both governmental and commercial roles under the PSC model. Pertamina was the holder of the mining authority and was also responsible for licensing and contracting with foreign operators, marketing the crude oil and gas produced, and supplying the domestic market with refined products. There was no independent agency to monitor its commercial activities. Pertamina was supposed to be an oil producer, but under this model it mainly served as a distributing agent.

In the aftermath of the 1997 financial crisis, the fall of the Suharto regime and the International Monetary Fund's Special Audit, the government was asked to reform the governance of oil and gas. One of the reforms was Pertamina's transformation into a limited liability company and the elimination of its monopolistic role. Under Law 22/2001, Pertamina was officially relieved of its role as the government's representative in the upstream oil and gas business, and was transformed into an ordinary limited liability state-owned enterprise operating in both the upstream and downstream oil and gas sectors. The mining authority was transferred to the government, which is represented by the Ministry of Energy and Mineral Resources. The government as the holder of the mining authority took over Pertamina's governmental role. It then established an independent, non-profit state-owned legal entity, BPMIGAS, to replace the contracting function of Pertamina. BPMIGAS replaced Pertamina as the state party to the PSC and was responsible for the management and supervision of the implementation of the PSC by contractors to ensure that oil and gas extraction provides the greatest benefits for the Indonesian people.

BPMIGAS was part of the national effort to reform the oil and gas legal framework. Its role was to produce accountable, transparent and predictable policies that would foster competition and efficiency in the upstream oil and gas sector. Unfortunately, however, its establishment failed to boost performance and oil production continued to decline. BPMIGAS was perceived as being slow to recognise the realities of both the world oil markets and Indonesia's hydrocarbon resources. However, this was not the reasoning of the Constitutional Court when it declared BPMIGAS unconstitutional in 2012; the entity was effectively abolished that year as a result. The Constitutional Court decision was based on the following reasoning:[4]

---

3 PN Pertamina was established in 1968 as a result of a merger between PN Permina and PN Pertamin. Under Law 8/1971, PN Pertamina changed its name to Pertamina. For more information on the history of Pertamina, see Pertamina, "Who we are", https://pertamina.com/en/who-we-are.

4 Constitutional Court Decision 36/PUU-X/2012, paras 3.11–3.14.

- The state was not directly involved in the upstream oil and gas sector, as BPMIGAS only had a supervisory function, whereas actual exploration and exploitation activities were carried out by private companies through a PSC with BPMIGAS. This arrangement did not provide the state with sufficient control of its own natural resources.
- The act of BPMIGAS entering into PSCs directly fettered the discretion and sovereignty of the state to issue new regulations and policies that would conflict with the PSCs.
- The existence of BPMIGAS resulted in greater bureaucracy and potential inefficiencies and corruption.

In order to fill the legal vacuum as a result of the abolition of BPMIGAS, the Constitutional Court expressly stated that BPMIGAS's powers would be vested in the Ministry of Energy and Mineral Resources. It further stated that its ruling should not take effect retroactively and therefore, all existing PSCs should in theory remain valid and binding. The government swiftly responded to this decision by establishing a temporary regulatory entity called SKK Migas (previously known as SKSP Migas) to administer the transition to the long-term successor to BPMIGAS as per the Constitutional Court decision. Although this short-term assumption of BPMIGAS's functions by SKK Migas was intended to minimise disruption, in reality, disruption and uncertainty remain ongoing, as Law 22/2001 is still in force. The amendment to Law 22/2001 under Law 11/2020 on Job Creation provided no clarity on who will be the long-term successor to BPMIGAS. Thus, the quest to find the right legal framework for the Indonesian petroleum industry continues, creating legal uncertainty for investors.

5. Analysis of the main clauses of the PSC

The main clauses of the PSC are as follows:

- exploration;
- development and commercial discovery;
- local content;
- operator;
- minimum work obligations;
- liability;
- environment;
- corruption;
- royalties;
- taxes;
- applicable law; and
- dispute resolution.

5.1 Exploration

The term of the PSC is 30 years, consisting of exploration and exploitation periods. The initial term of the exploration period is six years as from the effective date, with an option for the contractor to request a one-off extension to the end of the initial term of the exploration period by SKK Migas for a maximum period of four years.[5] SKK Migas will not unreasonably withhold approval of such a request, provided that the contractor has fully complied with the requirements of relinquishment of the contract area and has performed its firm commitments as set out under the PSC.

If the contractor fails to fulfil these requirements, SKK Migas may consider the following factors in evaluating and determining whether to approve the extension:

- the contractor's performance in conducting exploration operations during the initial six years of the exploration period;
- its fulfilment of financial obligations; and
- its efforts to discover hydrocarbons.

If, at the end of the initial six years of the exploration period or the approved four-year extension, no petroleum is discovered in commercial quantities in the contract area, the PSC will automatically terminate in its entirety and the contractor must relinquish all of the remaining contract area to the government through SKK Migas immediately after receipt of notification from SKK Migas.

However, the termination of the PSC will not release the contractor from its outstanding obligations, including the obligation to perform any necessary abandonment of any fields, remove any equipment and installations and undertake site restoration.

While the maximum exploration period under the PSC is 10 years, on occasion, the government has approved an additional exploration period beyond this 10-year period.[6]

5.2 Development and commercial discovery

If, during the exploration period or the additional exploration period, petroleum is discovered in the contract area in a quantity and quality which the contractor has reasonably determined make production commercially viable, the contractor will immediately report the discovery to SKK Migas and the government. Its report must specify in reasonable detail the estimated amount of the reserves and quality of the petroleum, supported by the relevant data,

---

5 This is in line with Article 14 of Law 22 and Article 27 of Government Regulation 35/2004 on Upstream Oil and Gas Business Activities.

6 Inpex Petroleum (Masela PSC) and Premier Oil (Tuna PSC) are some of the companies that have received an extension of the exploration period.

such as a certificate of the quantity and quality of the petroleum reserves discovered by the contractor. SKK Migas will not unreasonably withhold delivery of an acknowledgement letter to the contractor.

Upon receipt of SKK Migas' acknowledgement letter, the contractor must, as soon as practicable, but in no case later than three years thereafter, submit a proposed POD for the field to SKK Migas for evaluation. If, during this three-year period, the contractor does not submit a proposed POD and the exploration period expires, the PSC automatically terminates. There are some exceptions to this provision whereby the contractor may request a maximum two-year extension in relation to:

- the discovery of hydrocarbons in frontier or deepwater areas, or certain other areas whose development, in the view of SKK Migas, is technically difficult; and/or
- the discovery of a natural gas field (except a field containing associated natural gas), the sale and purchase commitment for which cannot be agreed by the contractor and the buyer(s) within this three-year timeframe, having negotiated in good faith.

If the government – in this case, the minister of energy and mineral resources – approves the contractor's proposed POD for the first field in the contract area, this approval will constitute the declaration of commerciality of the entire contract area, and the contractor must commence development of the field or fields in which the petroleum has been discovered.[7]

If the contractor receives POD approval to develop its first field in the contract area, but fails to conduct petroleum operations to develop it within five years of the end of the exploration period, in accordance with the schedules proposed in the approved POD, the PSC will automatically terminate on the expiry of this five-year period, unless the parties have agreed otherwise.

SKK Migas will notify the contractor of the expiry of this five-year period and the expiry of the contract. Upon receipt of the notification letter, the contractor must relinquish all of the remaining contract area to the government through SKK Migas.

Given the unique nature of the gas market, an exception to this five-year period may be made for the development of natural gas fields. If it is anticipated that the contractor may not have successfully entered into any commercial gas sales agreements within the five-year period, at the request of the contractor, SKK Migas may extend this for a reasonable period(s) of time, as determined by SKK Migas. If, on the expiry of this extension, the contractor remains unable to

---

7 Using POD approval as a declaration of commerciality of the contract area is enshrined in the latest model PSC. In previous model PSCs, the declaration of commerciality was separate from the POD approval.

enter into a commercial gas sales agreement, the parties will confer in good faith to determine all reasonable steps, including the possibility of granting an additional extension. If SKK Migas decides not to grant an additional extension to contractor, it will advise the contractor of its decision and the expiry of the term of the contract, and the contractor will be obliged to relinquish the remaining contract area to the government through SKK Migas.

5.3 Local content

The Indonesian model PSC includes no local content obligations other than a requirement for contractors to employ qualified Indonesian personnel and provide training once commercial production commences. The costs and expenses of training Indonesian personnel must be included in the operating costs. Although the contract is silent on local content requirements, this does not mean that contractors have no obligation to prioritise local goods and services. Under the PSC, the contractor is subject to local laws and regulations, including local content regulations.

Ministry of Energy and Mineral Resources Regulation 15/2013 on the Use of Domestic Products in the Upstream Oil and Gas Business Activities is the primary regulation on local content. It essentially requires the use of domestic goods and services in upstream oil and gas business activities by specifying a minimum level of local components that must be used by upstream oil and gas businesses.

The contractor must conduct its own assessment, which must be verified and validated by the director general of oil and gas and the Ministry of Energy and Mineral Resources. In addition, the director general has the authority to conduct audits to determine whether the contractor has achieved the required level of local content.[8] Contractors that fail to comply with the local content obligations are subject to sanctions imposed by SKK Migas,[9] including rejection of cost recovery in the case of cost recovery PSCs. In the case of gross split PSCs, the sanctions are somewhat unclear. However, under Regulation 8/2017, contractors that use local goods and/or services at a rate of between 30% and 100% will receive an additional split ranging from 2% to 4%.[10]

Domestic suppliers are also subject to financial sanctions by contractors if they fail to fulfil their local content obligation in rendering goods and services.[11]

5.4 Operator

Where there are two or more participating interest (PI) holders in a contract area, the PI holders must appoint an operator. The operator is authorised to

---

8 Article 17(3) of Ministry of Energy and Mineral Resources Regulation 15/2013.
9 *Ibid*, Article 21.
10 Part A, Point 9 of the Attachment to Ministry of Energy and Mineral Resources Regulation 8/2017.
11 Article 23 of Ministry of Energy and Mineral Resources Regulation 15/2013.

execute petroleum operations under the contract and to represent all PI holders in communicating and liaising with SKK Migas, the government and all other parties in relation to the PSC and its performance. SKK Migas will look solely to the operator for the performance of PI holders under the PSC.

As a general rule, the operator to be proposed to SKK Migas must have the necessary skills, experience, financial capability and qualified personnel to conduct petroleum operations. The initial appointment of the operator upon signing of the contract is recorded in the exhibit of the contract. The appointment of the operator in no way limits, restricts or discharges the other PI holders from their obligations, responsibilities and liabilities as PI holder(s) under the contract; and does not prevent SKK Migas from directly communicating and liaising with them, and enforcing their obligations, responsibilities and liabilities based on joint and several liability.

5.5 Minimum work obligations

The PSC requires the contractor to commence petroleum operations within six months of the effective date of the contract, failing which SKK Migas may recommend that the government terminate the contract.

Each PSC contains different level of work obligations. In general, there are two types of work obligations: firm commitments and work commitments. Firm commitments must be performed in the first three contract years and work commitments in the second three contract years. The contractor will be fined if it cannot complete the firm commitments, but this is not the case for the work commitments. In many cases, both the firm commitments and the work commitments are biddable.

Table 2 in the next page illustrates the firm and work commitments.

During the first three contract years, the contractor must carry out the work programme as set out above in respect of each of those years. If, during the first three contract years, the contractor performs less work than required, it may, with the consent of SKK Migas, carry forward such work not performed and add it to that to be performed in the following three contract years, without prejudice to its rights and obligations.

If, during the first three contract years, the contractor performs more work than required, it may subtract such excess from the work to be performed in the following three contract years.

In order to guarantee performance of the firm commitments, the contractor must submit a performance bond for the benefit of the government – in this case, the director general of oil and gas of the Ministry of Energy and Mineral Resources – for the sum as defined in the bid document. This submission must be made no later than the date of signing of the PSC. The value of the performance bond can be reduced if the value of the unperformed firm commitments is less than the value of the performance bond. Thereafter, the

Table 2. Firm and work commitments

Contract year	Work description	Activity		Budget	
		Unit	Amount	Unit	Amount
First three years (firm commitments)	Geological & geophysical (G&G)	Package	1	$	200,000
	Seismic 3D acquisition and processing	KM2	2,500	$	10 million
	Shipborne gravity and magnetic data	KM2	2,500	$	100,000
Second three years (work commitments)	G&G	Package	1	$	150,000
	Exploration well	Well	2	$	50 million

remaining value of the performance bond must at least equal that of the unperformed firm commitments.

5.6 Liability

Apart from tax liability, which is based solely on several liability, the contractor will be jointly and severally liable to SKK Migas and any other parties in connection with the petroleum operations under the PSC. That said, SKK Migas will first and foremost seek liability from the operator as the party appointed by the PI holders to represent them before SKK Migas.

5.7 Environment

Under the PSC, the contractor is responsible for preparing and executing the work programme in a conscientious manner and following good engineering practices. In addition, the contractor must, in conducting the petroleum operations:

- implement the applicable occupational health, safety and environmental protection standards in the oil and gas industry;
- take all reasonable and necessary precautions in order to prevent injury to or death of persons and damage to the environment and property; and
- comply with all applicable safety and environmental laws and regulations.

Furthermore, the contractor must:

- conduct an environmental baseline assessment at the beginning of its activities and thereafter conduct all obligations pursuant to the applicable law, such as analysis of environmental impact;
- take the necessary precautions to protect ecological systems, navigation and fishing, and prevent extensive pollution of the land, sea, rivers and other natural resources as a direct result of the petroleum operations undertaken under the work programme; and
- be responsible for the removal of all equipment and installations from such part of the contract area that is relinquished in a manner that is acceptable to SKK Migas and the government, and perform all necessary site restoration activities in accordance with the applicable government regulations to prevent hazards to human life and property or the environment.

5.8 Corruption

The Indonesian PSCs contain no provisions on corruption, but they require the contractor to comply with all laws and regulations in Indonesia, including those on anti-corruption. Indonesia has legislation that aims to prevent and prohibit the receipt and payment of bribes.[12] Under these laws, state apparatus, government officials and civil servants are prohibited from receiving or requesting gifts or payments for their personal benefit.

5.9 Royalties

In theory, Indonesian PSCs do not recognise the payment of royalties, but some may consider FTP as a kind of royalty. Under the FTP scheme, each year SKK Migas is entitled to take and receive a certain percentage of the petroleum production before any deductions for the recovery of operating costs and handling of production. Typically, this is:

- 10% of annual production when it is not shared with the contractor; or

12 Law 11/1980 on Bribery; Law 28/1999 on State Management that is Clean and Free from Corruption, Collusion and Nepotism; Law 31/1999 on Corruption Eradication (last amended by Law 20/2001); Law 30/2002 on the Corruption Eradication Commission; Law 46/2009 on the Corruption Court; and Law 8/2010 on the Prevention and Eradication of Money Laundering.

- 20% of annual production when it is split equally between SKK Migas and the contractor.

5.10 Taxes

The tax regime differs from one PSC to another. There are at least four regimes in this regard.

The first is the 'assume and discharge' PSC tax regime. These PSCs were signed before 2010 and contain 'assume and discharge' provisions, whereby SKK Migas – except with respect to the contractor's obligation to pay income tax and the final tax on profits after tax deduction – assumes and discharges all other Indonesian taxes of the contractor, including:

- value added tax;
- transfer tax;
- import and export duties on materials, equipment and supplies brought into or out of Indonesia by the contractor, its contractors and subcontractors; and
- exactions in respect of property, capital, net worth, operations, remittance or transactions, including any tax or levy on or in connection with operations performed under the PSC by the contractor.

The second regime applies to PSCs signed after 2010, under which the contractor must pay all taxes.[13] The assume and discharge privilege was eliminated under GR 79/2010. Consequently, investment in the oil and gas sector has slowed down since GR 79/2010 was introduced.

In an attempt to address this and improve the investment climate, the government issued GR 27/2017, amending GR 79/2010. Under this new regulation, the contractor may be granted tax facilities which are virtually equivalent to the old assume and discharge regime.[14] This is the third tax regime to be found in Indonesian PSCs.

The fourth tax regime is found in the gross split PSCs, under which the contractor is exempt from paying any tax during the exploration period. Tax obligations arise only once commercial production has commenced, at which point the contractor must pay all types of taxes (direct and indirect). This requirement is governed by GR 53/2017 on Tax Treatment for Upstream Oil and Gas Business Activities with Gross Split PSCs. While the tax regime under GR 53/2017 is not as good as the assume and discharge regime, it is better than the tax regime under GR 79/2010.

Law 22/2001 allows the contractor to choose the prevailing tax law or tax law applicable to it on signing of the PSC. However, contractors have

13 Articles 11 and 25 of GR 79/2010.
14 Article 14 of GR 27/2017.

consistently opted for the tax law applicable on signing of the PSC, known as the 'nailed-down' tax principle. Hence, such contractors cannot enjoy the lower tax rates that have been introduced by the government in recent years.[15]

5.11 Applicable law

The governing law of the PSC is Indonesian law and the contractor must comply with all applicable laws of Indonesia. The work programme must also be executed in a way that does not conflict with obligations under international laws that have been ratified by the Indonesian government.

5.12 Dispute resolution

Any disputes between SKK Migas and the contractor relating to the PSC or the interpretation and performance of any of its provisions should be settled amicably within 90 days of receipt by one party of notice from the other party of the existence of the dispute.

If the dispute cannot be settled amicably, it must be submitted to arbitration. SKK Migas on the one hand and the contractor on the other will each appoint one arbitrator, and these two arbitrators will appoint a third. If either party fails to appoint an arbitrator within 30 days of receipt of a written request to do so, that arbitrator will, at the request of the other party and as long as the parties have not agreed otherwise, be appointed by the president of the International Chamber of Commerce (ICC). If the first two arbitrators fail to agree on the appointment of a third arbitrator within 30 days of the appointment of the second arbitrator, the third arbitrator will, at the request of either party and as long as the parties have not agreed otherwise, be appointed by the president of the ICC.[16] If an arbitrator fails or is unable to act, his or her successor will be appointed in the same manner as the arbitrator whom he or she is succeeding. While the arbitral award is pending, the parties must diligently proceed pursuant to the provisions and terms of the PSC.

The arbitral award is final and binding upon the parties.

Arbitration will be conducted in English at a place to be agreed upon by both parties[17] and in accordance with the Rules of Arbitration of the ICC.

In addition, neither party will have the right to commence or maintain a suit or legal proceeding concerning the dispute, except as required to enforce execution of the arbitral award.

---

15 The corporate income tax rate has gradually reduced from 35%, 30% or 25% (depending on the year in which the PSC was signed) to 22% in 2021 and 20% from 2022 onwards. However, this latest reduction introduced by Law 2/2020 cannot be enjoyed by PSC contractors, as they have opted for the 'nailed down' tax regime in their PSCs.

16 In some PSCs, the parties must refer the appointment to the secretary general of the International Centre for Settlement of Investment Disputes.

17 Some PSCs pre-define the place of arbitration (ie, Indonesia).

6. Relationship of the PSC with the petroleum law

The legal and contractual foundation of the Indonesian PSC is the 1945 Constitution. From this flows the legislative authority that governs the tax and oil and gas regulations and outlines the authority and boundary conditions for relationships with investors. The Constitution is the cornerstone upon which all else stands, including the petroleum legislation and individual contracts. This means that Law 22/2001 and PSCs cannot contradict the Constitution – specifically Article 33, which provides that the state "controls and exploits the natural resources contained in the land and the water to the greatest benefit of the people".

Generally, a cooperation contract – which can be in the form of a PSC or a service contract – overrides the general principles of Indonesian income tax law, because such contracts have the status of *lex specialis*. Reference to the general tax laws and regulations will be made only on matters that are not specifically mentioned in the cooperation contract. The Indonesian PSC clause that deals with taxes falls under the rights and obligations of the contractor, but does not mention the income tax percentage or the additional withholding tax. However, in 2010, a dedicated regulation dealing with both tax and cost recovery arrangements for cost recovery PSCs was issued (GR 79/2010). A similar regulation (GR 53/2017) was then issued in 2017 to deal with tax arrangements for gross split PSCs.

As in many countries, Law 22/2001 provides the regulatory framework for a cooperation contract, which is usually in the form of a PSC. This serves as the basis for cooperation between the government and investors in the upstream oil and gas industry. Law 22/2001 authorises the Ministry of Energy and Mineral Resources to negotiate certain aspects of the cooperation contract, such as firm commitments, work commitments and bonuses. However, the following key principles are non-negotiable:

- Title to oil and gas remains with the government until the delivery point, which is the point of sale of oil and gas;
- All capital and risks of the oil and gas operations are to be borne by the contractor; and
- The management of operations is controlled by SKK Migas through the granting of approval of work programmes and budgets and PODs, and control over their realisation.

These key principles are also applicable to gross split PSCs, except the requirement to obtain SKK Migas' approval of the budget, as this type of PSC does not apply the cost recovery mechanism; instead, the contractor bears all capital and operational costs.

The cooperation contract is the official link between the government and contractors under Law 22/2001. Under the cooperation contract, the

Indonesian government contracts with an investor or a group of investors to engage their financial and technical capabilities to explore for, develop and produce oil and gas within the working area specified in the cooperation contract. The Indonesian government is represented by SKK Migas. The government signs a cooperation contract either following a competitive bidding round or based on bilateral negotiations with investors interested in a particular area through a joint study arrangement. The cooperation contract model is expected to improve the predictability and legal certainty of the process. This model contains provisions that the government expects to be followed by all contractors and leaves blank certain provisions that are more specific to the development of a particular geological field and are thus negotiable.

A regulatory framework that is consistent with the 1945 Constitution and a cooperation contract that is consistent with this regulatory framework are both important to ensure legal certainty for investors, which in turn should create a healthy environment for the upstream oil and gas industry in the long run.

7. Conclusion

The Indonesian PSC has undergone significant changes since its inception. Initially, the legal basis for the PSC was Law 44/1960, which raised a significant debate on whether the PSC could be considered as part of a COW. Law 8/1971 was then enacted to address this issue, providing that only PSC-type contracts may be entered into with foreign investors, and that all rights and obligations and consequences arising from an agreement between Pertamina and any other party would become rights and obligations of Pertamina.

Another major change to the concept of the PSC was introduced in 2001 through the issuance of Law 22/2001. While the cost recovery mechanism of the PSC was maintained by Law 22/2001, the assume and discharge principle was eliminated and consequently a PSC contractor most now pay all kinds of taxes (direct and indirect). Another major change introduced by Law 22/2001 was the replacement of Pertamina as the regulator by BPMIGAS. In 2012, however, the Constitutional Court declared BPMIGAS unconstitutional and mandated that PSCs be concluded by a state-owned company and a private (domestic or foreign) company (business to business).[18]

The most radical change to the PSC was introduced in 2017 through the issuance of Regulation 8/2017, which eliminated the cost recovery concept from the PSC. All existing PSCs remain valid and effective until the end of their lives, but new PSCs take the form of a gross split PSC. This latest move was intended to increase efficiencies in the oil and gas industry and remove the risk of cost recovery disputes with contractors. However, this new PSC model is less

---

18 It has been 10 years since the Constitutional Court decision, but PSCs are still signed by SKK Migas, representing the government, and a private company.

favourable to investors and is negatively perceived by many investors. Given this fact, the Ministry of Energy and Mineral Resources enacted Regulation 12/2020, providing flexibility for the contractor to choose between a gross split PSC or a cost recovery PSC. Since the issuance of Regulation 12/2020, the government has launched one new bidding round; but the process is still ongoing, so it is difficult to predict whether this new policy will increase investors' appetite to invest in Indonesia.

Despite these changes to the legal basis and the concept of the PSC, the following key concepts have not changed since its inception:

- Title to oil and gas remains with the government until the delivery point, which is the point of sale of oil and gas;
- All capital and risks of the oil and gas operations are to be borne by the contractor; and
- The management of operations is controlled by SKK Migas through the granting of approval of work programmes and budgets and PODs, and control over their realisation.

Kazakhstan

Sanzhar Amangeldy
Saniya Perzadayeva
Unicase Law Firm

1. Introduction to production sharing agreements

One of the most common types of contractual arrangements for the exploration and production of natural resources, production sharing agreements (PSAs) are very complicated and often cause disputes between states and exploration companies. PSAs in Kazakhstan have their own history, characterised by both success and failure. This chapter reviews the evolution of the PSA in Kazakhstan, briefly describes the most ambitious projects and summarises the issues encountered along the way.

1.1 History of PSAs

PSAs have been widely and successfully employed in more than 60 countries around the world for decades. They balance out the interests of the state in regulating access to its natural resources and those of extraction companies that possess various resources.

The fundamental principle that underpins the PSA is the distribution of the extracted oil between the government of the resource-rich country and the oil extraction company, which allows the latter to recover its capital and operational expenditures. The oil extraction company assumes all risks of exploration, pays taxes on its share of the extracted oil and transfers its proprietary rights to constructed infrastructure to the host state under the respective legislation and the terms of the PSA. This model is often used in countries that have fairly favourable resource potential, but a dearth of financial and technical assets.

The first PSA was developed in the early 1950s in Bolivia. However, the modern form of the PSA, as it still known today, was implemented for the first time in 1966 in Indonesia. The PSA diverged considerably from the existing models of oil and gas contracts at the time, under which oil companies carried out oil operations at their own expense and at their own risk, but received no rights to the subsoil.

At the time the PSA emerged, nationalistic sentiments prevailed which prevented the Indonesian government from granting rights for subsoil use and concluding the traditional types of concession agreements with international oil companies (IOCs). At the same time, the government could not afford to let its oil and gas sector stagnate, as national companies did not have the necessary expertise and capital to develop the industry. Thus, the concept of the PSA was introduced, and a precedent was established and was subsequently taken up in other developing world countries.

Although the main concept of the PSA remains unchanged today, the individual characteristics of these agreements may differ from country to country; and even the terminology is not necessarily consistent. Straddling both public and private law, PSAs have a controversial legal nature which is often the subject of intense debate among the legal community, the general public, governments and IOCs.

This chapter discusses the history, legal nature and current situation of the PSA in Kazakhstan. Section 2 outlines the history of the oil and gas sector, the introduction of the PSA, its relationship to the Kazakh petroleum regime and the latest developments.

The following sections discuss the legal nature and main features of PSAs and the regulatory bodies that govern them. They aim to provide the reader with a comprehensive understanding of the legal nature and essence of the PSA in Kazakhstan.

The final sections of this chapter discuss the main clauses of the PSA – such as terms of operation, taxation, applicable law and jurisdiction – as well as environmental protection. Finally, the conclusion summarises the main points discussed.

2. History of the oil and gas sector

2.1 Before the introduction of PSAs

According to BP's 2020 *Statistical Review of World Energy*,[1] the world's total proved oil reserves were estimated at more than 1.73 trillion barrels as of the end of 2019. Kazakhstan ranks 12th in the global rankings, with 30 billion barrels of proved oil reserves.

The first activity in the Kazakh oil and gas sector began in 1899, in the Karachunul field. At first, oil was extracted using the fountain method. This was a cheap and easy way to extract oil, but it was inefficient. The wellhead had to be sealed and the total pressure inside the well had to be guaranteed. As time went on, companies began to extract oil using depth pumps and compressors, and later rotary drilling. During that period, and until Kazakhstan gained independence, the subsoil and the lands of the Kazakh people were owned by the Communist Party. The Soviet government built some pipelines and, instead of rotary drilling, began to use rapid turbine drilling, which increased oil production. The Communists were extracting millions of tonnes of oil and gas

1 BP plc, *Statistical Review of World Energy 2020*, p14.

each year. However, the profits did not remain in Kazakhstan, but instead went directly to Moscow. The most significant discoveries were made in 1979, during the Soviet period: the Tengiz and Karachaganak fields in western Kazakhstan.

After the collapse of the Soviet Union, Kazakhstan gained independence and the right to use its subsoil, which had previously been the exclusive prerogative of the Communist Party. The question thus arose: how should the subsoil be used and regulated?

Although Kazakhstan lacked experience and resources, it still had a strong regulatory base. However, improvements to this legislation were needed in order to attract more international investors to the country, as the Soviet Union was no longer providing money and expertise. These legislative amendments and improvements resulted in a very weak position for the state. As a result, the government adopted the new Code of the Republic of Kazakhstan on Subsoils and Processing of Mineral Raw Materials dated 30 May 1992, which was the first of many laws in the oil and gas sector. This law was generally favourable for foreign investors, but less so for Kazakhstan. Two years later, the government adopted the Regulations on the Subsoil Use Licensing Procedure dated 8 August 1994, which required that subsoil use contracts comply with the respective licences. During the 1990s, Kazakhstan ratified several international conventions and treaties, including the Energy Charter Treaty, signed in Lisbon on 17 December 1994. At the time, the Kazakh government was keen to develop the legislation governing the subsoil. Accordingly, Kazakhstan adopted the Law of the Republic of Kazakhstan on Oil dated 28 June 1995 and the Law of the Republic of Kazakhstan on Subsoils and Subsoil Use dated 27 January 1996. These laws were significant and governed the Kazakh oil and gas sector until July 2010. They provided for a system of licences and contracts to use the subsoil, and a stabilisation statute guaranteed that the licences awarded and contracts concluded would remain unaffected by any legislative amendments or new laws which could potentially worsen the positions of investors in the future.

2.2 The PSAs in Kazakhstan and their relationship with the petroleum regime

As Kazakhstan lacked the necessary expertise, machinery and funds, it could never develop the full potential of its oil and gas sector without foreign investment. The introduction of the PSA was the only possible way to attract significant foreign investment to the country and develop vast oil fields such as Kashagan, Tengiz and Karachaganak.

According to some commentators, the PSA is the preferred model of field development contract among foreign investors.[2] As the conditions of the PSA

2 Speech by A Akkaisieva, "Analysis of Types of Oil Contracts: World Experience", Third Atyrau Legal Seminar, "Topical issues and analysis of the practice of applying legislation in the oil and gas industry of the Republic of Kazakhstan" (Atyrau, 15 April 2005).

establish a special regime, the agreement facilitates the proper calculation of the economic efficiency of specific projects by reducing the number of unknown variables in the equation and guaranteeing investors an acceptable level of risk and stability. Before the start of the project, the investors conduct a feasibility study of the PSA, in which the most important indicators are the internal rate of return, the net present value and the period of compensation for their investments. Given the complexity and size of the Kashagan, Tengiz and Karachaganak fields, foreign investors agreed to enter into these projects only on the basis of PSAs.

At present, 11 projects are still operating under the PSAs. For the purposes of this chapter, we will consider the three largest and oldest of these:

- the Karachaganak project;
- the North Caspian Project; and
- a joint venture called Tengizchevroil LLP, established by the first president of Kazakhstan, Nursultan Nazarbayev, and Chevron Corporation. This has all the features of a PSA, but the contract and their terms have not been disclosed to the public.

(a) *North Caspian PSA*

The North Caspian PSA (NCPSA) was concluded between Kazakhstan and the international consortium in November 1997, with a contract term of 40 years. According to the official website of North Caspian Operating Company BV (NCOC),[3] the current operator of the project is NCOC and the consortium consists of the following oil and gas companies:

- 'NC KazMunayGas JSC (KMG) – 16.88%;
- ENI SpA (Agip) – 16.81%
- Exxon Mobil Corporation – 16.81%
- Royal Dutch Shell plc – 16.81%
- Total SA – 16.81%
- China National Petroleum Corporation (CNPC) – 8.33%
- INPEX Corporation (Inpex) – 7.56%

In the course of time, an enormous oil field – the Kashagan field – was discovered in the northern part of the Caspian Sea in 2000. The oil reserves of the Kashagan field are estimated at 4.5 billion tonnes.

The parties to the NCPSA have also discovered:

- the Kalamkas Sea field (284 million tonnes of oil);
- the Aktoty field (156 million tonnes of condensate gas);
- the Kairan field (112 million tonnes of oil); and
- the Southwest Kashagan field (20 million tonnes of condensate gas).

3 www.ncoc.kz/en/ncoc/about.

(b) *Karachaganak Field Final PSA*

In 1979, the Soviet government discovered one of the largest oil fields and one of the largest gas condensate fields in the world – Tengiz and Karachaganak respectively. The condensate reserves of Karachaganak are estimated at nine billion barrels, while the gas reserves are estimated at 14 trillion cubic metres (m^3).

In 1997, the government of Kazakhstan and IOCs signed the Karachaganak Field Final Production Sharing Agreement (KFFPSA), with a term of 40 years.

According to the official website of Karachaganak Petroleum Operating BV (KPO),[4] the operator of the project is currently KPO and the consortium consists of the following IOCs:

- KMG – 10%
- Agip – 29.25%
- Chevron Corporation– 18%
- Shell – 29.25%
- Lukoil Oil Company JSC – 13.5%

By 2019, KPO had extracted 18 million tonnes of oil production and 8.7 billion m^3 of gas production. Half of the gas produced was reinjected to maintain reservoir pressure.

(c) *TengizChevrOil joint venture*

On 2 April 1993, a joint venture called TengizChevrOil LLP (TCO) was established by the first president of Kazakhstan, Nursultan Nazarbayev, and Chevron Corporation. This project has all the features of the PSA, but the contract is not a classic PSA. The parties to the contract have concluded numerous agreements, but the terms of those agreements are not disclosable to the public. The licence for exploration and production was issued for a period of 40 years.

According to the official website of NC KazMunayGas JSC,[5] which is currently the operator of TCO, the following IOCs are participants in this project:

- Chevron – 50%
- Exxon – 25%
- KMG – 20%
- Lukoil (through LukArco) – 5%

The oil reserves in the Tengiz field are estimated at 3.4 billion tonnes. By 2017, oil production by TCO had reached 28.697 million tonnes.

---

4 www.kpo.kz/about-kpo.html#:~:text=Located%20in%20north%2Dwest%20Kazakhstan,and%2016%20tcf%20of%20gas.

5 www.kmg.kz/self/annual_report_2017/en/013.html.

(d) *Law on PSAs*

Kazakhstan had great strategic plans to use the PSA to further the development of the Caspian Sea and attract IOCs to build infrastructure, discover and extract oil, and use local content at their own expense and risk. To realise these ambitions, the government adopted the Law of the Republic of Kazakhstan on the Production Sharing Agreements in Offshore Oil Operations dated 8 July 2005 ('PSA Law').

However, the PSAs also resulted in damage to the state economy and losses to the national budget. In a speech in 2008, former Prime Minister Karim Massimov stated that Kazakhstan needed to increase the tax burden for subsoil users and revise the procedure through which they paid taxes; he also highlighted the importance of excluding the PSA as a type of subsoil use contract. He assured investors that Kazakhstan would continue to fulfil its obligations under existing PSAs, but would not conclude any new PSAs because times – and Kazakhstan – had changed. Thus, the PSA Law was abolished in 2009.

2.3 Current situation

(a) *Kashagan and the NCPSA*

The commencement of commercial oil production in the Kashagan field was initially scheduled for 2008, but was postponed first to 2013 and then again to 2016. According to the consortium of IOCs, the delays were due to:

- problems with pipelines, machinery and equipment;
- the technical difficulties of the project;
- the harsh climate;
- the ecologically sensitive environment of the Caspian Sea; and
- strict regulatory requirements.

In November 2016 the NCPSA finally commenced commercial oil production in Kashagan; by the end of 2018, this had reached 22.5 million tons of oil, 13 billion m^3 of gas and 2.6 million tonnes of sulphur. As yet, however, this has not yielded dividends for Kazakhstan. Under the terms of the PSA, for the time being, the IOCs will retain almost 90% of the profits as compensation for their investments; Kazakhstan will begin receiving adequate profits and revenues in approximately 2027–2029.

There are several problems connected with Kashagan, as a result of which the government of Kazakhstan now regrets signing the NCPSA.

First, the government appreciates that oil extraction from the seabed is more complicated than on land. As previously mentioned, Kazakhstan did not have – and still does not have – the necessary resources to exploit the Kashagan field by itself. In order to extract the oil, the consortium must build artificial islands, bring machinery to those islands and endure the harsh winters of the Caspian Sea – not to mention addressing the related environmental issues. We also understand that NCOC made a number of engineering mistakes, which caused delays and budget increases. This means that Kazakhstan will not see any profits in the immediate future.

Second, the PSA concept requires the consortium to be compensated for its investments by the state. The state must thus strictly control the investors' expenses; if it does not, the investors may deliberately increase their costs. However, in the late 1990s and early 2000s, the government was poor in controlling these expenditures; and even today, it cannot adequately control the costs of the project. This has allowed the investors to export as much oil as they wish. Once again, this means that Kazakhstan will not see any profits for the foreseeable future.

The third problem is the controversial participation of KMG in the project. Between 2004 and 2008, KMG invested a stake of 16.81% in the project. KMG is the national company, which is owned by the government. As the state had always been a party to the NCPSA, this meant that the government was now represented on both sides of the PSA. As previously mentioned, this project has abundant potential, but has also required huge investments. NCOC has made large cash calls, which are quite acceptable for IOCs but not for KMG, which can barely pay them.

(b) Karachaganak and KFFPSA

Since development started in 1997, the IOCs have invested more than $14 billion in the Karachaganak field. In 2015, a dispute arose with the government over the costs of the project. The issue was resolved through arbitration in 2019, with a decision in favour of Kazakhstan. According to that decision, the consortium was ordered to pay an initial $1.305 billion to Kazakhstan and an additional payment of $600 million by 2037. Consequently, both parties to the KFFPSA approved the expansion of the Karachaganak field with an investment of $1 billion.

(c) Tengiz and TengizChevrOil LLP

On 5 July 2016, the participants of TCO reached agreement to finance the Future Growth Project/Wellhead Pressure Management Project. Under this project, TCO will build a refinery and crude gas reinjection facilities, a well-stream gathering system, pressure-boosting facilities, infrastructure and auxiliary facilities. The estimated cost of the project is $36.8 billion.

The participants in TCO have increased the budget and delayed the schedule several times. Currently, Chevron claims that the cost of the project is $45.2 billion. However, the government believes that the increased cost for Tengiz is too high and wants the investors to recalculate it.

In 2020, TCO planned to renovate the machinery used in the Tengiz oil field. However, due to the COVID-19 pandemic, the renovation was postponed to 2021.[6]

3. Legal nature of PSAs

As previously mentioned, it is vital to understand the legal nature of the PSA. The PSA is a type of contract with specific features which are essential to investment agreements. In Kazakhstan, the PSA does not specifically indicate the counterparty as a foreign entity. The participation of a foreign investor does not imply that international law will apply; in fact, the state only applies local law under the PSA. Moreover, sometimes the local company (KMG) participates alongside the investors. Thus, we would argue that the PSA is not specifically regulated by international public and/or private laws.

As some commentators point out,[7] all public elements of the PSA – such as taxation issues, environmental regulations and production sharing procedures – are resolved before the PSA is concluded. The investors have the right to choose whether to enter into the contract. Once the PSA has been concluded, both parties have equal rights and mutual obligations to perform the contract. Accordingly, we consider that the PSA is a civil contract.

4. Main features of PSAs

4.1 Cost oil versus profit oil

When an oil field is discovered, the state and investors negotiate on the proportions in which the oil will be shared. Once they have reached an understanding, the investors can start developing the oil field. As previously mentioned, the investors bear all capital and operating costs, and receive compensation in return. The investors calculate all of their investments and define the costs of the project, which the state must compensate by sharing oil with investors. It is thus very important for the state to monitor these costs; otherwise, the investors can increase the costs and can even provide fake invoices.

Once the oil field has been developed, the investors commence oil production. The start of commercial oil production means that investors can retain the produced oil as compensation for their investments. The proportion of this compensation is agreed between the investors and the state. This compensation is called 'cost oil', as it only compensates the investors for their investments. The remainder of the oil produced is called 'profit oil', and is divided between the parties in a certain proportion as agreed between the state and investors before the conclusion of the PSA.

---

6 According to the annual report of NC KazMunayGas JSC (2020).

7 ZS Yelyubayev, *Regulatory Problems of Subsoil Use: Local and International Practice* (OmniScriptum Publishing KS, 2010), p14.

5. Role of the authorised body

The history of Production Sharing Agreements Limited Liability Partnership (PSA LLP) – the authorised body for PSAs in Kazakhstan – begins in 1997, when the NCPSA and the KFPSA were concluded. Kazakhstan needed an authorised body in order to enter into these PSAs. Kazakhoil JSC was designated as the authorised body from 1997 to 2001, in accordance with a decree of the Kazakh government.

In 2001, the Ministry of Energy and Mineral Resources took over this role for one year. Then, in 2002, in accordance with a decree of the president of Kazakhstan and a decree of the government of Kazakhstan, NC KazMunayGas JSC was established, which assumed this role until 2010.

In 2010, the Ministry of Oil and Gas became the authorised body. That same year, KMG also transferred a 100% participation interest in the charter capital of PSA LLP to the Ministry of Oil and Gas.

In 2014, the Ministry of Oil and Gas was restructured as the Ministry of Energy, which then became the authorised body for the PSAs. Two years later, under Government Decree 355/2016, PSA LLP[8] was appointed as the authorised body, and it continues in this role today. The main task of the authorised body is to make decisions on behalf of the state regarding the transfer of cost oil and to monitor the invoices submitted by investors.

As previously mentioned, it is very important that the state monitors costs closely; otherwise, investors could increase the costs and could even provide fake invoices. For example, an investor could buy drilling equipment abroad for $1 million and resell it through an affiliated third company for $2 million. As a result, the investor could report that it has invested $2 million in the state economy. Thus, the amount of the cost oil doubles, which is negative for the state economy.

In this regard, it is questionable that KMG has certain shares in the Kashagan, Karachaganak and Tengiz projects, while an affiliated company, PSA LLP, is the authorised body in the respective PSAs. This presents a risk of corruption in the national oil company. We would argue that the authorised body of the PSA should be completely independent from the PSA operator that incurs the costs under the PSA, as a conflict of interest is otherwise inevitable.

6. Analysis of the main clauses of the PSA

6.1 Exploration, development and production

Once the investors have signed the PSA, the government approves the list of blocks/sections in order to implement the PSA. After accepting the designated contract area, the investors carry out the geophysical surveys. These operations

8 www.psa.kz/en/.

should take place only within the designated blocks. Under the PSA in Kazakhstan, the investors bear all risks and receive compensation through sharing in the oil produced. Without oil, there is no compensation. Based on the results of the survey, the investors choose a drilling site for the purpose of well exploration. If this is successful, the investors will announce the discovery of oil.

Technical and economic feasibility studies are then carried out. Based on the available data, the government will approve the field development programme. The development then begins: the investors commence construction and develop infrastructure and transportation networks. Once the necessary preparations have been made, oil wells are drilled, the development stage ends and the commercial production stage begins.

6.2 Local content

As the budgets of Kashagan, Karachaganak and Tengiz kept expanding, the government decided to impose a minimum 50% local content obligation on investors. In response, NCOC, the operator of the Kashagan field, increased its share of local content to 46.2% in 2014, 27.7% in 2015, 27.8% in 2016, 32% in 2017 and 48% in 2018. These fluctuating figures suggest that there is little stability or sustainable growth. Meanwhile, TCO, the operator of the Tengiz field, declared that in 2018 it purchased $2.5 billion of Kazakh goods and services. However, the percentage of local content that this represented was not disclosed. KPO, the operator of the Karachaganak field, issued a report in 2018 which stated that its share of local content was 56%.

However, operators do not treat local workers in the same way as they treat expats. Several incidents have resulted from these unequal work conditions. Workers have gone on strike numerous times, but the issues remain unresolved.

6.3 Operator

Under the PSA, the operator is responsible for the respective project and for all working processes. Usually, investors create a special legal entity for operating purposes. Although the operator is a separate legal entity, the investors bear joint responsibility to the state for the operator's actions under the PSA.

The operator usually does not possess funds itself. In order to maintain the project and working processes, the operator makes cash calls to the investors.

The operator of the Karachaganak field is a foreign legal entity, KPO. Similarly, the operator of the Kashagan field is also a foreign legal entity, NCOC. In Tengiz, the investors created a limited liability partnership, TCO, under Kazakh law.

6.4 Environment

In order to reduce environmental pollution, IOCs endeavour to upgrade and modernise their equipment and machinery. However, environmental disasters still frequently occur. Kazakhstan needs to rethink its attitude towards its natural resources. The most badly affected area is the Caspian Sea, which includes the Atyrau and Mangistau regions. The anthropogenic impact in these areas is catastrophic, encompassing millions of hectares of technogenic zones and degraded pastures, and millions of tonnes of spilled oil.

The companies that operate under PSAs in Kazakhstan experience similar problems, such as sulphur utilisation. The increase in sulphur reserves in Tengiz and Kashagan is another red flag. TCO and NCOC claim that they cannot utilise the amount of sulphur produced and thus most of it is blown away by the wind. Environmental specialists argue that the actions of the IOCs are insufficient. TCO and NCOC would rather pay billions of dollars in fines to the government than find a way to utilise the sulphur produced without environmental consequences.

The North Caspian Sea is a delicate ecological zone. Its flora and fauna are very sensitive, and there are a lot of rare species – such as sturgeon fish and the Caspian seal – which are included on the International Union for the Conservation of Nature Red List of Threatened Species. The development of the Kashagan field is proving difficult due to the limits of the existing technical capabilities.

However, KPO always fulfils its obligations to ensure safe working conditions and protect the environment in the region in which it operates.

6.5 Corruption

According to the United Nations Convention against Corruption and the Organisation for Economic Co-operation and Development, 'corruption' is the abuse by officials of their state powers for their personal benefit by pursuing the interests of third parties. According to Article 2, part 1 of the Anti-corruption Law, 'corruption' is:

- the acceptance of property benefits and advantages not provided for by law, in person or through an intermediary, by persons who perform state functions and persons equated with them, through the use of their official powers and opportunities linked to them, or such other use of their powers; and
- the bribery of such persons by individuals or legal entities through the illegal provision of benefits and advantages.

In the PSA context, corruption mainly arises in relation to oil extraction, tax collection, ecology protection, land use and goods procurement. Oil extraction is hard to control, as it involves ongoing examinations of licences, ecological indicators, land use, labour relations and tax payments.

6.6 Royalties and taxes

Under the existing PSAs in Kazakhstan, the tax burden on investors is inadequate. Currently, investors need only pay corporate income tax and value added tax. They do not pay property tax, land tax, excess profit tax, royalties, customs fees for exported crude oil and gas condensate, or excise duties for crude oil and other minerals. Moreover, the PSA members of the Kashagan, Karachaganak and Tengiz projects need not comply with the current Tax Code, as this does not have retroactive effect.

6.7 Applicable law and dispute resolution

As previously mentioned, the PSA in Kazakhstan possess no features of international law. As the subsoil has economic and strategic significance, the only applicable law is the law of Kazakhstan.

With regard to dispute resolution, we would suggest that the PSA is a civil contract. Disputes under such contracts may be addressed in accordance with the agreed conditions in the contract, whether through the Kazakh courts or through international arbitration. In general, such disputes are resolved through international arbitration, given that one party to the PSA is the state itself.

7. Conclusion

The PSAs currently used in Kazakhstan appear to have facilitated the effective colonisation of the country. Kazakhstan cannot cancel the existing PSAs and investors continue to operate based on them. According to these PSAs, Kazakhstan receives a small share of the profits from the exploitation of its natural resources once the investors have been reimbursed for their investments. IOCs purposefully overestimate their expenses. Investors are aware that the Kazakh government does not have the necessary expertise to check the implied costs.

On the other hand, Kazakhstan also does not have the necessary expertise, funds and technologies to exploit its natural resources itself; and without the IOCs, it would be unable to produce oil and exploit large oil fields such as Kashagan and Tengiz. For these reasons, the PSA is both a blessing and a curse.

Libya

Ebtissam El Kailani
Vestas
Asma Muttawa
International energy lawyer

1. Introduction

This chapter focuses on the exploration production sharing agreement (EPSA) in Libya. It provides an overview of the scope and structure of the contract, highlighting its main features and analysing the main clauses contained therein. It also defines the role of the Libyan National Oil Corporation (LNOC) in the negotiation and implementation of EPSAs, and examines the relationship of the EPSA with the Petroleum Law.

Since oil activity commenced in Libya, the oil and gas agreements used have gradually evolved from concession agreements to the more recent EPSAs. Libyan oil contracts are generally viewed as having evolved in favour of investors.

The current Libyan EPSA is Version IV, which is the main subject of analysis in this chapter. Over four generations, this has developed into an instrument that is negotiable between a bid winner and the LNOC, bearing in mind that substantial revisions to the model agreement are likely to be limited in nature and are unlikely to materialise. Amendments are possible to the extent that they enhance the effectiveness of the EPSA, subject to the approval of the Cabinet of Ministers.

2. Scope and structure of the EPSA

The EPSA is a unique type of oil investment agreement that was first used in the international oil industry in 1974. Since its introduction in Libya, four generations of EPSAs have evolved, in 1974, 1980, 1989 and 2005. Contracts for the exploration and production of oil and late gas entered into by the LNOC ('first party') and certain international oil companies (IOCs) ('second party') before the introduction of the EPSAs continue to be implemented and remain valid.

Under an EPSA, the IOC assumes all risks and expenses of the exploration operations, which are non-reimbursable if a commercial discovery does not materialise. However, if a commercial discovery is made, the predicted production oil is subject to allocation based on economic and technical specifications set out in the terms of the EPSA, as negotiated and agreed between the parties.

The validity of an EPSA is subject to endorsement of its terms by the Cabinet of Ministers and certification in accordance with Libyan law.

This chapter outlines the legal and technical progress that has shaped legal relationships in the Libyan oil and gas industry.

The first-generation EPSA (EPSA I) was introduced in 1974. The main characteristic of EPSA I was the radical change it introduced by exempting the IOC's share of production from taxation. By contrast, the concession deeds that prevailed until 1974 were based on a taxation system under which the IOC's share of production was subject to heavy taxation at a rate of over 50%, and in some cases up to 90%. Under EPSA I, the percentage of production assigned to the IOC was also reduced.

The second-generation EPSA (EPSA II) came into effect in the early 1980s. EPSA II introduced some changes as a result of protracted negotiations between the LNOC and IOCs, including the injection of capital investment for exploration by the IOCs. This eventually resulted in major and significant discoveries being made, mainly in the more challenging terrain in the south of the country.

The third-generation EPSA (EPSA III) became operational in the latter part of the 1980s and resulted from a national strategy to increase exploration activities and lobbying from the IOCs for improved conditions in investment contracts, due to the realities of such contracts and the need for foreign investment reassurances for new entrants. The most important change introduced by EPSA III was more flexible terms relating to the parties' respective share of production, based on a new formula which took into consideration variable factors such as oil prices, exploration costs and operating costs. This aimed to address the problems that had arisen in practice in relation to the existing EPSAs. EPSA III was concluded at the peak of the US and international sanction regime; all US companies had departed Libya by 1986 as a result of the US embargo. As a result, such EPSAs were negotiated and concluded only with European companies and a few small investors from Asia.

The fourth-generation EPSA (EPSA IV) came into effect in the early to mid-2000s, around the time when international and bilateral sanctions were lifted, and was based on an open bidding system. A committee was established to review the development of the Libyan oil industry over the previous 50 years and review practices and experiences in other oil producing countries in order to develop EPSA IV. In September 2004, the first round of presentations on the characteristics of EPSA IV was made in Tripoli to a large number of IOCs, attracting positive feedback and suggesting positive expectations for the future. This version of the EPSA remains operational today.

EPSA IV introduced major modifications to the EPSA regime, especially in relation to taxation and gas. The analysis in this chapter now turns to EPSA IV.

3. Main features of the PSA: cost oil versus profit oil

Most of the EPSAs concluded in Libya grant the second party the right to a share of crude oil production in accordance with the terms of the agreement, which is not subject to taxation as declared in the Petroleum Law (25/1955) or the Income Tax Law (64/1973), and is outside the scope of the national tax system.

Unlike more traditional PSAs, Article 12.1.1 of EPSA IV subordinates cost oil recovery below the LNOC's allocated share. This provision could result in the second party not receiving its entire cost recovery for petroleum operations expenditures. If the investor is granted the opportunity to explore and exploit from other sites in Libya, it may wish to recover such expenditures from production under the current agreement. The agreement could authorise such cross-recoveries. An acceptable discount rate should be allowed upon calculation of the project's return.

Article 15.1.1(b) of EPSA IV specifically provides that signature bonuses and production bonuses are not recoverable from cost oil as petroleum operation expenditures and cannot be recovered under EPSA IV. If cost recoverable, bonuses will be offset against a relevant portion of the minerals produced (ie, under Article 12.1.1 of EPSA IV, the portion allocable to the investor). For tax planning or other purposes, however, the investor may want to treat bonus payments as tax-deductible items. Indeed, profits tax is payable by the LNOC on the investor's behalf, affording the investor the opportunity to take a foreign tax credit. In this case, the tax deductibility of bonus payments may reduce the amount of tax credit that the investor can take. Nevertheless, depending on the tax regime of the jurisdiction in which the investment will be financed and accounted for, the investor may stipulate in the agreement that bonus payments are tax deductible.

This condition is referred to as the 'tax exemption of the second party's share in the production of oil'. This is the cornerstone of the economic accounts of EPSAs, which balance the relationship between the participating parties through the customary imposition of additional obligations on the activities of IOCs, and specifically with regard to taxation and customs, thus affording the government diverse income streams.[1]

4. The role of the competent authority in the contract: NOC, ministry or independent agency?

The regulations implemented under the Petroleum Law pursuant to Decree 10/1979 reorganised the LNOC and defined its scope of activities. Under this regulation, the LNOC is empowered to enter into new forms of oil petroleum exploitation agreements other than the concessions introduced by Petroleum

1 See Ibtisam Al Kalani, "Libya" in David Perks (ed), *Oil & Gas: Jurisdictional Comparisons* (Sweet & Maxwell, 2012).

Law 25/1955. Article 1 of Decree 10/1979 authorised the LNOC to engage in the exploration, production and marketing of oil and gas in Libya and overseas, whether through wholly owned subsidiaries or through participation with others by way of employed contractors or other forms of investment contracts.

Article 5 of Decree 10/1979 provides that the LNOC is considered to be the first party in all participation agreements and EPSAs, and any other agreements for investment in oil wealth, in accordance with the terms and conditions of such contracts and agreements.

Article 6 of Decree 10/1979 provides that the Cabinet of Ministers is responsible for approving and amending the contracts and agreements concluded between the LNOC and IOCs. Most of the EPSAs submitted for approval by the LNOC have been approved by the Cabinet of Ministers. On rare occasions where approval was denied, the Cabinet of Ministers determined that the investor was incapable of honouring its obligations or that a violation of approved procedures had occurred.

Further amendments were introduced to ensure the transparency and efficiency of the contractual relationship between the parties and the effective implementation of the agreements. These included the composition of management committees and their substructures, and definition of the roles and powers of the various entities involved.

The concept of the management committee was first introduced in Libya in 1973, when the LNOC was negotiating and executing participation agreements with various IOCs. That same year, Law 77/1973 was enacted, which nationalised 51% of the IOCs' rights and interests in Libya.

Article 3 of the participation agreement, entitled "Operation and Management", governs the composition, functioning and voting system of the management committee established between the LNOC as first party to the EPSA and the IOC as second party to the EPSA.

Paragraph 3/B states:

The management committee shall be composed of three members; two, including the chairman, shall represent the Government whilst the third member shall represent the Second Parties. Each such party is entitled to elect its members. They may also elect an alternate or replacement at any time... The members representing the Government shall maintain 51% of the voting power, whilst the member representing the Second Parties shall maintain 49% of the voting power. The members appointed by the Government shall each have a 25.5% vote, the member appointed by the Second Parties may split his vote to reflect the wishes of each of the Second Parties. The Resolutions of the Management Committee shall be adopted by a simple majority vote representing 51%.

The Committee shall settle all of the important matters relating to petroleum operation on the concessions and in particular all programs and budgets prepared by the operator for the exploration, development, and production operations. The resolutions of the Committee shall be considered as final and binding on both parties except as provided for in paragraph K below, and shall be executed by the operator.

Paragraph 3/K states:

Except with respect to the exploration program..., if the First Party or one of the Second Parties approves a program or a project to which one or more of the Second Parties is opposed, the Party or Parties recommending such program or project can proceed with it at its sole risk and expense. In this event, the Party or Parties undertaking such program or project will be entitled to all the benefits therefrom. The non-undertaking Party or Parties shall have no right to demand participation in such program or project thereafter.

The management committee was later restructured into two committees under the Libyan EPSAs. The first is the owners management committee, which is usually comprised of equal members representing the parties and owners of the joint venture, regardless of their participating shares in it. This committee usually takes all important decisions relating to the work programmes and budgets as prepared by the operator. The decisions of the committee are usually taken unanimously by the representatives of the parties to the joint venture, which are nominated and may be replaced any time by the parties.

Decree 10/1979 also provided for the creation of the operators management committee, whose powers and responsibilities relate to the day-to-day business of the operations, in addition to preparation of the work programmes and budgets, all under the control and supervision of the owners management committee. The operators management committee is usually composed of equal numbers representing the parties to the joint venture, with each member being responsible for a specific activity or division of the operating company. The resolutions of the operators management committee are usually taken by simple majority vote of the members; and the chair of the committee, as designated by the first party, has the casting vote.

Article 4/b of EPSA IV introduced the concept of the single management committee into the Libyan *lex petrolea* for the first time, as well as the simple majority vote principle. The management committee decides on all important matters relating to petroleum operations in the case of concessions, and in particular all programmes and budgets prepared by the operator for exploration, development and production operations. The potential damage that might occur to the 'non-undertaking' party or parties in the event of a simple majority vote that they believe goes against their interests is balanced by the principle of sole risk in favour of such party or parties, as introduced in Article 4/b.

The management committee is appointed no later than one month after final approval of the agreement to supervise all petroleum operations in the contract area. The management committee is comprised of four members: two members, including the chairman, are appointed by the LNOC and two by the IOC.

The IOC is appointed as operator during the exploration period to carry out exploration and appraisal operations, as well as abandonment relating to such operations, in accordance with the terms of the agreement between the parties, under the control and supervision of the management committee.

The operator is thus responsible for the procurement and/or lease of all material, equipment, machinery, articles and supplies that must be purchased or leased in preparation for the agreed work programme.

In reality, the unanimous voting mechanism included in the EPSAs resulted in a number of inconsistencies, mainly due to the wide scope of the management committee's authority, which includes not only the declaration of a commercial discovery and the adoption of the development plans, but also the approval of all work programmes and budgets. Without a deadlock-breaking mechanism, each party can block the petroleum operations. While this may be acceptable to some companies, particularly those that know the LNOC well, it is likely to cause problems for others.

5. Analysis of the main clauses of the contract

The main clauses of EPSA IV cover the following:

- exploration;
- development and commercial discovery;
- local content requirements;
- operator;
- minimum work obligations;
- liability;
- environmental requirements;
- anti-corruption provisions;
- royalties;
- taxes;
- applicable law; and
- dispute resolution.

The language of EPSA IV appears to be that of a purely commercial deal. However, apart from being a commercial arrangement, EPSA IV purports to award substantial rights to the production of natural resources which are not normally transferred pursuant to commercial arrangements. Therefore, EPSA IV has features of both a commercial transaction and an administrative licence. It would be helpful if EPSA IV stipulated more clearly the specific rights granted to the investor. These would include:

- the rights of exclusive exploration and production within the area;
- the right to use, free of charge, the land within the area (including the water surface and sea floor);
- the right to run the petroleum operations without the need to obtain any specific activity licences or permits;

- the right to freely export production;
- the right to freely use foreign currency; and
- other rights necessary for the proper conduct of the operations.

The Petroleum Law first introduced petroleum agreements in the form of a tax-royalty system, under which IOCs took full responsibility for petroleum activities and operations against arrangement royalties to be paid to the LNOC. However, four generations of EPSAs were subsequently developed, with the latest version issued in 2005. Generally, the Libyan EPSAs contain three important economic values:

- the participation of the LNOC in the development plan, operations and expenditures (through the joint management committee);
- the exemption of the second party's share of production from taxation, guaranteed by the LNOC through a tax exemption certificate – a radical change from the previous regime; and
- the concept of cost recovery and the profit oil split.

One of the major changes introduced by EPSA IV was the commercialisation of excess associated gas, which must be included in the development plan. Upon approval, the first and second parties must endeavour to conclude a long-term gas sales agreement for this purpose, before the operator implements the facilities required for production and delivery. The delivery point is either specified in the development plan or agreed in the gas sales agreement. Where a gas utilisation scheme is not available, the second party must offer the first party the option to its share of excess associated gas, free of charge, at the delivery point, which is specified as immediately after the gas oil separation point. If the first party is in agreement, it will be responsible for all costs relating to collection, transportation and compression. If the first party does not agree to the second party's offer, a meeting to discuss the alternative should be convened.

Article 15.1.1(b) of EPSA IV apportions bonus payments and specifically provides that signature bonuses and production bonuses are not recoverable from cost oil as petroleum operation expenditures, and cannot be recovered under EPSA IV post production.

If cost recoverable, bonuses will be offset against a relevant portion of the minerals produced (ie, under Article 12.1.1 of EPSA IV, the portion allocable to the investor). For tax planning or other purposes, however, the investor may want to treat bonus payments as tax-deductible items. Indeed, profits tax is payable by the LNOC on the investor's behalf, affording the investor the opportunity to take a foreign tax credit. In this case, the tax deductibility of bonus payments may reduce the amount of tax credit that the investor can take. Nevertheless, depending on the tax regime of the jurisdiction in which the investment will be financed and accounted for, the investor may want to stipulate in the agreement that bonus payments are tax deductible.[2]

The first article of the tax clause in EPSA IV provides that the first party's share of production is subject to tax. However, the following article immediately contradicts this by assigning all obligations relating to the second party's share of production to the first party for payment.

The total amount of royalties and income tax obligations is calculated by the second party, and is open for negotiation by both parties before it is processed by the first party and a tax certificate is issued by the competent tax authority in the name of the second party. To calculate the tax and royalty due on the revenue derived from crude oil, the official selling price of Libya is used. To calculate the tax and royalty due on the revenue derived from natural gas, the actual selling price according to the gas sales agreement is used. A defined price is set in Article 12 of EPSA IV to calculate the revenue derived from the disposal of liquid hydrocarbon by-products.[3]

Under Article 19.1.2 of EPSA IV, the investor has the right to raise objections to the LNOC's comments on the tax declaration. Disputes that arise in this regard should be decided by a reputable firm of accountants appointed to the mutual satisfaction of both parties. It is also prudent to stipulate that no tax on assignments pursuant to Article 24 of EPSA IV will be due from the assignor or assignee of the investor's share or share in a holding company.

Neither the Petroleum Law nor EPSA IV includes special environmental requirements relating to oil and gas investment operations. Instead, this is addressed in Law 5/1969 – the first environmental law to be issued in Libya. The law includes provisions on organisation, planning of environmental reforms and environmental protection. It also provides for the establishment of a responsible department for the operation and maintenance of public utilities to manage water and waste water.

In 1973, Law 130/1973 was enacted, authorising local councils to approve regulations issued by the municipalities. In the same year, Law 39/1973 was enacted, which:

- sets out the organisational structure for the respective ministry;
- establishes a number of general departments to supervise safe drinking water, sanitary requirements, waste and pollutant disposal and elimination; and
- provides for the supervision of environmental improvements.

Law 7/1982 on Environmental Protection was issued in 1982 and introduced numerous environmental protection principles.

Petroleum Regulation 8 /1972 and its three annexes also address health and

2 *Ibid.*
3 *Ibid.*

safety issues in detail. In addition, Decision 32/2012 provides for the establishment of a special Department of Technical Affairs and the Environment. The responsibilities of the department include:

- approving well-drilling permits, in addition to developing and deepening these wells according to the applicable laws;
- approving the grant of permission for the surrender of dry wells and non-economic production wells in compliance with the applicable standards;
- granting test certificates for the primary production of oil and gas wells;
- following up on plans and programmes concerning exploration, drilling and excavation in accordance with the applicable laws;
- approving oil production rates according to technical specifications and marketing requirements, and specifying the production period; and
- following up on the second recovery programmes for reservoirs.[4]

The local content provisions in EPSA IV are somewhat vague compared to those of other PSAs. EPSA IV does not include a cap on local content requirements, which many PSAs traditionally contain. The investor or second party will bear all training costs for Libyan nationals during the five-year exploration period.

The second party is exempt from paying customs duties, rentals and fees, as well as other governmental charges, if the second party can neither offset current agreement costs against those from other agreements nor consolidate income with that from other activities.

A major issue in all international contractual agreements is the governing law and the competent jurisdiction should any disputes arise in connection with the interpretation or implementation of the contract. Earlier concession agreements were governed by Libyan law, according to the principles of international law. Due to the commercial nature of EPSAs, the government decided that they should be exclusively governed by Libyan law, on the grounds that this would afford additional guarantees to foreign investors.

As a result of choosing Libyan law as the governing law of EPSA IV, foreign investors are entitled to certain legal entitlements. These include:

- the acceptance of international arbitration as an instrument of dispute settlement and the International Chamber of Commerce Arbitration Rules;
- specific acknowledgment of EPSA IV as an agreement governed by private law principles, which should reduce the ability of the LNOC to amend or terminate such agreements, except in accordance with the terms of EPSA IV, and which also reduces the likelihood of EPSA IV being characterised as a governmental licence; and
- the contract stability clause.

---

4 *Ibid.*

As commercial contracts which are governed by Libyan law, Libyan oil contracts incorporate the rules of such law in force at the time they are executed. With such rules being 'merged' into the contract, some commentators argue that the contract will thus be protected for the term of its validity against future changes in law. However, this view has not been conclusively tested in any judgment to date or enshrined in any binding source of law.

EPSA IV contains no explicit provisions that protect investments from future legislation adversely affecting them or from current laws that conflict with EPSA IV. Article 21 of EPSA IV states that it will be governed by, and interpreted in accordance with, the laws and regulations of Libya, including the Petroleum Law. Article 27.3 provides that EPSA IV will not be amended or modified in any respect except by the mutual consent in writing of the parties, executed and approved in the same manner as EPSA IV. This stability clause is intended to protect the foreign investor from any amendments to EPSA IV that may take place after its execution without the consent of the foreign investor.

The Petroleum Law permits the respective ministries to issue subordinate regulations applicable to EPSAs. To exclude the application of regulations that may have an adverse effect on investors, the law provides that such principles or any amendment to the contract must not include anything that "may forthrightly harm the contractual rights" granted in the contract. Accordingly, "any alteration to or repeal of … regulations" will not "affect the contractual rights of" the investor "without its consent".

Libya is not a party to the New York Convention on the Recognition and Enforcement of Foreign Arbitral Awards. Therefore, in order to enforce an arbitral award, the IOC must look to local law. Thus, if a case has been resolved by the courts of a foreign jurisdiction or an arbitral award has been issued in a foreign jurisdiction, the question may arise as to whether that decision or award can be enforced in Libya.

The Libyan courts tend to regard themselves as competent and Libyan law to apply in legal disputes arising from contractual agreements with foreign companies or bodies. For the courts to claim jurisdiction, it will suffice if:

- one of the parties is Libyan;
- the agreement was entered into in Libya; or
- in certain cases, both parties are foreigners and the contract was concluded in a foreign country, but is executed in Libya.

This applies even if the courts of a foreign jurisdiction were chosen in the agreement between the parties. In such situations, the Libyan courts will regularly regard Libyan laws as applicable in compliance with international laws.

The Civil Procedure Law treats foreign court orders and arbitral awards equally and allows them to be enforced in Libya under specified conditions and according to a certain procedure.

Unlike most other PSAs, EPSA IV does not include a specific waiver of sovereign immunity. Historically, the LNOC has never raised sovereign immunity as a defence; however, there is a risk that this could be used as a defence to the enforcement of remedies in the future.

In addition, all arbitration claims relating to nationalisation have been settled prior to judgment. Therefore, it is difficult to determine whether threats of the exercise of sovereign immunity have been raised by the LNOC. It is clear that the LNOC is aware that this is a concern of foreign investors, but this was not addressed in EPSA IV.

Clause 27 of the Petroleum Law specifies only five situations in which a concession or EPSA can be cancelled, as follows:

- failure to commence operations within the specified timeframe;
- failure to pay amounts due within six months of the date on which they are due;
- bankruptcy;
- failure to perform certain obligations; and
- failure to pay an arbitration award within 90 days of the date on which such payment is due.

While the definition of '*force majeure*' does not appear to be limiting in EPSA IV, acts of any Libyan governmental authority or persons controlled by the government that preclude the investor from performance under the agreement and that do not constitute a breach of contractual undertakings under the agreement will usually be specifically listed as a circumstance of *force majeure*.

EPSA IV severely limits assignments by the second party, which would make the investment illiquid and potentially difficult to finance. Assignments are:

- subject to the prior written consent of the LNOC; and
- specifically prohibited before the completion of all seismic commitments and drilling of a least 50% or more of the new field wildcat wells, as set out in the exploration programme as per Article 24.2.

Other provisions include a requirement that notices are due in English, as per Article 27.1.

6. Relationship of the PSA with the Petroleum Law

The first Petroleum Law (25/1955) was enacted on 21 April 1955 and the final text, along with two schedules, was published in the *Official Gazette* of 19 June 1955. Although the law was amended after oil production began, its basic structure remains unchanged today. The law contained several unusual features, which fostered the development of a competitive and prosperous oil industry throughout the 1960s.

The law refers to and governs Libyan oil contracts in general, including exploration agreements and PSAs. The law initially recognised the deed of concession as the sole contractual form for the exploitation of petroleum resources; but as a result of regulations issued in 1970 and 1979, it is generally accepted that EPSAs are now the appropriate contracts for the exploitation of petroleum resources.

Various initiatives have been launched to update the Petroleum Law. For example, a draft law was developed between 2005 and 2010 to update the legislation in line with international practices relating to energy investment. However, this law was never enacted. In 1996, a commission was formed by the secretary of energy in 1996 to review the Petroleum Law and make recommendations for improvements. Some of these recommendations included the following:

- updating the regulations to reflect recent developments in the international oil industry;
- updating the Petroleum Law to address all aspects of the oil industry, including refining, petrochemicals and exploitation of gas;
- providing means to encourage the full participation of qualified oil companies (eg, open bidding rounds);
- introducing legislative incentives for IOCs (eg, customs duties and administrative procedures pertaining to taxes and the employment of expatriate personnel);
- accommodating and encouraging foreign investment and participation in the refining and petrochemicals industries; and
- adopting flexible policies for training and developing manpower.

A new Petroleum Law has been drafted, but has not yet been enacted.

7. Conclusion

The language of EPSA IV appears to be that of a purely commercial deal. However, in addition to being a commercial arrangement, EPSA IV purports to grant substantial rights to the production of minerals which are not normally transferred pursuant to commercial arrangements.

Therefore, EPSA IV has the features of both a commercial deal and a governmental licence. In this respect, it would be prudent if the Libyan government issued a guarantee (performance, financial or both) to investors. The request for a guarantee would counterbalance the requirement for a guarantee from the investor (Exhibit D to EPSA IV). Among other things, the governmental guarantee would contain a list of warranties and representations with regard to the contract area and its undertakings pursuant to EPSA IV.

Additionally, EPSA IV could more clearly stipulate the specific rights granted to the investor. These would include:

- the rights of exclusive exploration and production within the area;

- the right to use, free of charge, the land within the area (including the water surface and sea floor);
- the right to run the petroleum operations without the need to obtain any specific activity licences or permits;
- the right to freely export production;
- the right to freely use foreign currency; and
- other rights necessary for the proper conduct of the operations.

It also appears that, to the extent that the LNOC grants rights to produce and own minerals in Libya or to conduct mineral exploration and production activities in Libya, it is acting on behalf of the Libyan government. Unless the respective language is included in the governmental guarantee, it would be prudent to stipulate in EPSA IV that, as well as being a commercial counterparty of the investor, the LNOC also represents the Libyan government.

Ultimately, investors will need to have EPSAs approved by the Cabinet of Ministers into law of the state of Libya.

Malaysia

Philip Teoh
Azmi & Associates

1. Introduction

In 1910, Malaysia discovered its first oil well, on top of Canada Hill in Miri, Sarawak. The discovery was made by Shell Company; and by 1914, Shell had constructed Malaysia's first oil refinery. In 1974, the national oil and gas company – Petroliam Nasional Berhad (PETRONAS) – was established to undertake exploration and production activities in Malaysia. The Petroleum Development Act 1974, which is the main statute governing the Malaysian oil and gas industry, conferred on PETRONAS all ownership, exclusive rights, powers, liberties and privileges to explore and exploit Malaysia's petroleum resources, whether onshore or offshore. The act abolished the concession system, whereby oil companies were granted the right to prospect for and extract oil resources under lease arrangements for periods of up to 40 years or more, in exchange for royalty payments to the Malaysian government.

The Petroleum Regulations 1974 gave PETRONAS the right to issue licences to qualified and competent oil and gas companies (contractors) to conduct upstream activities for the exploration, development and production of oil and gas. As a result, domestic and foreign oil companies that wish to participate in exploration and production activities must first obtain a licence from PETRONAS. The issuance of licences is coordinated by Malaysia Petroleum Management. The first production sharing contract (PSC) was awarded to Esso in 1976 for the Duyong oil field in Terengganu.

Unlike the old concession system, the key advantage of the PSC is that it allows PETRONAS to have input in strategic and operational decisions, ensuring that operations are aligned with its business objectives and Malaysia's nation-building agenda.

The contractor operates under the terms of a production sharing agreement (PSA) or production sharing contract (PSC) and a joint operating agreement with Petronas Carigali Sdn Bhd (PCSB), a wholly owned subsidiary of PETRONAS, in the development of Malaysia's petroleum blocks across the entire upstream value chain.

These contracts create contractual relationships between PETRONAS and oil exploration and prospecting companies (contractors). The contractors are authorised to develop new oil and gas fields in a defined area for a defined period. The contracts further specify the percentage of oil and gas production that will be received by each party once the parties have recovered a specific amount of costs and expenses.

2. PETRONAS companies

PCSB's wholly owned subsidiary, VESTIGO Petroleum Sdn Bhd, focuses on marginal oil fields through risk sharing contracts (RSCs). PETRONAS dominates the midstream and downstream segments of the oil and gas industry in Malaysia. It is involved in everything from refining to marketing, trading and retail operations. Subsidiaries PETRONAS Penapisan (Terengganu) Sdn Bhd and PETRONAS Penapisan (Melaka) Sdn Bhd operate refineries in Kerteh, Terengganu, and Sungai Udang, Melaka, respectively.

PETRONAS's involvement in the gas industry covers the whole range of activities, including processing and liquefaction, transmission pipeline operations, marketing and trading. PETRONAS Gas Berhad is responsible for gas processing and transmission operation and wholesale activities. It owns and operates the Peninsular Gas Utilisation System, which delivers gas to the power and non-power sectors in peninsular Malaysia, as well as the power industry in Singapore. PETRONAS LNG Complex in Bintulu, Sarawak, is one of the largest liquefied natural gas (LNG) production facilities at a single location, with a combined capacity of about 23 million tonnes per annum.

PETRONAS has also ventured into the petrochemicals industry, partnering with foreign multinationals such as BASF, BP Chemicals, Eastman Chemical, Idemitsu Petrochemical, Mitsui, DSM and Dow Chemical Company. PETRONAS has made a significant contribution to the development of support infrastructure, dedicated utilities and services in the petrochemical zones in Kerteh, Terengganu and Gebeng, Pahang – the respective locations of ethylene-based and propylene-based petrochemical plants.

PETRONAS's shipping subsidiary, MISC Berhad, provides transport and logistics support for its petroleum and LNG business in the international markets; while wholly owned subsidiary MISC Integrated Logistics Sdn Bhd fulfils the upstream and downstream logistics requirements of PETRONAS and the global energy industry.

The marketing of liquefied petroleum gas (LPG) and other petroleum products is undertaken by subsidiary PETRONAS Trading Corporation Sdn Bhd's LPG & Petroleum Products Group. These activities include:

- trading in LPG and petroleum products;
- supplying LPG and petroleum products to meet domestic requirements and meet the needs of PETRONAS's overseas marketing ventures; and
- marketing LPG and petroleum products produced by PETRONAS's gas processing plants and refineries.

Figure 1. Role sharing under the Petroleum Development Act

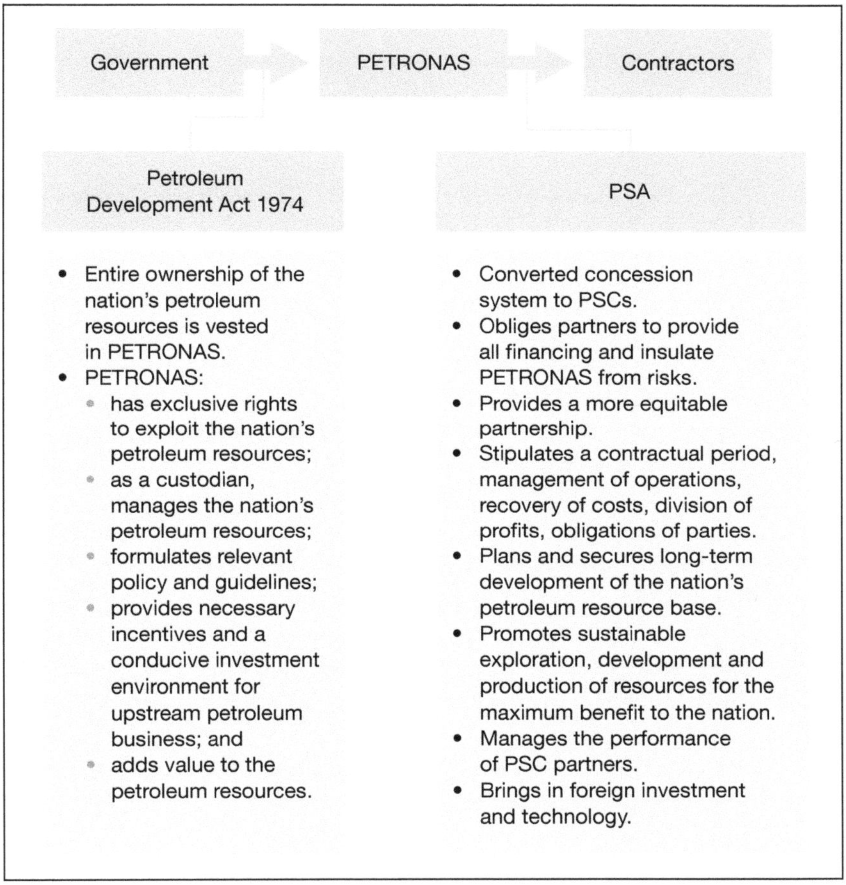

PETRONAS Dagangan Bhd is the subsidiary responsible for PETRONAS's domestic retail business. Currently, PETRONAS has over 1,000 petrol stations in the country. PETRONAS operates the only natural gas for vehicles service stations in Malaysia.

3. Scope and structure of the PSC

The PSC is a contract which governs oil and gas upstream activities in Malaysia. It sets out the terms, conditions, rights and responsibilities of the parties involved. A typical PSC specifies, among other things:

- the scope and duration of the contract;
- the fiscal terms;
- a map of the contract area;
- the minimum work commitments;

- the minimum financial commitments;
- the participating interests of the contractors;
- the management of operations;
- the requirements for work programming and budgeting;
- the methods of segregation and valuation of hydrocarbons; and
- the cost recovery mechanism.

The PSC is based on a simple formula. The contractor provides all capital associated with the exploration and development of petroleum resources. In return, if its efforts are successful, the government allows the contractor to recover its costs through the sale of the oil and/or gas and pays the contractor a fee based on a percentage of the remaining revenues. This fee is often subject to taxes and all production belongs to the government.

As the regulator, PETRONAS awards PSCs to qualified and competent contractors. Under the typical PSC terms, the contractor has the right to a carried interest in any exploration block; this interest is negotiable, but usually varies between 15% and 25%. Once a commercial discovery has been made, the contractor becomes a working partner in any development. The PSC obliges the contractor to provide all financing and bear all risks of exploration, development and production activities, in exchange for a share of the total production.

There are four types of exploration PSCs, as follows:

- the Revenue-Over-Cost PSC for water depths below 200 metres;
- the Deepwater PSC for water depths between 200 metres and 1,000 metres;
- the Ultra Deepwater PSC for water depths below 1,000 metres; and
- the High Pressure High Temperature PSC.

More than 70 PSC contractors are operational in Malaysia. The major players include:

- PCSB;
- ExxonMobil;
- Esso Production Malaysia;
- Shell Sabah Selatan;
- Lundin Malaysia;
- Sarawak Shell Berhad;
- Sante Fe Energy;
- Nippon Oil;
- Amareda Hess;
- Murphy Sarawak;
- Mobil;
- JAPEX;
- NORSK Hydro;

- Mitsubishi Corp;
- Petrofac;
- Newfields;
- Talisman; and
- ConocoPhillips.

PCSB, Shell and ExxonMobil dominate the Malaysian exploration and production sector, with shares of 43%, 22% and 16% respectively, and thus account for more than 80% of Malaysia's total production.

Since its inception in 1976, the PSC scheme has contributed to the discovery of 22.2 billion barrels of oil equivalent (BBOE) of oil and gas resources in Malaysia, of which 14 billion BBOE were produced from 132 fields. The scheme has also attracted $75.4 billion in total upstream investment, including the construction of 10 terminals, 320 offshore platforms and 7,000 kilometres of upstream pipeline.

Economically, the PSC scheme generated around 20% of Malaysia's gross domestic product in 2012. The 27 PSC contractors operating in the country that year created jobs for 20,000 people; while the scheme created business opportunities for more than 4,000 oil and gas services companies in Malaysia.

Malaysia's PSC scheme has evolved in accordance with the needs of the field operators. PETRONAS has introduced a variety of PSCs for different operating environments, including deep water contracts, revenue-over-cost contracts, high pressure/high temperature contracts and progressive volume-based contracts.

4. Main features of the PSA

The PSA will generally include the following features.

4.1 Basic information

The basic and essential clauses of the agreement relate to the following aspects, among others:

- the parties (ie, PETRONAS and the contractors/operators);
- the duration of the contract;
- the scope of operations; and
- the area and location of the oil field (eg, onshore, offshore, marginal, jungle).

4.2 Relinquishment clause

This clause specifies the percentage of acreage that the contractor must surrender to PETRONAS in order to sustain competition in the oil and gas industry. This is important in order to enable the swift and efficient development of oil and gas exploration.

4.3 National interest provisions

This clause is vital to protect the socio-economic wellbeing of the host country. It covers matters such as:

- the royalties for the federal and state government;
- taxes such as petroleum income tax;
- local content policy;
- technology transfer;
- protection of the environment; and
- capacity building.

For example, the ownership of machinery and technology used during exploration will be returned to the host country upon termination of the PSC.

4.4 Carry provision

Under this provision, PETRONAS is obliged to bear the host country's obligation of contributing towards the production costs. It provides that if there is no profit or return on the exploration investment, the host country will have no obligation to indemnify or reimburse the oil company.

4.5 Profit oil

This clause provides for the return on the exploration investment once the costs have been deducted. The return is shared between the host country and the oil company based on the agreed terms in the PSC. The profit share will also allocate a percentage of the petroleum income tax.

4.6 Cost recovery oil

The percentage of produced oil to recover the costs which have been defined and specified in the PSA will be determined on an annual basis. Although the oil company bears the costs of the petroleum operations, if there are incorrect costs of the oil produced, the oil company will be entitled to the results of those incorrect costs.

4.7 Dispute resolution

As in other types of contracts, a dispute resolution provision is vital. If a dispute arises between the parties relating to the interpretation or implementation of the terms set out in the PSA, the parties may attempt to resolve it through negotiation. If the negotiation fails, the dispute will be submitted to arbitration.

5. Oil and gas revenue distribution under Malaysian PSAs

Oil and gas revenues under the PSA are normally categorised as cash payments (royalties), cost and profit share. The amount of revenue allocation stated in Figure 2 is a general and typical illustration. The actual percentage of the distribution amount will depend on the complexity and maturity of the oil or gas field.

For cash payments (royalties), the amount of revenue allocated is 10%: 5% is payable to the federal government and the other 5% is payable to the state government. These royalties are deducted from the gross revenue.

Seventy per cent of the revenue is then allocated to the recovery of costs. Over the years, the cost recovery ceiling for contractors has risen, due to the increased complexity and higher unit costs required to monetise hydrocarbons.

The remaining 20% of the revenue will be split as a profit share between PETRONAS and the contractors, and will also go towards payment of the petroleum income tax. PETRONAS is normally allocated 3.7% of the profit share; the contractors normally get 8.7% of the profit share; and 7.6% of the profit share goes towards payment of the petroleum income tax.

Figure 2. Normal income sharing

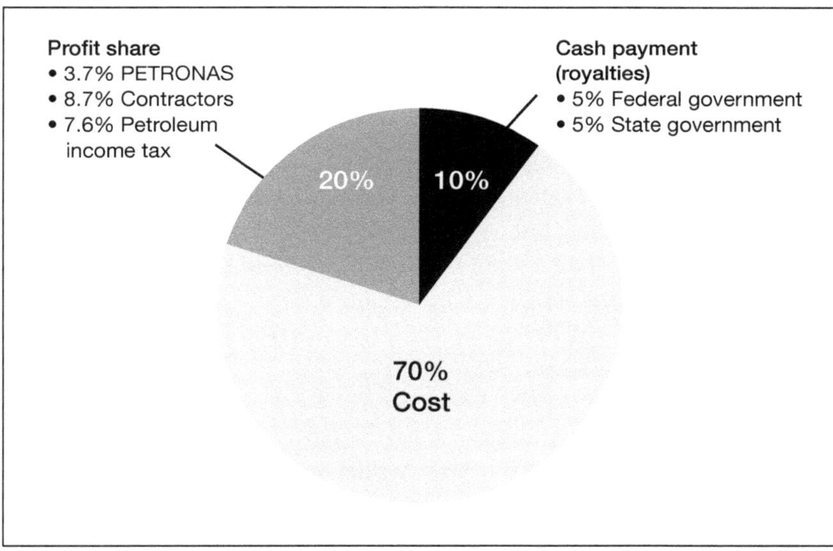

6. Relationship of the PSA with the petroleum law

6.1 Petroleum Development Act 1974

The Petroleum Development Act gives PETRONAS the exclusive ownership rights to Malaysia's oil and gas resources, and makes it the main regulatory body for upstream oil and gas activities. Under the Petroleum Development Act, upstream activities – that is, the exploration, development and production of resources – are carried out under a PSC.

(a) Section 2(1)

Section 2(1) of the Petroleum Development Act vests PETRONAS with the entire ownership of Malaysia's oil and gas resources, and the exclusive rights, powers, liberties and privileges to explore, exploit, win and obtain oil and gas, whether onshore or offshore, including in Malaysia's exclusive economic zone and its continental shelf.

(b) Section 4

Section 4 of the Petroleum Development Act provides that royalties (or 'cash payments') are payable by PETRONAS to the federal government and each of the 13 state governments to the extent that petroleum production is undertaken in the relevant state or offshore from its shore.

The royalty rates are set out in agreements between PETRONAS and the federal government and each of the 13 state governments. These agreements currently provide for 5% of the value of the petroleum obtained to be paid to the state in which the oil is found and 5% to be paid to the federal government. Instead of royalties, PSC and RSC contractors must pay export duty for the export of crude oil.

(c) Section 6

Section 6 of the Petroleum Development Act provides that any business that involves the processing or refining of petroleum, the manufacture of petrochemical products or the marketing and distribution of petroleum or petrochemical products may not be carried out by any party other than PETRONAS, unless that party has obtained permission from the prime minister.

6.2 Petroleum Regulation 1974

(a) Regulation 3

Regulation 3 of the Petroleum Regulations provides that applications for a licence must be submitted to the president of PETRONAS. A contractor that wishes to participate in oil exploration and production activities must apply for and obtain a licence from PETRONAS.

(b) Regulation 3(a)

Regulation 3(a) of the Petroleum Regulations provides that PETRONAS is the responsible authority for licensing third-party contractors that wish to participate in upstream petroleum activities, including exploration and exploitation activities.

(c) Regulation 3(b)

Regulation 3(b) of the Petroleum Regulations provides that PETRONAS is also responsible for licensing goods and service providers operating in the upstream sector, including providers of rigs and drilling services and suppliers of general goods and services related to upstream operations.

(d) ***Regulation 3A(1)***

Regulation 3A(1) of the Petroleum Regulations provides that the Ministry of International Trade and Industry is responsible for regulating the processing and refining of petroleum and the manufacture of petrochemical products from petroleum.

(e) ***Regulation 3A(2)***

Regulation 3A(2) of the Petroleum Regulations provides that the Ministry of Domestic Trade and Consumer Affairs is responsible for regulating the marketing and distribution of petroleum and petrochemical products in Malaysia.

(f) ***Regulation 5***

Regulation 5 of the Petroleum Regulations provides that the chairman and chief executive of PETRONAS will process applications and forward them to the prime minister for approval.

(g) ***Section 3***

Section 3 of the Petroleum Regulations provides that contractors bear all risks of the exploration activities, and will recover their investment only if a discovery is made and the relevant upstream assets proceed to production.

6.3 PETRONAS Licensing Guidelines

The PETRONAS Licensing Guidelines set out the general requirements for applying to PETRONAS for a licence to provide goods or services to the upstream sector and for registration with PETRONAS to participate in tenders and activities in the downstream sector. The respective equity requirements, where relevant, are based on the Standardised Work and Equipment Categories applied by PETRONAS. There is currently no official register setting out details of oil field ownership or operatorship that is available to the public.

6.4 Petroleum (Income Tax) Act 1967

(a) ***Section 23(1)***

Section 23(1) of the Petroleum (Income Tax) Act (PITA) provides that petroleum income tax is chargeable at a rate of 38% of the income derived by a chargeable person from petroleum operations.

(b) ***Section 23(2)***

Section 23(1) of the PITA provides that for petroleum operations derived from a joint development area (as defined under the Malaysia-Thailand Joint Authority Act 1990), provided that the prescribed conditions are complied with, the chargeable income is subject to petroleum income tax at the rate of:

- 0% for the first eight years;
- 10% for the next seven years; and
- 20% for the subsequent years of production.

6.5 Petroleum (Income Tax) (Exemption) Order 2013

(a) ***Sections 2 and 3***

Sections 2 and 3 of the Petroleum (Income Tax) (Exemption) Order define a 'marginal field' as a field in a petroleum agreement area which has potential crude oil reserves not exceeding 30 million stock tank barrels or natural gas reserves not exceeding 500 billion standard cubic feet, as determined by the minister of finance.

(b) ***Section 4***

Under Section 4 of the Petroleum (Income Tax) (Exemption) Order, one of the tax incentives applicable to petroleum operations is a tax exemption for a portion of chargeable income from marginal fields, which results in a reduction of the effective tax rate from 38% to 25% for petroleum operations in marginal fields.

6.6 Petroleum (Safety Measures) Act 1984 (PSMA)

The Petroleum (Safety Measures) Act 1984 (PSMA) sets out associated regulations which govern petroleum transportation, storage and handling.

(a) ***Section 19***

Section 19 of the PSMA applies to safety matters regarding the transportation, storage and utilisation of petroleum. It provides that no one may store or handle petroleum without a valid petroleum storage licence or a valid petroleum handling licence granted under the PSMA authorising the storage or handling of petroleum in accordance with such conditions, if any, as may be attached to the licence.

(b) ***Section 41***

Section 41 of the PSMA provides that whenever a party is liable to punishment under the PSMA or any other regulation for any act, omission, neglect or default, it will be liable to the same punishment for every similar act, omission, neglect or default of any agent or servant employed by it in the course of its business as a licensed party. Similarly, every agent or servant employed by a licensed party under the PSMA in the course of business under such licence will also be liable to all punishments and penalties prescribed for such acts, omissions, neglect or default contrary to the provisions of the PSMA as if it were the licensed party.

6.7 Petroleum (Safety Measures) (Transportation of Petroleum by Water) Regulations 1985

Among other things, Regulation 10 of the Petroleum (Safety Measures) (Transportation of Petroleum by Water) Regulations 1985 sets out a requirement for all vessels carrying prescribed classes of petroleum to be licensed by the surveyor general of ships.

6.8 Continental Shelf Act 1966

Section 6(1)(i) of the Continental Shelf Act 1966 provides that the Yang di-Pertuan Agong may make regulations on, among other things, the removal of installations or devices constructed, erected or placed in, on or above the continental shelf which have been abandoned or become disused

6.9 Environmental Quality Act 1974

The Environmental Quality Act is the primary statute governing the protection of the environment and the prevention of oil spills and pollutants on land and in Malaysian waters.

(a) Section 29

Section 29 of the Environmental Quality Act prohibits the discharge of oil and waste into Malaysian waters.

(b) Section 19

Section 19 of the Environmental Quality Act provides that written permission from the director general is required to occupy and operate prescribed premises and prescribed conveyances.

(c) Section 27

Section 27 of the Environmental Quality Act prohibits any unlicensed person from discharging or spilling any oil or mixture containing oil into Malaysian waters in contravention of the acceptable conditions specified under the act for the emission, discharge or deposit of oil or any mixture containing oil. Anyone that breaches this provision will be guilty of an offence and will be liable to a fine of up to RM 500,000, imprisonment for up to five years or both.

(d) Section 34A

Section 34A of the Environmental Quality Act provides that an environmental impact assessment (EIA) report is required for prescribed activities.

(e) ***Section 34A(8)***

Section 34A(8) of the Environmental Quality Act provides that anyone that carries out a prescribed activity without submitting an EIA report will be guilty of an offence and will be liable to:

- a fine of up to RM 500,000, imprisonment for up to five years or both; and
- a further fine of RM 1,000 for every day that the offence is continued after receiving notice from the director general requiring it to comply with the act specified in the notice.

6.10 Environmental Quality (Control of Petrol and Diesel Properties) Regulations 2007

(a) ***Regulation 7(1)***

Regulation 7(1) of the Environmental Quality (Control of Petrol and Diesel Properties) Regulations provides that a fuel supplier is responsible for the sampling and testing of each batch of fuel (ie, petrol and diesel) after distillation, blending or import for prescribed properties under the regulations.

(b) ***Regulations 7(6) and 7(7)***

Regulations 7(6) and 7(7) of the Environmental Quality (Control of Petrol and Diesel Properties) Regulations provide that samples and records collected must be kept for six months from the date of sampling; and that such information must be provided to the director general or any authorised officer as and when requested.

(c) ***Regulation 7(8)***

Regulation 7(8) of the Environmental Quality (Control of Petrol and Diesel Properties) Regulations provides that anyone that fails to perform the obligations stated above will be guilty of an offence and will be liable to a fine of up to RM 50,000, imprisonment for up to two years or both.

6.11 Environmental Quality (Clean Air Regulations) 2014

Regulation 5 of the Environmental Quality (Clean Air Regulations) provides that written approval is required for the installation of incinerators, fuel burning equipment and chimneys.

6.12 Environmental Quality (Prescribed Activities) (Environment Impact Assessment) Order 2015

(a) ***First Schedule***

The First Schedule to the Environmental Quality (Prescribed Activities)

(Environment Impact Assessment) Order provides that the development and construction of petroleum-related facilities are listed as prescribed activities

(b) ***Section 9***

Section 9 of the Environmental Quality (Prescribed Activities) (Environment Impact Assessment) Order prohibits the construction of product depots for the storage of petrol, gas or diesel with a combined storage capacity of 60,000 barrels or more (excluding service stations) within three kilometres of any commercial, industrial or residential area.

(c) ***Section 485A***

Section 485A of the Environmental Quality (Prescribed Activities) (Environment Impact Assessment) Order provides that the minister of transport may make regulations to ensure the safety of and control over offshore industry structures, offshore industry mobile units and vessels.

6.13 Exclusive Economic Zone Act 1984

(a) ***Section 3(1)***

Under Section 3(1) of the Exclusive Economic Zone Act, Malaysia's exclusive economic zone extends to 200 nautical miles from the baselines from which the breadth of its territorial seas is measured.

(b) ***Section 4(a)***

Section 4(a) of the Exclusive Economic Zone Act provides that Malaysia has sovereign rights for the purpose of exploring and exploiting natural resources in its exclusive economic zone.

(c) ***Section 23***

Section 23 of the Exclusive Economic Zone Act provides that the owner of a submarine cable or pipeline which has fallen into disuse or is beyond repair must inform the government and remove that cable or pipeline where it is directed to do so by the government.

6.14 Occupational Safety and Health Act 1994

The Occupational Safety and Health Act covers the safety, health and welfare of persons at work, and the protection of others against risks to safety and health in connection with the activities of persons at work.

6.15 Competition Act 2010

Section 3(3) of the Competition Act provides that all commercial activities regulated under the Petroleum Development Act which are directly connected with upstream petroleum operations, whether onshore or offshore, are exempt from the Competition Act.

Mozambique

Nuno Frota
Clyde & Co LLP

1. Country overview

1.1 Mozambican laws

Mozambique's legal system is a hybrid system – although essentially based on Portuguese-Roman civil law – inherited from pre-independence times prior to 1975. Legislation remains the primary source of law in Mozambique. The courts base their judgments on legislation; there is no binding precedent *per se*, as is the case in common law jurisdictions. The Constitution of the Republic of Mozambique recognises the existence of legal pluralism – in other words, other normative systems intertwine with the formal civil law-based system,[1] such as customary rules, to the extent that these are not *contra constitucionem*.[2]

The General and Specific Legislative Framework in Annex 1 of this chapter sets out tables of legislation detailing the broader legal framework applicable to the Mozambican oil and gas industry. This well-established legislative matrix encompasses laws, decrees, orders, resolutions, ministerial diplomas and contractual models, which work together seamlessly under directives of the Ministry of Mineral Resources and Energy[3] (MIREME), national oil company (NOC) Empresa Nacional de Hidrocarbonetos EP (ENH)[4] and the National Institute of Petroleum[5] (INP), in their capacity as the main institutional[6] stakeholders and regulatory bodies for the sector.

1 Paula Rainha, "Update: Republic of Mozambique – Legal System and Research", update by Orquídea Massarongo Jona , Hauser Global Law School Programme, New York University Law School, April 2013.
2 "Law and Customs in Mozambican Law", lecture by Professor Jorge Bacelar Gouveia, ISCTEM, Maputo, 11 July 2007.
3 Established by Presidential Decree 1/2015.
4 Established by Decree 39/97.
5 Established by Decree 25/2004.
6 The High Authority for the Extractive Industry was intended to be one of the key regulatory bodies overseeing the sector, but to date it is not known whether it has been materially established and it is unclear what concrete and formal regulatory powers it holds.

1.2 Investment climate

(a) *Exploration and production*

Mozambique has the longest stretch of Indian Ocean coastline in Africa and its proved natural gas reserves are estimated at over 100 trillion cubic feet. The country is ranked third for proved natural reserves in Africa, behind Nigeria and Algeria.[7]

In 2018, Mozambique produced 212 billion cubic feet (bcf) of natural gas and exported 148 bcf of natural gas. Although it is not known for crude oil exploration and production (E&P) compared to other African producing nations such as Nigeria and Angola, Mozambique has the potential to become a global player in the E&P of liquefied natural gas (LNG).

Due to the capital-intensive nature of E&P activities, significant debt financing arrangements are necessary over the life of each concession. Raising these funds is subject to specific underlying guarantees from project sponsors. In the case of Mozambican LNG, the financial commitments agreed to date have been the largest in Africa. Mozambique's investment climate, respect for the rule of law and the stability and consistency of the actions taken by the regulators are conditions for actual and future investments.

Independent of the legal structures of choice designed to document foreign direct investment (FDI) in the sector, the economic viability of Mozambican LNG concessions relies on specific internal and external conditions precedent and minimum conditions for investment.

(b) *Stability*

External relationships have contributed to the country's stability – or at least, to perceptions of stability. Mozambique is a member of several international and regional organisations,[8] including the Southern African Development Community and the Community of Portuguese Speaking Countries. It is a signatory to the 1958 New York Convention on the Recognition and Enforcement of Foreign Arbitral Awards, having signed the Reciprocity Agreement; and to the 1965 Washington Convention on the Settlement of Investment Disputes between States and National of Other States. From an LNG investment perspective, this provides the security afforded by clear internal legal, regulatory and fiscal regimes.

On the financing side, the African Development Bank has been active in the country since 1977; and Mozambique is also a valued member of the

---

7 Independent statistics and analysis from the US Energy Information Administration, "Mozambique, Natural Gas" (July 2020).

8 A Bouene, "Occasional Paper series, Pre-assessment report of the Mozambican energy sector under the principles of the international energy charter and the energy charter treaty", Energy Charter Secretariat Knowledge Centre (2016), p10.

International Monetary Fund, the International Finance Corporation, the Multilateral Investment Guarantee Agency and the Islamic Development Bank.

A strong relationship with the European Union through the Economic Partnership Agreement[9] makes the bloc Mozambique's second most important partner. Mozambique is also a member of the Commonwealth of Nations.

At a transparency level, and as a major commodities producer, Mozambique has adhered to the Extractive Industries Transparency Initiative[10] principles since 2012.

While Mozambique's political and military stability are conditions for successfully raising funding, exposure to and risk from external factors such as extremist violence remain a major concern.

Moreover, although Mozambique experienced economic growth and generated considerable international interest up to 2016, large unreported external borrowing has caused governance and transparency concerns more recently.

Meanwhile, a series of natural events between 2017 and 2020 has had a significant impact on E&P activities,[11] both onshore and offshore. The COVID-19 pandemic and the associated state of emergency followed by a state of calamity, as well as cyclones Idai and Kenneth in 2019, also significantly reduced the country's general economic growth, with repercussions for the investment climate.

From a *force majeure* point of view, most of these events have had a significant impact on contractual commitments and the progression of existing development efforts.

(c) State of emergency

Under Article 282.1 of the Constitution of the Republic of Mozambique, Presidential Decree 11/2020, extended by Presidential Decree 12/2020, Presidential Decree 14/2020 and Presidential Decree 21/2020, declared a state of emergency in 2020 in response to the outbreak of the COVID-19 pandemic. A state of emergency was declared twice over a period of months, followed by a state of calamity.

The state of calamity was established under the legal regime of management and disaster risk reduction approved by Law 10/2020. This legal regime is regulated by the Regulations on the Disaster Risk Management and Reduction Law, approved by Decree 76/2020.

The immediate impact of these measures on contractual arrangements was the limitations they imposed on the lives of both foreigners and nationals, such as their employment, their freedom to enter and exit the country, and in some

9 The Economic Partnership Agreement – which includes Botswana, Lesotho, Namibia and Swaziland – provides for duty-free and quota-free access to the EU market. See *ibid.*

10 Extractive Industries Transparency Initiative official website: https://eiti.org/mozambique.

11 Namely, in the LNG, metals and minerals sectors.

cases their freedom to circulate. The supply of basic state commodities such as water and refined products was also limited due to logistics constraints. Although Mozambique has a well-established legal framework for local content, LNG concessions still require significant foreign manpower; this proved problematic during the pandemic in terms of the rotational servicing of the industry. This was the first time that a state of calamity was declared in Mozambique.

2. Economic outlook drives contractual options[12]

Exporters of natural resources such as Mozambique rely on external and internal factors to successfully manage their commodities. From a practical point of view, the risks are geological, fiscal and related to pricing fluctuations. These risks inform the state's options for individual E&P contractual proposals.

Mozambique's decisions to propose and/or enforce model production sharing contracts, E&P concession agreements, joint ventures, service agreements, direct assignments of exploratory rights and hybrid contractual solutions are mainly predicated on striking a balance between risk and reward in the oil and gas value chain. The level of acceptability of a contractual arrangement can be measured by identifying the challenges or risks associated with the development of specific projects, from the perspective of income (and subsequent distribution) or investment attraction[13] and, as a result, the greater or lesser revenue participation of host governments. "Whichever the model of contract, States usually issue public auctions in order to give to the exploration and production companies the opportunity to compete for the best fields."[14]

In the case of Mozambique, bearing in mind the sovereignty principles enshrined in the Constitution and the state's ownership of the soil and of all commodities extracted therefrom, the choice of model agreement has long been based on the following factors:

- the short to long-term development of Mozambique's resources;
- the limited availability of public funds[15] and the natural risk associated with E&P activities;
- the level of control and management of the assets (or concessions) by

12 See the Constitution of the Republic of Mozambique, Law 22/2004, amended by Law 26/2007 and Law 1/2008 on the state sovereignty aspect; the Petroleum Law (21/2014); the National Strategy for the Development of the Market of Natural Gas in Mozambique; Decree 64/2009 on the principles behind the relationships established with E&P majors for the purpose of carrying out their activities; the Regulations on the Hiring of Citizens of Foreign Nationality in the Petroleum and Mining Sector; and Decree 63/2011 on the local content aspect.

13 K Bindemann, "Production-Sharing Agreements: An Economic Analysis", Oxford Institute for Energy Studies, WPM 25, October 1999, p11.

14 *Revista Espacios*, Vol 38 (Nº 31), 2017, p8.

15 It is commonly accepted that countries with a gross domestic product that is mostly dependent on successful E&P rely on external investments to develop their fields. The idea that national state budgets could accommodate the financial requirements for the development of the sector is not accepted in most developing nations.

international oil companies (IOC), production levels and the marketing of production;
- access to new technologies;[16]
- the efficient promotion of the country's reserves and the enhancement of local content;[17] and
- the promotion of health, safety and the environment.[18]

From the state's perspective, whether the adoption of production sharing agreements (PSAs) or other agreements is favoured in particular comes down to which model will satisfy the state's needs first. These needs tend to diverge from the objectives of the profit-based financial modelling calculations of IOCs.

Striking a workable balance involves agreeing and adopting a competitive arrangement that will justify the investment of an IOC over time, taking into account all factors discussed above.

3. A comparative analysis of the Pande and Temane PSA[19] and the E&P concession contract for Area Z5-C[20]

This section undertakes a comparative analysis of the Pande and Temane PSA and the E&P concession contract (EPCC) for Area Z5-C of the Zambezi Delta in order to identify the benefits of each model. Both of these are used in Mozambique, although the EPCC agreement has been predominant.

We have previously discussed the relevance of conditions precedent and minimum conditions for investment,[21] and the qualifying conditions that must be met. The satisfaction of these conditions will lead to an informed decision

---

16 Access to new technologies becomes unavailable to host states when barrel of oil market pricing falls or when the reserves are located in very deep waters. The fiscal terms of existing contractual arrangements (subject to stabilisation clauses such as Article 31 of the PSA) have been designed to accommodate the price per barrel at higher price points.

17 National Institute of Petroleum of Mozambique, "Local Content" (www.inp.gov.mz/en/Local-Content): *Local Content corresponds to the portion or proportion of the value of the national production factors applied in the production of a particular good or provision of a given service. The special legal and contractual regime applicable to the Rovuma Basin Liquefied Natural Gas (LNG) Project defines the Local Content requirements to be observed by the oil companies operating there. For example, Decree-Law 2/2014 from 2nd December establishes in its Art 10, among other provisions, that there should be preference in the contracting of supply of goods and services to national companies, owned by Mozambican citizens or legal entities and/or held by Mozambican citizens. Visit our Policy and Legal Regime window to access this other relevant Decrees.* Copyright © 2014 INP.

18 Points (i) to (iv), various, *International Petroleum Transactions* (Rocky Mountain Mineral Law Foundation, 3rd Edition 2010), p507.

19 National Institute of Petroleum of Mozambique, "Pande-Temane PSA Area", www.inp.gov.mz/en/Exploration-Production/Current-Areas-of-Exploration-and-Production/Pande-Temane-PSA-Area.

20 National Institute of Petroleum of Mozambique, "Area Z5-C", www.inp.gov.mz/en/Exploration-Production/Current-Areas-of-Exploration-and-Production/Area-Z5-C.

21 The comparative approach is therefore based on:
- the respective positions of the host state and the IOC in relation to the country;
- the legal, regulatory and fiscal regimes in place;
- an identifiable path to development and production after discovery;
- the level of securitisation required by sponsors;
- the level of government grant of concessionary rights or E&P titles, and the value of the rights granted; and
- the level of potential environmental liabilities.

on whether the PSA or the concession model is more attractive for a particular project.

In general, the main distinctions between the two models include:

- the ownership of the resources;
- the title transfer point;
- the percentage of entitlement;
- the ownership of the facilities;
- the operational management and/or control;
- the state participation; and
- ring-fencing provisions.[22]

Another key differentiator concerns the cost and risk allocation. The PSA applies the cost recovery principle based on a predetermined share of production; while the concession model is traditionally based on a tax and royalty calculation mechanism, with exclusive rights owned by the contractor and a high percentage of production allocated to the contractor (and generous lifting rights). However, this does not mean that a hybrid system of production sharing and tax and royalties would not be satisfactory from the state's perspective in the medium to long term, depending on the particular circumstances or factors prevailing in the country.

3.1 Pande and Temane PSA

This PSA was entered into on 26 October 2000.[23] It covers E&P activities in the light oil and gas reservoirs[24] of the Pande and Temane fields in the northern province of Inhambane. These fields are among the oldest discoveries in Mozambique, dating back to 1961 and 1957 respectively; they are the only fields in Mozambique that are subject to a PSA structure *per se*.[25]

The minimum conditions for investment include:

- promising geology (optimistic systemic surveys);
- security of tenure;
- a competitive fiscal regime;
- fiscal and regulatory stability;
- foreign exchange retention;
- freedom to export the investor's share;
- freedom of operation and commercial structure;
- stability in environmental management;
- access to international arbitration; and
- physical security.

Professor Dr HZ Harraz, "Petroleum Laws: Types of International Petroleum Contracts", Geology Department, Faculty of Science, Tanta University, 2016.

22 *Ibid.*

23 This PSA was entered into under the PSA dated 15 May 1998 related to the Temane block and the legal rights granted to ENH by Law 3/81 for E&P in this area.

24 Both reservoirs are located onshore, as defined by Annex B of the PSA, establishing the contract area. South African SASOL IOC (via its limited liability company incorporated in Mozambique, Sasol Petroleum Mozambique Limitada) remains the operator, with a 100% participating interest.

25 Article 1.1 of the PSA, entitled "Scope of the Contract", provides that: "This is a Production Sharing Agreement whose scope is the exploration, appraisal, development, production and exploitation."

As is generally the case with this type of production sharing structure between an IOC and host state – which in this case is represented by ENH[26] and MIREME – the IOC bears all risks and development and production costs for a stipulated share of the production, in accordance with Article 11 of the PSA on cost recovery and production sharing (establishing the cost oil/profit oil model).

(a) *Ownership of the resources*[27]

The preamble to the PSA states: "the Petroleum existing in the soil and subsoil of the Republic of Mozambique and its territorial waters and continental platform, is sole proprietary of the Republic of Mozambique." Under Article 18 of the Petroleum Law (21/2014), it is clear that Mozambican sovereignty extends to the ownership of its extracted resources.[28]

(b) *State participation, cost recovery and production entitlement*

Under the Pande and Temane PSA, Sasol Petroleum Mozambique (SPM) is the operator, holding a 100% participative interest. ENH is a party to the agreement, but has no participative interest *per se*, except regarding management and authority in its capacity of NOC.

The calculation of the Mozambican share is based on a predefined sliding scale established in Article 11.9 of the PSA. This allows the host state to increase its profit share in line with the progression of production levels once all recoverable costs have been recovered.

The roles and participations of the parties are clearly established in the PSA. The host is not required to share the costs, but has a supervisory and/or investigative role in relation to auditing, inspection, health, safety and the environment.

The cost recovery and production entitlement is based on a sliding scale calculated according to the R factor, as follows:

$$\textbf{\textit{R factor}} = \frac{\textit{IOC cumulative cash inflows } n^{29}}{\textit{IOC cumulative cash expenditure/costs}^{30} n}$$

---

26 ENH as the state-owned company (representing the state in petroleum operations) and the government itself, represented by MIREME.

27 E&P rights are transferred only under particular contractual conditions for a limited period, subject to pre-established financial conditions and subject to a phased operational term sheet.

28 Although any commodity extracted from the soil or subsoil is owned by the Republic of Mozambique, which crystallises the principle of sovereignty over the country's natural resources, we understand that it is the monetisation of the process of oil and gas extraction itself that is subject to contract under this PSA and is intrinsically its *raison d'être*. At a given time, title passes to the contractor (either at the well head or at the export point) pursuant to the applicable laws, and the general and share production terms in particular. As mentioned previously, the materialisation of title and ownership influence the contractual options for hosts and IOCs.

29 With 'n' corresponding to per annum.

30 PSA, Annex C, section 3 on cost recoverability and non-recoverable costs (for the purpose of calculating the entitlement of the IOC). Production bonuses paid to ENH pursuant to Article 14.2 will be considered as recoverable costs according to Annex C.

Cumulative cash inflows n = *Cumulative cash inflows (n-1)*[31] + *concessionaire's portion of profit petroleum+ concessionaire's cost petroleum – operating costs – computed corporate income tax n*
Cumulative capital expenditures n = *Cumulative capital expenditures (n-1) + exploration costs n + development and production capital expenditures n*

The PSA establishes a 65% floor for annual cost oil pursuant to Article 11.4; however, according to the progressive scale and depending on the variables of the R factor set out in Article 11.9, this could reach up to 95% of profit oil for the IOC (the scale ranges from 65% to 95%, depending on the R factor). In this case, ENH's share could reach up to 35% of profit oil, depending on the R factor, as this could range between 5% and 35%. The benefits of this method for the IOC include:

- the capital and the right to recover operational costs;
- a pre-agreed cost oil percentage; and
- the ability to carry forward costs which are not recovered in a particular year to the following year, if the operational costs in that year exceed the agreed annual limit.

(c) ***Fiscal provisions***

Pursuant to Article 13 of the PSA, on "Fiscal Terms and Other Charges", and in accordance with Decree 14/82, the IOC and its subcontracted entities benefit from fiscal exemptions relating to consumption tax and custom duties, circulation tax, property tax, withholding tax and petroleum export duties.

Foreign manpower hired to service the PSA's scope of works also benefits from income tax and personal duties exemptions. Local manpower, by contrast, does not qualify for such exemptions and is subject to general taxation.

Under the PSA, the IOC is liable for petroleum tax which corresponds to an oil and gas production royalty as follows:

- a 5% cash payment applied to natural gas produced and collected in the area of the contract; and
- 8% of crude oil produced and lifted in the area of the contract.

The contractor must also submit monthly statements to the Tax and Audit National Directorate evidencing regular quantity measurements at the delivery point.

In additional to royalties, the IOC will be subject to the following:

- industrial tax (corresponding to corporate tax) at a rate of 35%, according to the detailed conditions of applicability set out in Article 13.7 of the PSA;

---

31 With 'n-1' as the following year.

- customs duties and other levies and taxes not otherwise exempted under Article 13.2;
- consumption tax applicable to local consumables and/or imported goods to be used outside the scope of the PSA; and
- value added tax (except on the petroleum operations).

The PSA thus combines a typical production sharing mechanism and a fiscal system composed of taxation, notwithstanding relevant exemptions, together with a petroleum production royalty.

In comparative terms, and benchmarking to international practices at the time, the higher conditional percentage in the sharing scale up to 95% of profit oil was potentially an unbalanced formula, and was mostly found in concession agreements rather than PSAs. In addition, ENH was not an active player on the operational side of E&P activities and thus any investment would have had a limited beneficial impact on local content.

3.2 Area Z5-C EPCC

The EPCC for Area Z5-C, offshore of the Zambezi Delta,[32] mirrors the EPCC Model Agreement published in Resolution 25/2016, approving the E&P concession model.[33] It is also defined by Article 30 of the Petroleum Law.[34]

The contract was entered into in October 2018 between ExxonMobil as the operator, Rosneft[35] (via subsidiary RN-Exploration) and ENH, following Mozambique's fifth licensing round, which was led by the INP. The EPCC was later novated to include ENI Mozambico SpA and Qatar Petroleum, with a change in the initial partners' respective participating interests.

The EPCC Model Agreement was designed to formalise the terms of the Petroleum Law. It provides that ENH "is the national entity responsible for the

---

32 Please see Annex 1.

33 Please see Annex 1.

34 Article 30 on the EPCC reads as follows:

1. An exploration and production concession contract grants an exclusive right to carry out petroleum exploration and production, as well as a nonexclusive right to construct and operate oil pipelines or gas pipelines systems for transportation of crude oil or natural gas or infrastructure for liquefaction of gas produced from the concession contract area, except where access to an existing oil pipeline or gas pipeline system or other existing infrastructure is available on reasonable commercial terms.

2. The contracts entered into between legal entities with the purpose to submit a request for rights or for carrying out petroleum operations are subject to the approval of the Government.

3. The exclusive right to petroleum exploration, under an exploration and production concession contract, will not exceed 8 years and shall be subject to the provisions regarding abandonment of areas.

4. In the event of a discovery, the holder of an exploration and production right may maintain the exclusive right to complete the operations initiated within a specified area, in relation to the exploration period, for completion of the work schedule and commercial value assessment or determination and to allow the petroleum development and production.

5. The holder of an exploration and production right may maintain, in accordance with the development plan approved by the Government, the exclusive right to develop and produce oil and gas in the development production area, subject to renewal for equal or shorter periods, as it is more beneficial for the national interest.

35 Rosneft press release, Information Division, 22 August 2019, www.rosneft.com/press/releases/item/196635/.

prospecting, exploration, production and commercialisation of petroleum products and represents the State in petroleum operations";[36] and that its responsibility is to "participate in all petroleum operations and the respective stages of the activities, from prospecting, exploration, production, refining, transport, storing and commercialisation of oil and gas and their derivatives, including LGN and GTL inside the country or abroad".[37]

(a) ***Ownership of the resources***

In line with the preamble to the Pande and Temane PSA, the preamble to the EPCC states that: "the applicable law provides that all Petroleum resources in the soil and the subsoil of the land territory, in the seabed of internal waters and the territorial sea, in the exclusive economic zone and on the continental shell of Mozambique, are property of the Republic of Mozambique." These terms reproduce the constitutional terms on land ownership set out in the Constitution and mirror Article 18 of the Petroleum Law: "All petroleum resources located in the soil, subsoil, inland waters, territorial sea, and continental shelf and in the exclusive economic zone, are the property of the State."

(b) ***State participation, cost recovery and production entitlement***

Article 2 of the EPCC defines the notion of 'state participation' as: "the share of the participating interest owned by an entity holding such share on behalf of the State." This is followed by Article 3.2(b), which provides: "On the Effective Date the respective Participating Interest of: Exxon Mobile is sixty percent (60%), Rosneft is twenty percent (20%) and ENH is twenty percent (20%)." Effectively, the state via ENH has agreed a participating interest – referred to as a 'carry' – of 20% in the initial agreement, as per Article 9.8, which states that the concessionaires, excluding ENH, must pay all costs incurred in relation to the state's participating interest.

The cost recovery and production entitlement is defined in Article 9, which differs from the Pande and Temane PSA in terms of the limits agreed. The EPCC establishes a recovery potential of up to 60% against costs (cost petroleum/recoverable cost), as agreed in Annex C. The entitlement itself is subject to a calculation method established by the Special Tax Law,[38] the Regulation approved by Decree 32/2015 and the Corporate Tax Code.

Under Article 9.7 of the EPCC, the profit oil is calculated according to a more balanced scale than under the Pande and Temane PSA. It takes into account a maximum R factor whereby the concessionaires' percentage would be

36 Petroleum Law (21/2014), Article 24.1.
37 *Ibid*, Article 24.2.
38 Law 27/2014, as amended by Law 14/2017.

40% and the government's 60%; whereas in a minimum R factor situation, the government would be entitled to 15% as against 85% for the concessionaires,[39] excluding ENH.

(c) *Fiscal provisions*

According to Article 25.1 and 25.2 of the Petroleum Law on Taxes, the concessionaires are subject to specific and identifiable tax liabilities.[40] Pursuant to Article 11 of the EPCC, each concessionaire, excluding ENH, must pay the government in cash a petroleum production tax or royalty, based on the value at the delivery point as follows:

- *In respect to Natural Gas produced from Petroleum Deposits in the EPCC Area, an amount in cash corresponding to 6% of Natural Gas extracted, but not reinjected;*
- *In respect to Crude Oil produced from Petroleum Deposits in the EPCC Area, an amount in cash corresponding to 10 % of Petroleum extracted.*

The royalty on petroleum is due in cash and not in kind, as is the case for the Pande and Temane PSA, which is explained by ENH's 20% carry.

In addition to the above, the government has a legal requirement to participate in all projects.

The taxes, charges and contributions payable under the EPCC include an applicable 32% of the contractor's gross revenue for income tax purposes.

4. Observations

The production sharing mechanism has proved effective in Mozambique since the legislative initiatives of 2014. The country has adopted a hybrid contractual model, which means that E&P rights are subject to a structured system for the exploitation of the country's resources. The balance achieved through the model EPCC is beneficial overall, bearing in mind the government's carry, the stabilisation clause and the local content and environmental elements.

Mozambique is well placed to maintain its status as a global player in the gas

---

39 This is justifiable taking into account the risks, investment levels and carry. Article 9 is relevant to confirm this agreement as adopted, further to the enactment of the model EPCC, a PSA model entitlement or production sharing mechanism, and thus does not solely rely on taxes and royalties. It is effectively a PSA that includes taxes and royalties.

40 In addition to specific taxes, the holders of petroleum operations rights are subject to the payment of:
- income tax;
- value added tax;
- municipal tax, where applicable; and
- other taxes established by law.

They are also subject to the following special regimes:
- the Specific Regime of Taxation and Fiscal Benefits of Petroleum Operations (Law 27/2014);
- Decree 32/2015 amending the Specific Regime of Taxation and Fiscal Benefits of Petroleum Operations; and
- Law 14/2017 on the Regulation of the Specific Regime of Taxation and Fiscal Benefits of Petroleum Operations.

industry once the current instability in the northeast of the country has been addressed. The northern offshore natural gas fields have an estimated $60 billion in reserves. The model agreements that are currently in force make generous provision for increasing local manpower under the auspices of stronger local content laws.

Mozambique's privileged Indian Ocean coastline should suffice to strengthen the country's environmental policies, even though the model EPCC and major concessionaires implement their own risk management policies. Audits, supervision and transparency are key factors.

Mozambique is ahead of most countries in terms of clean energy. It is not a major oil producer or consumer, but is rather one of the few African nations that make full use of their renewable resources: 90% of the hydropower generated from the Cahora Bassa dam is consumed. The LNG sector should further contribute to this record by attracting additional inflows of FDI and continuing to empower local manpower through balanced and beneficial contractual terms.

Annex 1: General and specific legislative framework*

The general and specific legislative framework applicable to the oil and gas industry in Mozambique is established by the following legislation.[41]

Laws applicable to the oil and gas sector

Law	Number/date
Legal Regime for the Management and Disaster Risk Reduction regulated by the Regulations of the Disaster Risk Management and Reduction Law	Law 10/2020 of 24 August approved by Decree 76/2020 of 1 September
Amendment of the Specific Regime of Taxation and Fiscal Benefits of Petroleum Operations	Law 14/2017 of 28 December
Specific Regime of Taxation and Fiscal Benefits of Petroleum Operations	Law 27/2014 of 23 September

continued on next page

41 The proposed framework, which is reproduced in a sequential manner, is intended to be comprehensive, but not exhaustive. It refers to the main legal instruments and how these should be considered holistically to understand the complexity of the oil and gas industry in Mozambique. National Institute of Petroleum of Mozambique, "Legislation and Regime", www.inp.gov.mz/en/Policies-Legal-Framework/Legislation-and-Regime.

Law	Number/date
Petroleum Law	Law 21/2014 of 18 August
Mega Projects Law	Law 15/2011 of 10 August
Law Establishing the Principles and Rules for the Licensing, Manufacture, Storage, Commerce, Traffic, Destruction and Transport and Safety Measures for Users of Explosive Substances	Law 6/2011 of 11 January
Law Establishing the Governing Rules for Contracting, Implementing and Monitoring Procedures of Large Public Private Partnerships and Business Concessions	Law 15/2011 of 10 August
Constitution of the Republic of Mozambique	Law 22/2004, amended by Law 26/2007 of 16 November and Law 1/2008 of 12 June

Decrees applicable to the oil and gas sector

Decree law	Number/date
Regulation for the Licensing of Facilities and Petroleum Operations	Decree 84/2020 of 18 September
Presidential Decree declaring the State of Emergency (2020)	Decree 11/2020 of 20 March, ratified by Law 1/2020 of 31 March and extended by Presidential Decree 12/2020 of 29 April, Presidential Decree 14/2020 of 28 May and Presidential Decree 21/2020, of 26 June

continued on next page

Decree law	Number/date
Decree approving the Regulation on the Importation and Marketing of Petroleum Products and revoking Decree 45/2012 of 28 December	Decree 89/2019 of 18 November
Petroleum Operations Regulation	Decree 34/2015 of 31 December, amended by Decree 48/2018 of 6 August
Regulation of the Specific Regime of Taxation and Fiscal Benefits of Petroleum Operations	Decree 32/2015 of 3 December
Decree Approving the Regulation for the Management of Hazardous Substances and Respective Annexes	Decree 83/2014 of 31 December
Decree Amending Recital (a) of Article 17.1, Articles 21.1, 52.2, 65, 76.1, 82 and 89.1 and 89.2 of the Regulation on the Law of Explosive Substances	Decree 35/2014 of 1 August
Regulation of the Mega Projects Law	Decree 16/2012 of 4 June
Regulations for the Hiring of Citizens of Foreign Nationality in the Petroleum and Mining Sector	Decree 63/2011 of 7 December
Decree Approving the Regulation for Hiring Foreigners in the Oil Petroleum and Mining Sector	Decree 63/2011 of 7 December
Decree Approving the Regulation for Environmental Auditing Procedure	Decree 25/2011 of 15 June
Environmental Regulation for Petroleum Operations	Decree 56/2010 of 22 November

continued on next page

Decree law	Number/date
National Strategy for the Development of the Market of Natural Gas in Mozambique	Decree 64/2009 of 2 November
Decree Approving the Regulation for Technical Safety and Health for Geological and Mining Activities, Revoking All Legislation Contrary to This Regulation	Decree 61/2006 of 26 December

Orders applicable to the oil and gas sector

Order	Number/date
Ministerial Order establishing the Regulation on Licensing of Petroleum Installations and Activities	Ministerial Order 272/2009, of 30 December

Resolutions applicable to the oil and gas sector

Resolution	Number/date
Resolution Approving the Development Plan for Golfinho/Atum	Resolution 5/2018 of 7 February
Resolution Approving the E&P Concession (Model) Contract (CCPP)	Resolution 25/2016 of 3 October
Resolution on the Social and Business Responsibility Policy for the Extractive Industry Sector of Mineral Resources	Resolution 21/2014 of 18 May
National Strategy for Petroleum Operations Concessions	Resolution 27/2009 of 8 June

Specific legislation[42]

Legislation for specific assets	Decree
Law approving the inclusion of Total E&P Mozambique Area 1, Limited, in the financing structure of the LNG project Golfinho/Atum and approving the Long Term Sheet for Common Terms of Area 1 UVJ Senior Debt Financing, dated 15 May 2020	Decree 39/2020 of 12 June
Law approving the terms and conditions of the 2nd Complementary of Area 4, to the Exploration and Production Concession Contract of Area 4 Offshore, in the Romuva Block (EPCC), and amendment to its Annex C, related to the accounting and financing procedures, approved by Decree 68/2006 of 26 December	Decree 47/2019 of 5 June
Law approving the terms of the Exploration and Production Concession Contract for Area Offshore Angoche (A5 – A), to Eni Mozambico SpA, Sasol Petroleum Mozambique Exploration Lda. and Empresa Nacional de Hidrocarbonetos, EP (ENH, EP), as concessionaires	Decree 52/2018 of 3 September
Law approving the terms of the Exploration and Production Concession Contract for Area Offshore Zambezi Delta (Z5-D), to ExxonMobil Moçambique Exploration and Production, Limitada, RN Zambezi North PTE LTD and to the Empresa Nacional de Hidrocarbonetos, EP (ENH, EP), as concessionaires	Decree 53/2018 of 3 September
Law approving the terms of the Exploration and Production Concession Contract for Area Offshore Zambezi Delta (Z5-C), to ExxonMobil Moçambique Exploration and Production, Limitada, RN Zambezi South PTE. LTD and Empresa Nacional de Hidrocarbonetos, EP (ENH, EP), as concessionaires	Decree 54/2018 of 3 September

continued on next page

42 Mozambican-specific legislation involving onshore and offshore concession areas.

Legislation for specific assets	Decree
Law approving the terms of the Exploration and Production Concession Contract for Mazenga "Onshore" Area to Empresa Nacional de Hidrocarbonetos, EP (ENH, EP), as concessionaire	Decree 55/2018 of 3 September
Law approving the terms of the Exploration and Production Concession Contract for Area Angoche (A5 – B), to ExxonMobil Moçambique Exploration and Production, Limitada, RN Angoche PTE. LTD and Empresa Nacional de Hidrocarbonetos, EP (ENH, EP), as concessionaires	Decree 56/2018 of 3 September
Law approving the terms of the Exploration and Production Concession Contract for Area Onshore Pande Temane (PT5 – C), to Sasol Petroleum Mozambique Exploration Limitada, and Empresa Nacional de Hidrocarbonetos, EP (ENH, EP), as concessionaires	Decree 57/2018 of 3 September
Law approving the terms and conditions of the Complementary Agreement to the EPCC of Area 4 of the Rovuma Basin	Decree 56/2017 of 27 October
Law approving the terms of the combined sale of the LNG from the Initial Project between the concessionary Parties of Area 1 of Romuva Block aiming at guaranteeing large volumes of LNG to secure price competitiveness and maximisation of revenues and other marketing, transport and trade LNG benefits	Decree 78/2016 of 30 December
Law approving the complementary terms to the Exploration and Production Concession Contract, for Area 4, in Romuva Block, approved by Decree approved 68/2006, of 26 December, aimed at the development of the FLNG Coral Sul project, located in the southern part of Coral Eoceno 441 reservoir	Decree 74/2016 of 30 December

continued on next page

Legislation for specific assets	Decree
Law approving the terms of the Exploration and Production Concession Contract for Area 1, in the Rovuma Block, approved by Decree 67/2006 of 26 December, aimed at the construction and operation of two initial units for the production and commercialisation of LNG in the Afungi Peninsula, Province of Cabo Delgado	Decree 75/2016 of 30 December
Law approving the terms and conditions of the LNG contract for Area 1, in the Romuva Block aimed at guaranteeing large volumes of LNG for sale, price competitiveness and maximisation of revenues of the marketing and transport operations of LNG while avoiding trading competition arising from the same development and production area	Decree 76/2016 of 30 December
Law approving the terms and conditions of the LNG contract for the initial LNG project of Area 1, in the Romuva Block aimed at achieving price competitiveness, maximisation of revenues and other scalable economic benefits in marketing, transport and trade of LNG produced by the first two units of liquefaction of natural gas in the Afungi Peninsula, Province of Cabo Delgado, using the government's share of LNG for combined sales	Decree 77/2016 of 30 December
Law on the special legal and contractual regime applicable to the LNG project of Blocks 1 and 4 of the Rovuma Basin	Decree 2/2014 of 2 December
Legislative Authorisation Law for LNG projects in Areas 1 to 4 of the Romuva Basin	Law 25/2014 of 23 September
Amendments to the Pande and Temane LNG Development Plan	Decree 10/2009 of 1 April
Law approving the terms of proceedings for Production, Transport and Sale of Natural Gas from the Unified Blocks of Pande and Temane	Decree 27/2002 of 19 November

Exploration and production model contracts[43]

Model agreement	Current phase	Designation/ location	Concession operator	Concessionaires/ partners
PSA	Development	Pande and Temane (Mozambique Basin)	Sasol Petroleum Mozambique (SPM)	SPM (100%)
PPA[44]	Development	Pande and Temane deposits	Sasol Petroleum Temane (SPT)	SPT (70%), CMH (25%), IFC (5%)
EPCC	Development	Area 1 (Rovuma Basin) and Addendum to Area 1 EPCC	Total Exploration Production Mozambique	Total Exploration Production Mozambique (26.5%), Mitsui (20%), ENH (15%), BPRL (10%), Oil India (10%), ONGC Videsh (10%), PTT (8.5%)

continued on next page

43 Exemplification models; this table is not intended to be exhaustive, but sets out most of the live concessions, petroleum production agreements (PPAs) and PSAs.

44 This PPA is the only agreement construed as such in the sector in Mozambique. According to the INP, the PPA:

> *was signed on 26th October 2000 by Sasol, Empresa Nacional de Hidrocarbonetos (ENH), Companhia Moçambicana de Hidrocarbonetos (CMH) and the Government of Mozambique with the aim to develop and produce gas resources from Pande and Temane reservoirs.*
>
> *As part of the Sasol "Mozambique to South Africa Natural Gas Project", the agreement envisages the construction of: a Central Processing Facility (CPF) to process initially 120 MGJ per annum; a Pipeline with an extension of 865 km to transport the produced gas from Temane (Mozambique) to Secunda (South Africa).*
>
> *This pipeline has five Off-take points to supply gas to the Mozambican market. The PPA covers the reservoirs in the Pande and Temane gas fields, the Upper Cretaceous Lower Grudja formation, in Grudja 6 (G6) and Grudja 9 (G9) reservoirs, respectively. The two reservoirs have an estimated total gas initial in place of about 4.5 tcf as a base estimate. The natural gas production started in 2004 in the Temane field, and in 2009 the Pande field was coupled to the CPF. The total amount of gas produced from 2004 to 2018 is 2,087 MGJ (Million Giga Joules) (equivalent to about 1.8 tcf or 50,250 million Nm*^{3} *– normal cubic meters gas), and condensate produced is 7.1 MMbbl (Million barrels). On each of the two gas fields about 30 wells have been drilled in previous contracts and in the PPA, including both appraisal and development wells. The two fields are covered by 2D seismic data of different vintages (six 2D seismic surveys from 1990 to 2005, in addition to older seismic). In 2016 Sasol acquired 42 square km 3D seismic in the central part of the Pande field surrounding the well Pande-4, and in 2018 drilled the first infill horizontal well in the G6 reservoir in the Pande Field.*

National Institute of Petroleum of Mozambique, "Pande-Temane PPA Area", www.inp.gov.mz/en/Exploration-Production/Current-Areas-of-Exploration-and-Production/Pande-Temane-PPA-Area.

Model agreement	Current phase	Designation/ location	Concession operator	Concessionaires/ partners
EPCC	Development	Area 4 (Romuva Basin; Initial EPCC)	Mozambique Rovuma Venture (MRV)	MRV [Italy/USA] MRV (70%), ENH (10%), Galp (10%), KOGAS (10%)
EPCC	Development	Area 4 (Rovuma Basin) Complementary Agreements (I & II)	Total Exploration Production Mozambique	Mozambique Rovuma Venture (MRV) [Italy/USA] MRV (70%), ENH (10%), Galp (10%), KOGAS (10%)
EPCC	Exploration	Buzi Block (Mozambique Basin)	Buzi Hydrocarbons	Buzi Hydrocarbons Indonésia Buzi Hydrocarbons (75%), ENH (25%)
EPCC	Exploration	Area Z5-D (Zambezi Delta)	ExxonMobil Moçambique Exploration and Production Ltd	ExxonMobil Moçambique Exploration and Production Ltd (40%), Qatar Petroleum (10%), ENH (20%), Rosneft (20%), Eni (10%)
EPCC	Exploration	Area Z5-C (Zambezi Delta)	ExxonMobil Moçambique Exploration and Production Ltd	ExxonMobil Moçambique Exploration and Production Ltd EUA ExxonMobil (40%), Qatar Petroleum (10%), ENH (20%), Rosneft (20%) + (10%)
EPCC	Exploration	Area PT5-C (Pande and Temane)	Sasol PetroMoz	Sasol PetroMoz (70%), ENH (30%)

continued on next page

Model agreement	Current phase	Designation/ location	Concession operator	Concessionaires/ partners
EPCC	Exploration	Area A5-B (Angoche)	ExxonMobil Moçambique Exploration and Production Ltd	ExxonMobil Moçambique Exploration and Production Ltd (40%), Qatar Petroleum (10%), ENH (20%), Rosneft (20%), Eni (10%)
EPCC	Exploration	Area A5-A (Angoche)	Eni Mozambico SpA	Eni Mozambico SpA (34%), ENH (15%), Sasol (25.5%), Qatar Petroleum (25.5%)

* *Tables in Annex 1 are the author's creation.*

Nigeria

Ngutor S Jato
Serenity Legal Union and Partners

1. Introduction

A production sharing contract (PSC) is a petroleum exploitation arrangement between a state and an oil company (contractor), under which the oil company provides the financial and technical services needed for the exploration and development of the state's petroleum resources in return for a share in the profit oil after payment of royalties, cost and tax oil. By its nature, a PSC affords the state the opportunity to retain ownership of its unexploited resources while achieving its economic objectives. The contractor has no title to the oil deposits. A major feature of the PSC is that the state assumes no risk in the exploration and production of its resources. Therefore, if oil is not discovered, the contractor alone bears the losses of the exploration project and cannot be reimbursed by the state. Although the state has the option to participate in different aspects of exploration and development, it is not required to do so.

The first PSC was executed in Indonesia in 1966. The introduction of PSCs in the Indonesian oil industry was necessitated by the disadvantages of the traditional concessionary arrangements that were used in the country, which usually covered large areas and were granted for long terms (50–90 years). These concessions also gave international oil companies (IOCs) full discretion and control over petroleum exploration and development, and the IOCs could choose whether to develop a particular oil field. This caused the development of Indonesia's petroleum resources to stagnate.[1] As a result, the government refused to grant new concessions to IOCs. It found the PSC model more suitable, as this upholds the state's ownership of resources, imposes all risks on the IOC and affords the state the opportunity to participate in the management of the exploration and development operations.

Due largely to its inability to meet funding obligations under existing joint venture (JV) arrangements, the Nigerian government executed its first PSC on 25 March 1973. This was concluded between the Nigerian National Oil Corporation (NNOC), now the Nigerian National Petroleum Corporation

1 Kristen Bindemann, *Production-Sharing Agreements: An Economic Analysis* (Oxford Institute for Energy Studies, 1999), p1.

(NNPC), and US oil company Ashland Oil for two oil prospecting licences.[2] However, due to implementation challenges, in 1979 the government abandoned the PSC and adopted a risk service contract for the award of 11 oil blocks.[3] In 1993, in order to increase its petroleum production by exploring and developing resources in the deep offshore and inland basin areas, the government once again reverted to the PSC. Both the 1973 and 1993 PSCs were not backed by any specific legislation, as none existed at the time the contracts were executed. This presented problems regarding the legal enforceability of contract terms – especially fiscal incentives guaranteed by the government under the agreements. This necessitated the enactment of the Deep Offshore and Inland Basin Production Sharing Contracts Decree 9/1999 as the first formal statute dealing with PSC arrangements in Nigeria. The commencement date of the decree was backdated to 1 January 1993, so as to make it retroactively applicable to the 1993 PSCs. This decree has since been amended as the Deep Offshore and Inland Basin Production Sharing Contracts Act 2019 ('PSC Act').

The following section will assess the essential legislative and contractual features of PSCs in Nigeria.

2. Legislative and contractual framework

A 'PSC' is defined by the PSC Act as any agreement between the corporation (NNPC) and another petroleum exploration and production company for the exploration and production of oil in the deep offshore and inland basin areas.[4] This definition narrows the application of the PSC Act to PSCs executed in respect of exploration and production in these specific areas.[5] Consequently, any PSC executed in respect of oil fields outside the deep offshore and inland basin areas is presumably not enforceable under the PSC Act. Apart from the 1973 PSC executed with Ashland, all PSCs executed since 1993 are in areas covered by the PSC Act; exploration and production in respect of oil fields outside those areas are governed by other contractual arrangements, such as JVs or service contracts. While the PSC has been hailed as a key milestone in the efforts of the Nigerian government to open up the sector to greater foreign participation,[6] it appears that the government may be slow to achieve these aims due to the current area limitation inherent in the PSC Act.[7]

2 Maxwell M Gidado, *Petroleum Development Contracts with Multinational Oil Firms: The Nigerian Experience* (Ed-Linform Services, 1999), p160.

3 Taiwo Adebola Ogunleye, "A Legal Analysis of Production Sharing Contract Arrangements in the Nigerian Petroleum Industry" (2015) 5 (8) *Journal of Energy Technologies and Policy*, p1.

4 See Section 17 of the Deep Offshore and Inland Basin Production Sharing Contracts Act 2004.

5 See Ogunleye (n 3), p6.

6 Francis Kweku Samanhyia and Solomon Samanhyia, "Fiscal Regime of Ghana's Oil and Gas Industry: A Pre-Commercial Production Review" (2016) 4 (9) *European Journal of Business, Economics and Accountancy* 65, p72.

7 This statement is also reflected on the website of National Petroleum Investment Management Services at www.napims.com/dynamic.html.

The limitation of the scope of application of the PSC Act to the deep offshore and inland basin areas is unique to the Nigerian PSC legal regime. In Angola, for example, PSCs can be executed in respect of oil fields in the surface and subsurface areas of the Angolan national territory, inland waters, territorial waters, the exclusive economic zone and the continental shelf.[8]

The PSC Act as originally enacted in 1993 aimed to grant certain incentives – such as reduced royalties and tax rates – to companies operating in the deep offshore and inland basin areas. This objective has been maintained in subsequent amendments, which principally afford statutory backing and effect to both the revenues accruable to the government and the fiscal incentives afforded to oil and gas companies. The 2019 amendments to the PSC Act aim to increase the government's revenues from the oil and gas industry.

2.1 Royalty oil

From the oil produced, a quantum which, if sold, would generate an amount that would suffice to cover the actual royalty payable each month will be allocated as royalty oil by the contractor to the NNPC.[9] From the allocated royalty oil, the NNPC will pay all royalties on behalf of itself and the IOC to the government of Nigeria.[10]

The royalty rates payable in respect of deep offshore and inland basin PSCs depend on the type of field and the price of crude oil, condensates and natural gas.[11]

Until the 2019 amendment, the royalty rates payable in respect of deep offshore PSCs were calculated on the basis of the water depths of the oil fields. These ranged from 201 metres to more than 1,000 metres, and were charged rates of between 12% and 0%, as the case may be. The royalty rate for inland basin PSCs was fixed at 10%. Since the 2019 amendment, royalty rates now depend on the type of field in which the royalty payments are to be calculated, with different rates applicable to deep offshore fields and inland basin fields. Thus, the percentage of the chargeable volume of crude oil and condensates produced from any deep offshore field at a water depth of more than 200 metres is 10%; while the rate applicable to crude oil and condensates produced from the frontier or inland basin field is 7.5%. The 2019 amendment eliminated the 0% rate and reduced the maximum 12% to 10% for deep offshore PSCs. The amendment also reduced the percentage payable for inland basin PSCs from 10% to 7.5%.

The 2019 amendment further eliminated the need for a periodic review of the royalty rates where the price of crude oil at any time exceeds $20 per barrel

8 See Articles 1 and 14 of the Petroleum Activities Law (10/2004).
9 See Section 7 of the 2019 PSC.
10 *Ibid*, Section 11.
11 *Ibid*, Section 5.

(pb) in real terms.[12] There is therefore a provision for an additional royalty which is based on the price of crude oil, condensates and natural gas. As opposed to royalty rates based on the type of field, royalty rates based on the price of crude are identical for deep offshore and frontier or inland basin PSCs. Thus, whenever there is an increase in the price of crude in excess of $20pb, the royalty rates for any PSC will be determined as follows:

- From $0 to $20pb: 0%
- From $21 to $60pb: 2.5%
- From $61 to $100pb: 4%
- From $101 to $150pb: 8%
- From $151pb upwards: 10%

Royalty rates based on the price of crude are additional royalty rates and are not meant to replace the royalty rates based on the field. If the price of crude oil increases to $30pb, the royalty payable will not be solely determined by the price to arrive at a rate of 2.5%; it will be determined based on the field and, in addition, on the price of crude. If the field is in the deep offshore area (ie, a water depth of more than 200 metres) and the applicable royalty is 10%, because there is an increase in the price of crude above $20pb to $30pb, the applicable royalty will be 12.5%.

2.2 Cost oil

Once the applicable royalty oil has been paid from the actual oil produced, a quantum of the available crude oil which, if sold, would generate an amount that would suffice to cover all operating costs is allocated to the IOC as cost recovery oil.[13] The allocation of cost oil is further regulated by the PSC,[14] which usually allows the contractor to recover all its operating expenses within five years in accordance with the method prescribed under the Petroleum Profit Tax Act 1999. The 2005 and 2006 PSC rounds capped cost recovery at 80%. Operating costs are recovered in the year of expenditure; while capital costs are recoverable in equal instalments over a period of five years, with cost recovery capped at 80%.

2.3 Tax oil

After the allocation of royalty oil and cost oil, a quantum of oil that would suffice to cover the petroleum profit tax payable each month is allocated to the NNPC as tax oil.[15] The NNPC then pays the tax oil to the Federal Inland Revenue

12 See Section 16 of the 2004 PSC.
13 *Ibid*, Section 8.
14 Although there have been many PSC rounds and models in Nigeria, their main elements remain the same.
15 See Section 9 of the PSC 2004.

Services on behalf of itself and the IOC. Petroleum profit tax under a PSC is levied at a flat rate of 50% of chargeable profits for the duration of the PSC.[16] It is split between the parties in the same ratio as the profit oil as defined by the PSC.[17]

2.4 Profit oil

Once royalty oil, cost oil and tax oil have been allocated in accordance with the provisions of the PSC and relevant laws, the remaining oil is shared between the NNPC and the IOC in accordance with the terms of the PSC.[18] In Nigeria, profit sharing may be based on cumulative levels of production, known as the 'production-based sliding scale', whereby the level of production determines in whose favour the profit sharing rates may increase or decrease.[19] Where production is at lower levels, the profit sharing rate for the IOC increases; but where the levels of production increase, the profit sharing rate of the NNPC increases.

Profit sharing may also be based on the 'R factor sliding scale', whereby profit sharing between the parties is based on the profitability of the project.[20] The profitability of the project may be influenced by various factors, such as:

- an increase in oil prices;
- low project costs;
- the relevant production profile; or
- the level of oil reserves.

As the profitability of the project increases, so too does the NNPC's share of profit oil. This is also known as the 'progressive system'.[21]

2.5 Essential provisions of PSCs

(a) Contract term

Since the first PSC in Nigeria was introduced, the term of these contracts has changed over time. The initial term of the contract under the 1973 PSC model was 20 years, renewable for an additional period of five years. The PSC was terminated if oil was not discovered in commercial quantities within five years of the effective date. Under the 1993, 2000, 2005, 2006 and 2007 PSC models, the term of the contracts was a period of between 25 and 30 years. The

16 *Ibid*, Section 3.
17 *Ibid*, Section 12.
18 *Ibid*, Section 10.
19 See Bindemann (n 1), p18. See also Trian Hendro Asmoro, "PSC Sliding Scale as a Fiscal Model for Marginal Fields in Indonesia" (Proceedings, Indonesian Petroleum Association – 40th Annual Convention & Exhibition, May 2016), p2.
20 *Ibid*.
21 Where the project's profitability decreases and NNPC's take of the profit oil decreases, this will be a regressive system; and where NNPC's take remains flat, this will be a proportional system.

exploration phase (oil prospecting licence) is for a minimum period of five years and an aggregate period of 10 years; and if oil is found in commercial quantities, the production phase (oil mining lease) is for a period of 20 years. Currently, the term of a PSC spans a period of approximately 30 years (10 years for exploration and 20 years for production).

(b) Management committee

With the exception of the 1973 PSC, all subsequent PSCs have provided for the establishment of a management committee within 30 days of the effective date of the contract. The committee is tasked with providing orderly direction on all matters pertaining to the petroleum operation and work programme under the contract. The NNPC is primarily responsible for the management of petroleum operations, which it undertakes through the National Petroleum Investment Management Services; while the IOC is responsible for the work programme. The committee is composed of 10 members, with five each representing the NNPC and the IOC. The NNPC appoints the chairman, while the IOC appoints the secretary. The committee meets regularly and makes decisions unanimously.

(c) Work programme

Under all PSCs, the IOC is contractually responsible for preparing the work programme and budget for approval of the management committee.[22] Further, the IOC must provide the necessary funds for execution of the work programme. Because the 1973 PSC did not provide for a management committee, the IOC was simply required to prepare a work programme and budget and submit it to the then NNOC for approval within one month of the effective date of the contract and thereafter at least two months prior to the beginning of each year. The 1993 PSC, however, provided for a three-phase minimum work programme and specified the minimum amount required to be spent by the IOC in the different phases over the 10-year exploration period. On the one hand, if the IOC spends less than the budgeted operating expenditure, an amount equal to that expenditure will be carried forward and added to the amount to be expended in the following year. On the other hand, the 2000 and 2005 PSCs provide for a two-phase minimum work programme without specifying any amount to be spent by the IOC. Instead, these PSCs specify the number of wells to be drilled during each phase of the minimum work programme. The contracts further require the IOC to submit a performance bond for each of the two phases, so that if the IOC performs less than the required minimum work programme, the outstanding amount under the performance bond will be forfeited and paid to the NNPC.

Currently, every work programme is secured by a performance bond

22 See Ogunleye (n 3), p4.

covering the entire budget of the work programme. The amount that must be expended on the minimum work programme during the 10-year exploration period is:

- $24 million for the first to third years;
- $30 million for the fourth to sixth years; and
- $60 million for the seventh to tenth years.

Where the IOC spends less than the required amount in any contract year, an amount that is equal to what has been spent will be carried forward and added to the amount that must be expended in the following period.

(d) ***Employment and training of Nigerian personnel and local content***

The PSCs require the IOC to recruit and train Nigerians in all aspects of petroleum operations. For non-specialised positions, the PSCs require the IOC to employ Nigerians only. For specialised positions – such as exploration, drilling, engineering, production, environmental safety and finance – the IOC must employ qualified Nigerians as well as foreigners. However, the IOC must recruit and train Nigerians to fill specialised positions in order to keep the number of foreign employees to a minimum.

(e) ***Governing law, stabilisation and arbitration***

PSCs are governed by the laws of the Federation of Nigeria and all disputes arising therefrom are construed and determined in accordance with the laws.

In order to protect the contractor from the legislative and administrative powers of the state to unilaterally change the fiscal regime and terms relied upon by the contractor when entering into the agreement, a stabilisation clause is often included in PSCs. This clause serves to ensure that, should the state revise its legislative or regulatory framework in a way that alters the existing fiscal regime or materially affects the commercial benefits of the contractor under the PSC, the contractor will be restored to its original position.[23] The 2019 amendment to the PSC Act, which aims to increase the Nigerian government's revenues through incremental royalties, has altered the royalty regime applicable to existing PSCs. IOCs must now rely on the stabilisation clauses to renegotiate and modify the provisions on royalties to reflect the additional royalties based on the price of crude oil, condensates and natural gas. This may, insofar as is practicable, restore the IOCs' commercial benefits under the contracts. If a review of the altered terms is not conducted within a specified period from the date on which the change took effect, the IOC may have recourse to arbitration. This dispute will be determined in accordance with the

---

23 Tade Oyewunmi, "Stabilization and Renegotiation Clauses in Production Sharing Contracts: Examining the Problems and Key Issues" (2011) 9 (6) *Oil, Gas & Energy Law*, p8.

Arbitration and Conciliation Act 2004 and other laws of the Federation of Nigeria.

2.6 Other notable amendments introduced by the 2019 PSC Act

(a) Review of contracts

As opposed to the old PSC acts, which required a review of the PSC at any time the price of crude oil exceeded $20 pb in real terms, the 2019 amendment prescribes that all PSCs will be reviewed every eight years.

(b) Offences and penalties

The provision in the 2019 PSC Act on offences that result from failure to comply or neglect in complying with obligations under the PSC is a recent innovation in the Nigerian PSC regime. Section 18 of the PSC Act now makes it an offence not to comply with obligations imposed under the law. This offence attracts a fine of at least N500 million or imprisonment for at least five years, or both.

3. Conclusion

Given the Nigerian government's inability to meet cash call obligations over time and the diminishing revenues available to it, PSCs represent a preferable oil and gas exploration and production model for the government. Although they only cover exploration and production in the deep offshore and inland basin areas, the PSCs relieve the government of the associated financial burden and give it a degree of control over the operations of IOCs.

The establishment of the PSC Act to give legislative backing to the fiscal terms of the PSCs has made the Nigerian PSC regime more welcoming to investors. The act includes clear provisions on government take and the contractor's take, including royalties, cost oil, tax oil and profit oil. The 2019 amendment to the PSC Act will increase the government's revenues and should thus have a positive impact on the Nigerian economy. However, the new royalty regime will have a significant impact on existing PSCs and necessitates their renegotiation. IOCs may request an increase in the initially agreed cap on cost oil or have recourse to arbitration as a result.

Russia

Aaron M Cooper
Coventry University

1. Introduction

Russia is the world's largest transcontinental country, spanning 11 time zones.[1] It has played and continues to play a crucial role in the global energy and resources market. Its economy is primarily built on the exploitation of natural resources: Russia has the world's largest natural gas reserves,[2] second-largest coal reserves and eighth-largest oil reserves.[3] However, where resource development is concerned, Russia can prove to be a risky venture for foreign investors. Over the decades, the dynamics of energy have changed and Russia has struggled to adapt to the increasing emphasis on efficiency and green technologies. Thus, on the whole, it is now being left behind.

However, Russia is opportunistic. In light of the move away from more polluting fossil fuels, natural gas and liquefied natural gas (LNG) have been promoted as 'bridge fuels' to wean nations off their reliance on fossil fuels and invest in the development of renewables (although this approach is somewhat controversial).[4] Due to its large gas reserves, Russia is only too happy to meet this increased demand. However, changing dynamics have forced Russia to focus more on security of supply and the preservation of its status as an energy power.[5] This has required it to encourage the growth of further investment opportunities; and as such, the focus is now more on the protection of international oil companies (IOCs) from the risks associated with unstable and developing states (which can range from political to monetary – that is, taxes and other arbitrary economic penalties). To protect developing states from exploitation by IOCs, protection is afforded through the development of a regulatory framework for production sharing agreements (PSAs). In general, some of the more attractive features of the PSA include the following:

1 Organisation for Economic Co-operation and Development (OECD), "Russian Federation – OECD Data" (2021), https://data.oecd.org/russian-federation.htm.
2 Statista, "Global Natural Gas Reserves by Country 2020" (2021), www.statista.com/statistics/265329/countries-with-the-largest-natural-gas-reserves.
3 OECD, "Energy – Crude Oil Production – OECD Data" (2021), https://data.oecd.org/energy/crude-oil-production.htm.
4 T Powell, "Calling natural gas a 'bridge fuel' is alarmingly deceptive" (Sightline Institute, 2019).
5 C Sørensen and E Klimenko, *Emerging Chinese-Russian Cooperation in the Arctic* (Stockholm International Peace Research Institute, 2017), p16.

- The risks associated with exploration are borne by the IOC;
- The costs are recovered during the cost oil phase of production;
- The profit oil is then shared between the company and the state; and
- Further benefits can be drawn from profits and tax.

Compared to other resource-dependent states, Russia was comparatively late in its adoption of a PSA regime. However, since the early 1990s, it has adopted a comprehensive set of laws to encourage the conclusion of PSAs between the state and investors. The PSA regime applies similar standards to those utilised across the sector and affords protection against legal and political risks in order to justify large-scale investments. It was thought that these developments would play a part in shaping Russia as an energy power – even more so in the present day.

However, modern Russia is very different from the Russia of the 1990s, when the PSA regime was conceived. Politics and priorities have changed, and exports of natural gas have decreased – Russia is now the world's fourth-largest exporter of LNG. As it copes with changing dynamics and seeks to maintain its status as an energy power, Russia has welcomed the growing economic influence of China – in particular, in the form of the 'Belt Road' initiative and increased economic cooperation in the Arctic through projects such as Yamal LNG, designed to meet China's growing energy demand, and to increase its energy mix and wean the state off its over-reliance on coal.[6] In November 2017, Novatek – one of the largest independent natural gas producers in Russia – signed a strategic cooperation agreement with the Chinese National Petroleum Company, which owns 20% of Yamal LNG. Production in 2019 was expected to be around 16.5 million tons;[7] however, it exceeded this by 11%, with 18.4 million tons of LNG produced.[8] Yamal LNG was not expected to operate at full capacity until late 2020; and although the outbreak of the COVID-19 pandemic and the stalemate between the Organization of the Petroleum Exporting Countries and Russia proved to be significant economic obstacles, it ultimately exceeded this goal.[9]

It would seem that overall, since the 1990s, the PSA has fallen out of favour in Russia. As it has been used in few projects to date, its relevance is dwindling. However, the PSA regime and its implementation serve as proof that Russia still has a unique ability to adapt to the changing dynamics of the industry.

---

6 Yamal LNG shareholders include PAO NOVATEK (50.1%), Total (20%), CNPC (20%) and the Silk Road Fund (9.9%).

7 Novatek, "Novatek and the Silk Road Fund Conclude Framework Agreement on an acquisition of a stake in Yamal LNG" (2019), www.novatek.ru/en/press/releases/index.php?id.4=984.

8 M Schuler, "Yamal LNG Crushes output capacity in 2019", GCaptain (2020), https://gcaptain.com/yamal-lng-crushes-output-capacity-in-2019/.

9 A Cooper, "Energy Development in the Russian Arctic: Examining the Russian Energy Strategy and the Development of the Northern Sea Route in the Context of Geopolitical competition", *Oil, Gas and Energy Law* (2021), www.ogel.org/article.asp?key=3947.

2. Scope and structure of the PSA

In Russia, at its core, the exploitation of natural resources is based on the Constitution of the Russian Federation.[10] At least in theory, PSAs are one of the more favourable methods of regulating petroleum development. Nearly every country has a legal and administrative framework which regulates agreements such as PSAs.[11] In Russia, since the early 1990s, three main instruments have been developed which constitute the framework for the exploitation of natural resources (although the focus here is on the PSA):

- the Subsoil Law 1992;
- the PSA Law 1995; and
- the Law on the Gas Supply in the Russian Federation 1999.

The PSA Law is the main focus of this chapter, as it established a special regime for PSAs. In place since 1996, the law marked a leap forward for the former socialist economy.[12] This introduced a degree of legal certainty for foreign investors, which had historically viewed Russia as unstable due to its shifting political dynamics and ever-changing legislation. This was especially the case as the adoption of the PSA afforded more advantages to foreign investors than the previous method of regulation under mineral licences. Mineral licences in Russia were vulnerable because no protections were afforded against future changes in law, bureaucratic whim and political volatility. Because of how Russia regulates its petroleum activities, investors could find themselves caught in the crossfire both between the regions and within the state itself. Therefore, for foreign investors, insulation from this volatility made Russia a more attractive prospect.

However, there were substantial delays in the enactment of additional legislation and the state subsequently adopted what seemed to be an unfavourable approach to the PSA. Very few projects have since proceeded on production sharing terms. Since 1993, only the Sakhalin-1, Kharyaga and Sakhalin-2 PSAs have been agreed. In 1995, the law was harmonised and it was agreed that PSAs would be treated under Russian law as civil law contracts subject to a special statutory regime entered into between the Russian Federation and the investor(s). This was a significant step forward in the reform of the Russian energy markets, which are a vital part of the Russian economy. Still, even with this legislation in place and the potential clarity afforded by the adoption of the PSA regime, Russian PSAs have primarily been reserved for remote regions only and have thus been all but killed off, apart from the legacy fields.

10 Specifically, Article 24 of the Russian Law on the Production Sharing Contracts.

11 Although there is no uniform approach, there are commonly agreed standards that are implemented in order to achieve a degree of protection for foreign investors.

12 T Walde and M Freidrich, "Russian Federation: Law on Production Sharing Agreements", *International Legal Material* 35(5) 1996.

3. Main features of the PSA

In Russia, the development of the PSA was influenced by international standards which are common throughout the sector. In essence, these aim to protect investors which are seeking assurances that any payments made to the state will not be subject to any arbitrary decisions or influences – that is, they will not be altered or amended in the future. However, these international norms were not exactly replicated in Russian law. Nevertheless, the PSAs concluded in Russia have some features to consider and lessons can be learned from them. The PSA Law contains three chapters comprising 26 articles; and while there are similarities with international standards, there are also certain unique features, some of which are tailored to the Russian environment. These changes must be taken into account by investing IOCs to ensure the feasibility of a venture.

A PSA is entered into between the IOC and the Russian Federation using the 'one box, two key' procedure.[13] This procedure was previously used for joint licensing under the Subsoil Law.[14] This is where the production sharing licence and the PSA diverge from international norms. Under the Russian PSA regime, once an agreement has been reached, the operator both obtains the mineral rights and has a contract with the government. This is defined under Article 2(1) of the PSA Law as follows:

> *The production sharing agreement (hereinafter the agreement) shall be an agreement under which the Russian Federation shall grant to the subject of entrepreneurial activity (herein the investor), on a chargeable basis and for a specified period exclusions rights to prospect, explore for and extract mineral raw materials in the subsoil plot specified in the agreement and to perform operations connected therewith, where the investor shall determine all necessary terms and conditions connected with the subsoil use including terms and conditions of and procedure for sharing the extracted products between the parties to the agreement in accordance with the provisions of the present Law.*

This places an emphasis on civil law and thus reduces the PSA to a simple contract – the preferred option for investors, as opposed to the administrative approach, which is subject to wider governmental control and potential interference. This emphasis on civil law (while unclear) is favourable to foreign investors, even though it creates a '*lex specialis*' with a claim for precedence over all past and future legislation.[15] Therefore, if there is any need for a claim to be made on the basis of the contract, for this to succeed, a degree of political agreement is still required, which can be difficult to achieve.[16] Section 1(1) of the general provisions specifies the areas in which the PSA Law will take

13 Referring to the agreement on one hand, and then to the Russian authorities on the other.
14 Article 2-4 of the Subsoil Law.
15 With reference to Article 1(4) of the PSA Law.
16 Walde and Freidrich (n 12).

precedence in the event of any disagreements. This is an unusual characteristic within a contractual arrangement, which illustrates the dominance of the PSA Law insofar as the implementation, conclusion and termination of the agreement are concerned. This gives the added benefit of insulation from Russian administrative interference. Further, some protection is offered in the form of one of the 'safety nets' set out Article 1(4), which states that: "legal acts of the Russian Federation set rules other than those provided for by the present Law, the rules of the present Law shall apply to the domain of the regulation of relations specified in para. 1 of the present Article."

However, regardless of these contractual protections, Russia's energy politics can be difficult to navigate for foreign investors and the expectations can be very different from the realities of operating in the country. For all the benefits afforded at the international level, Russian PSAs are a very different beast from the international norm. Although the PSAs aim to protect investors, Russia has proved reluctant to completely relinquish its control and influence. For example, it still regards the Sakhalin-2 development as being detrimental to the Russian state.

Sakhalin-2 was one of the earliest PSAs to be concluded – the initial exploration phases were set at 25 years, which could have been extended if, upon further exploration, more economically viable discoveries were identified. This somewhat unusual extension feature is more reflective of the oil concession contracts to be found in Middle Eastern states. Further, all proceeds from oil and gas sales are treated as cost oil until the operator has received its capital investment and an internal rate of return. Thereafter, the operator (in the case of the Sakhalin-2 PSA, Sakhalin Energy Investment Company Ltd (SEIC)) receives 10% of the hydrocarbons for the following two years. Once these two years have elapsed, the Russian party to the agreement receives 50% of the hydrocarbons until SEIC has received 24% of the profits; thereafter, 70% of the hydrocarbons are shifted to the Russian party. These particular features showcase exactly why the Russian Federation has had a less than favourable view of PSAs. The architecture of the PSA is constructed in such a way that if there is any cost overrun, it will fall upon the state to address this issue. This is characteristic of Russia, in that the state and the PSA itself are still highly politicised. As such, the state can still push for more domestic involvement and investment without the necessary fair competition rules in place. This is further reflected in the domestic preference rule, which is highly questionable under existing international law.[17]

Since 2003, further amendments to the PSA legal framework have meant that this model is essentially restricted to use in remote regions, essentially relegating the value of the PSA within the Russian energy system because of the

17 Specifically, the Energy Charter Treaty and the World Trade Organization Rules.

resulting economic detriment to the Russian state. However, in these circumstances, Russia can still benefit from transfers of technology: Russia still hopes to use the PSA as a means of generating investment in Russian companies throughout the production cycle. However, as the PSA will only be used in frontier situations, whether investors will still seek to venture into Russia remains to be seen.

4. The role of the competent authority

The Ministry of Natural Resources and Environment[18] is the executive body responsible for drafting and implementing government policy relating to natural resources (including water bodies, woodlands, flora and fauna). Where minerals and natural resources are concerned, it also implements government policies and develops regulations in the fuel and energy industry, including in relation to:

- oil and gas development;
- refining;
- trunk oil;
- oil products and gas pipelines;
- the development of hydrocarbons on the basis of PSAs; and
- petrochemicals.

Actual operations and development are overseen by the ministry, while environmental matters are overseen by the Federal Environmental, Industrial and Nuclear Supervision Service. There is a perception that the minister of energy has a certain degree of influence in this position, as the minister frequently features in the global media in relation to Russia's efforts to stabilise the global oil market and balance oil prices. However, the ministry's powers in relation to the oil and gas sector are limited primarily to controlling the fuel and energy balance of Russia and its regions, and overseeing the development of gas supply programmes and gasification plans.

5. Analysis of the main clauses of the contract

5.1 Exploration, development and commercial discovery

The exploration and development phases of the PSA state that the costs are borne by the foreign investor and are subsequently recovered from the cost oil. When the initial phases of development and exploration take place, the costs are recovered from the cost oil profits (which are usually taxed at a favourable rate). This is usually appropriate in developing states that lack a comprehensive tax system, but this is not the case for Russia. Russia has a comprehensive

---

18 www.mnr.gov.ru/en/.

finance system; and investors are often invited to operate in fields which have proven reserves, which reduces the exploration costs.

Article 7(2) of the PSA provides that: "The investor, within the framework for the fulfilment of works under the agreement, shall have the right to construct facilities for the storage, processing and transportation of mineral raw material, the title to which stall be determined…" In this case, the fields will contain proven reserves and thus there will be no need for extensive exploration and commercial discovery works. Further, with reference to Article 7(2), any works carried out must be in line with general international practice. Primarily, when fields are developed, three main regulations must be adhered to:

- the Safety Regulations for the Oil and Gas Industry;[19]
- the Safety Regulations for Complex Offshore Oil and Gas Facilities;[20] and
- the Industrial Safety Regulations for Oil Processing Works.[21]

In terms of the standards that must be adhered to during these phases from a health and safety perspective, it is perhaps a stereotype that Russian health and safety standards are not strictly observed. However, in general, the provisions in the contracts have moved towards a risk-based system, resulting in stronger adherence to the standards outlined in the provisions. Further, the fines levied for breaches of health and safety standards can be quite steep.

5.2 Local content and operations

A number of key stipulations require that at least a certain percentage of developments involve Russian personnel (eg, at least 80% of employees must be Russian citizens, with foreign employees restricted to the initial stages of the project or where no appropriately qualified Russians are available) and equipment; and that sufficient legal protections be offered to indigenous groups where relevant.

These stipulations are reflected in in Article 7(2) of the PSA, which provides: "In the agreements the parties shall stipulate the condition that the investor must purchase locally manufactured products up to a specific percentage of all technological equipment which is utilised for the production of mineral resources and their processing…"

However, while this is beneficial for the development of Russian technological knowledge, it is not without its problems. For example, the Sakhalin-2 project was marred by issues concerning the selection of local contractors and suppliers. According to the terms of the PSA, the operator (SEIC)

---

19 Adopted by the Federal Service for Environmental, Technological and Nuclear Supervision in 2013.
20 Adopted by the Federal Environmental, Industrial and Nuclear Supervision Service in 2014.
21 Adopted by the Federal Mining and Industrial Inspectorate in 2016.

was required to allocate 70% of the construction costs to Russian companies. However, as costs spiralled, the development served to reduce the profits made by the Russian state. The State Audit Chamber expressed its extreme displeasure and sought compensation, but to no avail.[22]

Perhaps one of the more straightforward provisions in the PSA is the requirement that the appropriate protections be afforded to indigenous groups and traditional activities. These standards supplement the protection available under International Labour Organization Convention 169 and the United Nations Declaration on the Rights of Indigenous Peoples. Article 7(3) of the PSA Law provides that: "When carrying out works under the agreement at sites located in territories of traditional residence and economic activities of exiguous ethnic communities, the investor shall take all necessary measures to protect their environment and traditional way of life..." This guarantee of protection allows for the inclusion and dissemination of indigenous knowledge. Even though it seems that international norms have been adopted, the practical realities of implementation of and adherence to this guarantee are somewhat inconsistent.

5.3 Environment

The environment is protected under the Russian Constitution[23] and at both the federal and regional levels. Within the terms of the PSA, it is covered by Article 7(2), which provides as follows:

> *works under the agreement shall be accomplished in compliance with requirements stipulated by the legislation of the Russian Federation as well as in compliance with standards (norms, rules), approved in the established procedure concerning the safe conduct of works and the protection of the subsoil, the natural environment and the health of the population. In this respect, the agreement shall stipulate the investor's obligations concerning:*
>
> - *granting Russian legal entities, with all other conditions being equal, preferential rights for the participation in the performance of the work carried out under the agreement as contractors, suppliers, transporters;*
> - *taking measures aimed at the prevention of harmful effects of the said works on the natural environment, as well as the elimination of consequences of such effects;*
> - *insurance against liability to compensate for damage in the event of accidents resulting in harmful effects on the natural environment;*
> - *dismantling of all installations, units and other property upon the completion*

22 Russian government officials estimate that the project has cost up to $2.5 billion in revenue. "Record High Oil & Gas Project Costs Expected for 2007", 12 February 2007.

23 Article 42 of the Constitution of the Russian Federation provides: "Everyone shall have the right to favourable environment, reliable information about its state and for a restitution of damage inflicted on his health and property by ecological transgressions."

of the works under the agreement as well as the clean-up of pollution in the territory in which the works were conducted.

The inclusion of this article essentially ensures adherence to the Environmental Protection Law 2001 and the Environmental Expert Review Law 1995. Prior to the implementation of the project, once the PSA has been concluded, an environmental impact assessment must be carried out, the costs of which are borne by the foreign investors. This can be a lengthy process, due to the need to obtain approval from the federal authorities.

During operations, like many other environmental protection regimes, the Russian regime relies on the grant of permits insofar as extraction, processing and waste are concerned. In the event of any spillage or industrial pollution from oil or gas activities, liability is based on the polluter pays principle – or rather, a 'pay to pollute' principle. Each type of pollution is assigned a tariff; and once a particular load is exceeded, it will result in higher payments – for example, gas flaring violations can result in stiff penalties. This follows the issue of Decree 1148/2012, which called for a substantial increase in penalties. Between 2012 and 2014, the penalty for breach of the emissions regulations was subject to a multiplier of 12 and, in the absence of adequate equipment, to a multiplier of 120.[24]

As well as being covered by the Environmental Protection Law, any waste produced is covered by Federal Law 89.[25] This imposes controls on the transportation and removal of waste. While at face value, it appears that environmental protection within the context of the PSA has a solid foundation, there are recurring issues that detract from the credibility of the regime and can result in added costs for foreign investors. The Sakhalin-2 project has been marked by numerous environmental violations, drawing worldwide criticisms from environmental groups, and has served as a basis for government intervention. The construction of offshore facilities and transportation pipelines has interfered with the fragile marine environment in the Okhotsk Sea. Pipeline construction has also resulted in deforestation and pollution of local waterways.[26] The damage was estimated to be in the region of $30 billion, which was a contributing factor to Shell selling its controlling stake in the project, which was then purchased by Gazprom.

5.4 Taxes

The tax burden is one of the most significant issues for oil and gas producers in

24 Decree 1148 on the structure of the executive power central bodies (Text 2279).

25 Federal Law 89-Fz of 24 June 1998 on Production and Consumption of Waste (with the amendments and additions of 29 December 2000, 10 January 2003, 22 August, 29 December 2004, 9 May, 31 December 2005, 18 December 2006 and 8 November 2007).

26 "Gazprom, Sakhalin Energy Work to repair Eco-Damage on Sakhalin-2", RIA Novosti (2007).

Russia. Generally, tax rates in the Russian Federation are controlled by the appropriate regional authority.

Article 13(1) of the PSA provides as follows:

With the exception of the profit tax and payments for the use of the subsoil and with due regard to the provisions of para. 3 of this Article the investor shall, within the duration of the agreement, be exempt from taxes, charges, excise levies and other obligatory payments (except those stipulated by para. 6 of this Article) stipulated by the legislation of the Russian Federation. The said taxes, charges and other obligatory payments to be collected shall be replaced by the production sharing arrangement of the agreement in compliance with the present Law.

If a general PSA regime is used, it will be largely similar to international norms. For example:

- certain expenses incurred by the investor are subject to reimbursement through compensation production (during the performance of the contract);
- the value added tax (VAT) on natural resources is reimbursed by the state; and
- the costs of goods imported (and exported) during the performance of the contract are covered by the state, as well as property and transport taxes.

Where exports are concerned, export customs duties apply. These are controlled by the central Russian government. Further, all oil producers are subject to corporate profit tax at a rate of 20%; 2% of this goes to the federal Treasury and 18% to the region. However, in some circumstances, rebates can be issued (usually at a rate of around 2.5%). The tax regulations have been fairly consistent since the introduction of the PSA in 1995; but in January 2015, an initiative to introduce upstream and downstream reforms was launched, with the aim of increasing the taxes for mineral extraction and reducing export customs duties. The reforms were completed in 2018. As a result, export duties have been reduced from 30% to 0% since 2019, while the mineral extraction tax was increased up until 2021.

5.5 Dispute resolution

The PSA Law provides that the parties to the PSA may elect to resolve disputes through international arbitration. Article 22 provides: "Disputes between the state and the investor which are related to the fulfilment termination and invalidation of the agreements shall be resolved in accordance with the terms and conditions of the agreement by litigation, arbitration or court of arbitration (including those of international arbitration institutions)."

This provision allows any dispute to be the subject of international arbitration, although in practice, this will often depend on the nature of the dispute – for example, whether the disagreement requires straightforward termination or can be resolved through arbitration without termination of the contract. International arbitration generally tends to adopt a broad approach to jurisdiction. However, if a dispute under the PSA is brought before the Russia courts, the focus may potentially relate to the subsoil licence. Regardless of the outcome, under Article 23 of the PSA Law,[27] the Russia Federation can waive its sovereign immunity with respect to methods of dispute resolution; although in practice this is unlikely and Russia will generally press for a resolution more favourable to the state oil company. Meanwhile, Article 24[28] ensures that rules are implemented which provide some form of guarantee that international provisions such as the Energy Charter Treaty will prevail. However, the practical realities of the situation mean that this is potentially a weak provision, given the state of the PSA in Russia.

6. Relationship of the PSA with the petroleum law

Since 2003, the PSA regime has been significantly curtailed. PSAs are available only if a block is put out to auction and the auction fails. This means that the PSA is the second choice of the state, used only where the relevant blocks are of no interest to subsoil users under standard licence terms. Hence, the most lucrative blocks are awarded on the basis of the general subsoil licensing regime (which is still subject to administrative interference). Moreover, the changes implemented in 2003 marked a definitive change in the Russian approach towards PSAs and resulted in a slowdown in foreign investment. This in turn was mirrored in the Russian policy, which signalled the country's desire to rely less on foreign innovation and become more self-reliant. However, this did not affect the existing PSAs (Sakhalin-1 and 2 and Khargaya). During his first term, President Putin took steps to make PSAs less attractive to IOCs. Then, during Putin's second term, the Russian government increased the regulatory pressure on foreign-owned energy assets, which was a hammer blow for the PSA and the safety it offers foreign investors.

7. Conclusion

It is difficult to say how long the Russian iteration of the PSA will last; or indeed, whether it will remain a feature of civil law in the development of Russian resources. Only three PSAs are currently in operation, none of which has found favour with the Russian government. The reality is that the PSA was introduced to the legal system merely to pay 'lip service' to international norms. It is questionable whether foreign investors will ever again see such favourable terms

---

27 The agreements to be concluded with foreign citizens and foreign legal entities under Russian law may provide for the waiver of the state's judicial immunity – that is, immunity with regard to interim measures for the protection of the claim and execution of the court and (or) arbitration ruling.

28 If an international treaty of the Russian Federation establishes rules other than those provided for by the present law, the rules of the treaty will prevail.

as those included in the Sakhalin-2 PSA. As Russia has adopted an independent approach in its efforts to remain an energy power, it has turned its attention to the east. Chinese demand and the changing climate have buoyed Russian's plans as it seeks to pursue its strategies along the northern sea route and develop its LNG resources.

One thing is certain: the Russian *Duma* has failed to agree on how the PSA regime should operate and who should benefit therefrom. Regardless of the protections it offers, the PSA in Russia is still exposed to the posturing and influence of the Russian government – and the attitude towards PSAs is unlikely to change in the near future. The combination of excessive governmental influence, poor legal structure and the battle between the Russian oil majors – LUKoil, Rosneft and Gazprom – for a dominant position has left each of the major PSA projects facing various issues. When also considered in light of the imposition of unfavourable tax terms and provisions for IOCs, it is clear that the PSA will remain an unfavourable instrument for years to come. The 2003 reforms effectively killed off the instrument. In these circumstances, Russia may be a favourable destination for investment, but investors should be prepared for tough negotiations and should approach such ventures at their own risk.

Trinidad and Tobago

Terrance Ali
Risa J Mark
Indira Rampaul-Cheddie
Ministry of Energy and Energy Industries

1. Scope and structure of the production sharing contract

The Republic of Trinidad and Tobago is the largest producer of crude oil and natural gas in the Caribbean and has been involved in the industry for over 100 years. Production sharing contracts (PSCs) were first introduced into Trinidad and Tobago in 1974. The then minister of petroleum and mines signed two such contracts: the first with a consortium comprising Tenneco Oil Company of Trinidad and Texaco Trinidad Inc and the second with Texaco Trinidad Inc, for Block 6 and Block 1 respectively.

Thereafter, several PSC models have been used. In 1995, a model PSC was developed for the Ministry of Energy and Energy Industries by the World Bank and used for the 1996 and 2002 bid rounds. In 2006, this model was changed in order to achieve the new policy objectives of the then government; however, the bid round based on this model was unsuccessful. In 2010, Trinidad and Tobago returned to a version that more closely resembled the 1995 model, and has been improving on this model with each successive bid round as government policy and the global environment evolve.

In Trinidad and Tobago, there are three distinct zones: land, shallow water and deep water. Trinidad and Tobago currently uses slightly different model PSCs for each zone. The differences between these models lie mainly in the allowances for cost recovery, the contract term and the relinquishment requirements. These will be considered in further detail below.

The PSCs have detailed provisions encompassing exploration, development and production with reference to a market development phase in the case of a natural gas discovery. PSCs are governed by the Petroleum Act,[1] which allows the minister to enter into a PSC for the carrying out of petroleum operations relating to the exploration, production and disposition of petroleum in accordance with such contract, upon such terms and conditions as the Cabinet may approve. The Petroleum Act further provides[2] that:

so much only of this Act and the Regulations as are not excluded by the contract

1 Petroleum Act, Ch 62:01 (Act 46/1969), Laws of the Republic of Trinidad and Tobago.
2 *Ibid*, Section 6(4).

shall apply to any person carrying on petroleum operations under such contract, and where any provision of this Act or the Regulations is modified by the contract for the purposes of such contract, this Act and the Regulations shall be read and construed accordingly, and where there is any conflict or variance with reference to any matter between the provisions of the contract and this Act or the Regulations, the provisions of the contract shall prevail.

The main features of the PSC are discussed in more detail below.

2. Main features of the PSC

2.1 Cost recovery petroleum versus profit petroleum

Provisions for 'cost recovery petroleum' and 'profit petroleum' are detailed in Article 18 of the PSC. This article is arguably the crux of the PSC to the government, given that the majority of revenue is gleaned from profit petroleum.

Article 18.7 provides that the contractor will recover costs and expenses duly verified in respect of the petroleum operations to the extent of, and from a stipulated percentage of, all available crude oil and/or all available natural gas from the contract area, or 'cost recovery petroleum'. The cost recovery cap is a percentage which varies from contract to contract depending on the bid round in which it was awarded and the zone to which it relates. The PSCs for the deep water blocks in unexplored territory – which entail greater risk and greater capital investment than the shallow water and land blocks – tend to have a higher cost recovery cap to make the blocks more attractive. Some costs are not recoverable under Article 18 of the PSC according to Article 5 of Annex C of the PSC, such as:

- interest on financing charges;
- costs incurred before the effective date of the PSC;
- costs of expert determination or arbitration; and
- fines and penalties imposed by any authority.

The remaining available petroleum not required to cover costs, known as 'profit petroleum', is allocated between the government and the contractor. The contractor may export any available petroleum received. Test or experimental production, to the extent not required for petroleum operations, will be deemed profit petroleum and will be allocated between the government and the contractor.

Article 18.14 is a critical provision, in that it provides for the calculation of the government's share and the contractor's share of the profit petroleum, which are determined using a matrix based on daily production tiers and crude oil price classes. The matrix is generated from the submitted bid for each block and is one of the most heavily weighted criteria in the bid evaluation process.

Annex C of the PSC details how the daily production rates are to be determined.[3]

Costs and expenses are allocated to the applicable recoverable crude oil cost account or recoverable natural gas cost account on a first in, first out basis, subject to costs incurred in development operations, exploration operations and other costs, as identified in Annex C of the PSC. Any excess is carried forward for recovery in succeeding calendar years until costs are fully recovered.

Articles 17 and 20[4] of the PSC are closely aligned with Article 18. Article 17 requires the contractor to maintain records of costs incurred, as well as the quantity and value of all petroleum produced and saved from the contract area which is not used in petroleum operations. The contractor must also submit a statement of expenditure to the minister who will verify the claimed costs for cost recovery under the terms of the PSC (Article 17.6), which would be influenced by the fair market value of crude oil and natural gas as provided for in Article 20. This verification is done by the PSC Audit Unit, which was created in January 1999 to enable the minister to fulfil his responsibility under Article 17.6 of the PSC.

3. The role of the competent authority in the contract

The oil and gas industry in Trinidad and Tobago is regulated by the Ministry of Energy and Energy Industries. The ministry is responsible for the execution of PSCs and the monitoring of the petroleum operations conducted thereunder.

The state petroleum company, Heritage Petroleum Company Limited, also represents the interests of the country in some PSCs. In recent times, the majority of the competitive bidding orders published have given a compulsory interest in the PSC to its predecessor company, the Petroleum Company of Trinidad and Tobago. The deep water bid rounds did not include this stipulation. This participating interest entails a carried interest during the exploration period. Heritage participates in the development phase by paying the equivalent of its participating interest percentage of the development costs. This participating interest was vested in Heritage by virtue of the Miscellaneous Provisions (Heritage Petroleum, Paria Fuel Trading and Guaracara Refining Vesting) Act, 2018.[5]

The details of this participating interest are laid out in a model joint operating agreement which is issued as part of the competitive bidding order and the successful bidder must execute same with Heritage with no or very minimal negotiation. The purpose of this participating interest is to enable

3 The daily production rate is determined by dividing the respective total measurements of available crude oil and available natural gas attributable to each field for the month by the number of days on which crude oil and/or natural gas was produced in such month.

4 Article 17 makes provision for "Books of Account, Financial Reporting, Audit, and Cost Verification". Article 20 makes provision for "Valuation".

5 Act 17/ 2018, Laws of the Republic of Trinidad and Tobago.

technology transfer, development of the state company and financial gains to the state. It is also envisaged that Heritage will play the important role of ensuring that environmentally friendly and sustainable practices are used in the petroleum operations conducted thereunder.

4. Analysis of the main clauses of the contract

4.1 Exploration and minimum work obligations

Article 7 of the PSC, on the minimum exploration work programme (MEWP), contains the obligations which the contractor must fulfil during the exploration period. It outlines the work needed to ensure effective exploration of the contract area with additional work being executed by the contractor in many cases. The PSC provides that exploration work must commence within 90 days of the effective date.

The duration of the exploration phase varies based on the location of the contract area. For land and shallow water PSCs, the duration of the exploration period is usually shorter than that for deep water PSCs. The exploration period is typically divided into a mandatory first phase and optional second and third phases. To progress to the next phase, the contractor must complete all obligations of the current phase.

During each phase of the exploration period, there are usually obligations for three disciplines: geological, geophysical and drilling. The specific obligations listed under these disciplines arise from the competitive bidding process which is governed by the issuance of a competitive bidding order in accordance with the Petroleum Act.[6] Through this process, companies submit bids comprising, *inter alia*, technical work which they plan to perform and the associated cost. PSCs may be executed outside of a competitive bidding order through direct application to the minister, but this has seldom been the practice.

Geological obligations are standard across the PSCs, with the contractor being required to evaluate, integrate and map all data relating to the contract area. The data elements vary, but may comprise sedimentology, sequence stratigraphy, geochemistry and biostratigraphy studies. The geophysical obligations typically include the acquisition and processing of 3D seismic data. If there is existing 3D seismic data, the obligation may simply require the reprocessing of such data. If an area is considered to be high risk, geological and geophysical obligations are usually satisfactory. However, if preliminary analysis reveals potential leads, multiple drilling obligations may be incorporated into the MEWP. The drilling obligation details the minimum true vertical depth to which the contractor must drill an exploration well.

---

6 Chap 62:01 (Act 46/1969), Laws of the Republic of Trinidad and Tobago.

Should the contractor seek a revision to the MEWP, the PSC allows for the contractor to propose a revised MEWP for the consideration of the minister. The minister will usually approve the revised programme once the value of the work proposed is equal to or greater than the original obligations and the revisions are technically justified.

If, during the course of the drilling of an exploration well, the contractor attains the minimum depth in a prospective zone, the PSC mandates that the contractor continue drilling beyond the minimum depth to ensure proper evaluation of the entire prospective zone. The additional drilling will be credited against any other outstanding obligation of the current phase. If, however, the contractor has proven that an exploration well cannot be drilled to the minimum depth for technical reasons, the contractor may stop the drilling of that well. The minister may consider a payment in cash or other work equivalent to the cost of the drilling of the well in order to permit the contractor to proceed to the next phase of the exploration period.

Article 8 of the PSC provides for an irrevocable guarantee to cover the value of work to be performed during the then current phase of the exploration period. Upon completion of the works contained within the applicable section of the MEWP, verification of those works by the minister and the submission to the minister of all technical data related to that work, the guarantees will be reduced by the value of the work performed.

4.2 Commercial discovery and development

If, during the drilling of an exploration well, the contractor makes a discovery, the evaluation of that discovery will depend on the hydrocarbon discovered. However, the steps at the start of the evaluation process are common to all hydrocarbon types. The contractor must immediately notify the minister of the discovery, following which the discovery will be preliminarily classified as either a crude oil or natural gas discovery. The contractor must determine whether the discovery has commercial potential within 90 days of the discovery; if so, Article 13 of the PSC outlines the mechanism by which the discovery will be evaluated, based on the classification previously provided.

For a crude oil discovery with commercial potential, the contractor submits an appraisal programme to the minister for review and approval, which details the appraisal work, including but not limited to seismic, drilling of wells and studies to be conducted. Upon completion of the appraisal programme, the contractor must submit to the minister a comprehensive evaluation report outlining the findings of the work executed within the appraisal programme, as well as a written declaration indicating whether the discovery is a commercial discovery.

For a natural gas discovery with commercial potential, the contractor must submit an assessment plan to the minister for review and approval. The assessment plan should include the works needed to determine a market for the natural gas, in addition to the technical studies, similar to those which would have been conducted for a crude oil discovery. Upon completion of the assessment plan, the contractor must also submit a comprehensive evaluation report to the minister summarising the works conducted during the assessment plan.

The contractor must then indicate whether the natural gas discovery is to be retained for a market development phase. Due to the logistical challenges of transporting natural gas, additional time is provided to ensure that the contractor can source a market for the discovered natural gas. The market development phase has a fixed period, as prescribed in each PSC. Within this market development phase, the contractor is also afforded the opportunity to conduct further assessment of the natural gas discovery to inform on its commerciality. To serve as an incentive for the expeditious conduct of work, the contractor must pay an annual holding fee, from which the cost of technical and marketing studies conducted can be deducted.

The contractor may choose not to enter into a market development phase and proceed directly to declare whether the discovery is commercial or not. Irrespective of a crude oil or natural gas discovery, once notice is provided by the contractor that the discovery is not commercial, relinquishment of the area in which the discovery was made is required.

If the contractor has declared a commercial discovery, within 90 days of such declaration, the contractor must submit a development plan for review and approval by the minister. The definition of the production area should be clearly stated within this development plan. Should disputes arise in the review process, the determination of the dispute could be resolved through dispute resolution, as discussed further below.

Upon resolution of all issues pertaining to the development plan, the minister may grant approval for the execution of the works contained within that plan. For drilling or workover operations, the contractor must seek separate approval from the minister for the execution of those operations on a well-by-well basis, as guided by the Petroleum Act. Furthermore, as per the Petroleum Act, the contractor must apply for and seek approval for the construction and operation of any pipelines which are routed out of the contract area. Any significant changes to an approved development plan, such as the extension of a field or the implementation of enhanced recovery projects, must be submitted to the minister for review and approval.

Upon approval of the development plan, the contractor must submit, on an annual basis, a development and production work programme and budget which details, on a quarterly basis, all aspects of the petroleum operations which are proposed to be carried out for the year being considered, together with a forecast for development and production activity as well as expenditure for the following four years.

4.3 Environment

The conduct of petroleum operations requires a certificate of environmental clearance (CEC) from the Environmental Management Authority according to the Certificate of Environmental Clearance Rules, 2001 as detailed in the Environmental Management Act.[7] When conducting a geophysical survey or drilling a well, a CEC must be submitted to the minister when applying for approval for the execution of those operations.

Furthermore, the PSC requires that, as part of the process for submission of the development plan, the contractor submit a comprehensive environmental impact study covering the proposed development and any related facilities or infrastructure inside or outside of the contract area. Moreover, the PSC states that evidence must be provided indicating that the contractor has complied with the applicable legislation in respect of the approvals required by environmental authorities.

The contractor must also establish an interest-bearing escrow account in the name of the minister to accumulate cash reserves for decommissioning and abandonment activities, as well as possible pollution. The amount payable is tied to the quantum of petroleum produced. The minister can withdraw funds from this account should the contractor fail to conduct environmental clean-up or abandonment and decommissioning activities to the satisfaction of the minister. The contractor must replace any funds utilised by the minister. These contributions are cost recoverable under most of the PSC models used.

Additionally, the contractor must submit an abandonment programme and budget prior to the expiration of the PSC or the anticipated end of life of the fields under the PSC for the review and approval of the minister. Within 60 days of the cessation of production or the relinquishment of the contract area, the contractor must carry out, to the satisfaction of the minister, an abandonment programme for all installations and pipelines that the minister does not elect to take ownership of. The funding for the execution of this work comes from the escrow account previously mentioned, with the contractor responsible for any shortfall. Upon determination of the PSC and completion of all works to the satisfaction of the minister, any funds remaining in the escrow account will be left with the minister.

4.4 Local content

The PSC defines 'local content' as the "local component of goods, services and human resources employed in the conduct of Petroleum Operations under this Contract". It also defines 'local enterprise' with reference to the place of incorporation, ownership and control. Article 10.4 requires that the contractor comply with the local content policy of the government in place. The local

7 Chap 35:05 (Act 3/2000), Laws of the Republic of Trinidad and Tobago.

content and participation policy and framework[8] set out the government's goal of maximising local content and participation through the following steps:

- identifying where local value-added opportunity capture exists from the sector;
- determining how to enable delivery of maximum local value-added; and
- ensuring delivery of local value-added.

The Permanent Local Content Committee directs efforts by defining local content and participation and requesting preferential treatment of local suppliers. Additionally, local content efforts are sought for maximisation via people development in key areas and technology and business know-how.

Throughout the PSC, the contractor must maximise the utilisation of local goods, services, materials and facilities, and must employ with priority nationals in all aspects of petroleum operations to the satisfaction of the minister. In its work programme and budget submissions, the contractor must estimate local content in its petroleum operations.

The contractor must use procurement processes that provide local enterprises, in competition with foreign entities, with opportunities to provide services or equipment required in connection with the petroleum operations. As such, the contractor must ensure that all tenders are advertised, evaluated and awarded in Trinidad and Tobago, unless the minister permits otherwise; and must give preference to local enterprises where bids placed by such are competitive with foreign bids in skills, resources, availability and price, while meeting the technical and financial requirements of the contractor. Additionally, the contractor must size subcontracts, insofar as is economically feasible and practical, to match the capability (time, finance and manpower) of local enterprises and manage the risk to allow their participation. The contractor must also include high weighting on local value added in tender evaluation criteria.

The contractor is also mandated to contribute to local development by imparting to nationals technology and business expertise in all areas of energy sector activity, including but not limited to certain areas that have been identified as priority, such as fabrication. The contractor must also train nationals to fill more value-added, managerial, analytical and decision-making roles.

The contractor must maintain records to facilitate the determination of the local content of expenditure incurred in respect of the petroleum operations, including supporting documentation, which is subject to audit by the minister. The contractor must prepare and submit annual local content reports with the required details to the minister in accordance with the specified timeframe.

---

8 Ministry of Energy and Energy Industries, *Local Content & Local Participation Policy & Framework for the Republic of Trinidad and Tobago Energy Sector* (7 October 2004), www.energy.gov.tt/wp-content/uploads/2013/11/Local_Content_&_Local_Participation_Framework.pdf.

4.5 Liability

In accordance with Regulation 42 of the Petroleum Regulations, the licensee is to "keep the Minister indemnified at all times against any action, claim or demands of whatever nature which may be brought against the Minister by any third party in relation to any matter arising out of the exercise of the rights granted by the licence".

Article 10.12 of the PSC notes that the contractor must indemnify the minister and the government against all claims and liabilities in respect of any loss or damage to third parties caused by its employees' or subcontractors' wrongful or negligent acts or omissions.

Article 24.1 of the PSC provides that where the ownership of any assets passes to the minister, from the date of such transfer, the contractor will have no further rights in, and will be released from, all responsibility and liability for the asset, unless it can be proven that liability arises from a defect that existed at the date of the passing of such ownership. Additionally, Article 26.2 stipulates that the president must indemnify the contractor in full for the duration of war or grave national emergency.

Annex C of the PSC also states that the cost of insurance may be carried by the contractor. However, if no insurance is carried for a particular risk, all such charges are to be charged to the appropriate expenditure account. The proceeds of any insurance or claim are to be credited to the contractor's statement of expenditures.

4.6 Corruption

The PSC does not specifically contain clauses designed to combat corruption. However, several salient pieces of legislation fill this gap and thus it is not necessarily a weakness in the model.

The Prevention of Corruption Act[9] contains several provisions that prohibit a wide description of acts of corruption in respect of any transaction in which the state or public body is involved. These include, among other things:

- corruptly soliciting or receiving any advantage;
- corruptly giving advantage; and
- corruptly using official information.

The penalties under this act includes fines, imprisonment and repayment of the value of the amount received, if applicable.

The Integrity in Public Life Act[10] adds another layer of protection against corruption. It provides for the establishment of the Integrity Commission and contains provisions for the prevention of corruption of persons in public life by providing for public disclosure. It also regulates the conduct of persons who

9 Chap 11:11 (Act 11/1987), Laws of the Republic of Trinidad and Tobago.
10 Chap 22:01 (Act 83/2000), Laws of the Republic of Trinidad and Tobago.

exercise public functions and preserves and promotes the integrity of public officials and institutions. The Integrity Commission is given wide powers, such as the power to:

- receive and investigate complaints regarding any breaches of this Act or the commission of any offence under the Prevention of Corruption Act;
- investigate the conduct of any person falling under the purview of the Commission which, in the opinion of the Commission, may be considered dishonest or conducive to corruption; and
- examine the practices and procedures of public bodies, in order to facilitate the discovery of corrupt practices.

4.7 Royalty and taxes

The PSC provides that – apart from royalty payments, property tax, withholding tax and stamp duty, which are to be paid by the contractor – the minister must pay on behalf of the contractor, from the government's share of the profit petroleum, the contractor's liability under the applicable law for petroleum impost, petroleum profits tax (PPT), supplemental petroleum tax (SPT), the petroleum production levy, the Green Fund levy, the unemployment levy and any other taxes or impositions whatsoever measured upon income or profits arising directly from the petroleum operations under the PSC.

The contractor's taxable income is calculated as gross income less the deductions allowed in connection with petroleum operations under the tax laws of Trinidad and Tobago, including any losses carried forward from previous financial years. The minister causes the appropriate tax authority of Trinidad and Tobago to furnish the contractor with the proper official receipts evidencing such payments. The gross income of the contractor is calculated as the total of "the sums received by Contractor from the sale or other disposition of all Petroleum acquired by Contractor pursuant to Article 18; and an amount equal to Contractor's Gross-up Value calculated in the manner shown in Annex C, Article 13". Some PSC models allow for limited consolidation with the contractor's other operations in Trinidad and Tobago outside the contract area.

Royalty and petroleum impost payments are governed by the Petroleum Act. By Legal Notice 163/2017, the government of the Republic of Trinidad and Tobago amended the Petroleum Regulations issued under the Petroleum Act to apply a 12.5% royalty to production from PSCs. Previously, a royalty was applied only to production obtained from exploration and production licences. The petroleum impost is calculated based on the contractor's production and the amount of funds needed to cover the administrative charges of the Ministry of Energy and Energy Industries.

Petroleum production levy payments are governed by the Petroleum

11 Chap. 62:02 (Act 14/1974), Laws of the Republic of Trinidad and Tobago.

Production Levy and Subsidy Act.[11] The petroleum production levy was initially used to offset the subsidy on petroleum products sold to the domestic market.

PPT and SPT are governed by the Petroleum Taxes Act.[12] PPT is applied to the net profits from operations. Special deductions are allowed for signature and production bonuses, dry holes, work-overs and qualifying side-tracks. The SPT refers to a charge imposed on income generated from production of crude oil and is applicable only when the oil price is above $50 per barrel.[13] SPT operates on a sliding scale, with varying rates for marine and land operations.

The Green Fund levy came into effect in January 2001, under the Miscellaneous Taxes Act (Chap 77:01). It was increased from 0.1% to 0.3% of the gross sales or receipts effective January 2016, and it is not tax deductible. This levy is used in the maintenance, reforestation, restoration and conservation of the environment.

The unemployment levy is governed under the Unemployment Levy Act[14] and is intended to provide funds to assist in the government's social programmes. Initially, the levy was applicable to individuals and all businesses, but this was amended in 1989 to apply only to companies that were charged PPT.

There are other financial obligations which are found in PSCs and are to be paid by the contractor, such as:

- minimum payment;
- annual charge;
- production bonuses;
- technical assistance/equipment bonus; and
- the funding of scholarships.

The PSC specifies the rate at which the minimum payment is calculated and is based on the active contract area within the PSC, with payments due on a quarterly basis. The quantum of any applicable royalty payments relating to the contract area are reduced by any minimum payments made for the royalty payment period being considered. The annual charge comprises an administrative charge, a training contribution and a research and development contribution. Production bonuses become payable when the rate of petroleum production from the contract area meets the threshold for the bonus as defined in the PSC. The technical assistance/equipment bonus is a one-time payment, payable upon execution of the PSC.

12 Chap. 75:04 (Act 22/1974), Laws of the Republic of Trinidad and Tobago.

13 A recent policy decision adjusted the oil price to $75/bbl. The recently assented Finance Bill (22/2020) made provision for the adjustment.

14 Chap. 75:03 (Act 16/1970), Laws of the Republic of Trinidad and Tobago.

4.8 Dispute resolution and applicable law

The validity, interpretation and implementation of the PSC are all governed by the laws of Trinidad and Tobago.

In the event of a dispute, the parties must first use their best efforts to come to a decision through consultation. Failing this, within 90 days of the start of the dispute, either party may, by written notice, propose arbitration or determination by a sole expert. Thereafter, the parties may, by mutual agreement, submit the dispute to a sole expert who is a relevant subject-matter expert. If the parties cannot agree on an expert, they may request an agreed upon internationally recognised organisation to appoint one.

Alternatively, the dispute may be referred to arbitration by an agreed sole arbitrator. If neither alternative is chosen, the dispute will be referred to arbitration by three arbitrators. Any arbitration will be conducted in accordance with the Arbitration Rules of the United Nations Commission on International Trade Law in effect of the effective date of the PSC.

All expert or arbitral proceedings hearing materials, statement and award will be in English. All proceedings must be conducted in Trinidad and Tobago.

If the dispute relates to the allowance of a disputed charge for cost recovery and the parties are unable to agree on a subject-matter expert within 30 days of the request for determination by a sole expert, the expert will be named by the International Chamber of Commerce.

Any decision by an expert or arbitration is final and binding, and the judgment for execution thereof may be entered by any court of competent jurisdiction without a review of the merits of the award.

The decision must be rendered within 60 days of completion of the proceedings of sole determination or arbitration.

5. Conclusion

The PSCs executed within Trinidad and Tobago are unique in the landscape of the global oil and gas industry. Each bid round hosted by the government results in improvements to the PSC which factor in the exigencies of the global environment. Aspects of the PSC that are unavailable are supplemented by several existing pieces of legislation. The intricacies of the PSC presented above represent only a snapshot of the entirety of the document that exists.

Vietnam

Ha T Nguyen
Airports Corporation of Vietnam
Umut Turksen
Centre for Financial and Corporate Integrity, Coventry University

1. Introduction

Vietnam has considerable oil reserves,[1] and the oil and gas industry is thus a key sector of the national economy and a significant driver of economic growth and energy security.[2] Although extraction activity began relatively recently, in the 1980s, Vietnam has since substantially increased its overall production (in terms of both volume and quality), and has thus become an important oil and gas producer in Southeast Asia.[3]

Vietnam National Oil and Gas Group (PetroVietnam (PVN)), the national oil company (NOC), has played a vital role in increasing the contribution of the oil sector to the state budget and maintaining high volumes of exports.[4] Over the years, revenues from the sale of crude oil have consistently accounted for over 20% of the overall state budget, while revenues from other state-owned sectors accounted only for about 15%–16%.[5]

In tandem with market liberalisation, Vietnam has attracted foreign direct investment (FDI) in numerous sectors of its economy. In order to increase extraction activities and optimise production, the oil and gas industry has attracted not only FDI, but also modern technology from leading energy companies.[6] Between 1988 and 2014, more than 40 international oil companies (IOCs) – from the United States, Japan, Russia, the United Kingdom, Malaysia,

---

1 In 2019, Vietnam's oil reserves and natural gas reserves were estimated at both 0.3% of the global total. BP, *Statistical Review of World Energy* (69th edition, 2020), pp14, 32, www.bp.com/content/dam/bp/business-sites/en/global/corporate/pdfs/energy-economics/statistical-review/bp-stats-review-2020-full-report.pdf.

2 Vietnam has enjoyed an impressive economic growth rate over the past decade. Gross domestic product (GDP), for example, is estimated to have grown by about 7% in 2019, close to the rate reported in 2018. World Bank, "The World Bank in Vietnam", www.worldbank.org/en/country/vietnam/overview.

3 In 2019, Vietnam ranked 34th worldwide in terms of oil production, with approximately 236,000 barrels per day. Statista, "Oil production in Vietnam from 2009 to 2019" (26 June 2020), www.statista.com/statistics/608982/oil-production-in-vietnam/#:~:text=Most%20of%20Vietnam's%20crude%20oil,stood%20at%204.4%20billion%20barrels.

4 VT Le, QV Tran and VC Pham, "An Overview of Vietnam's Oil and Gas Industry" (2016) 10 *Journal of Petroleum Economics & Management* 56, p64. See also CEIC Data, "Vietnam Crude Oil: Exports (1987–2019)", www.ceicdata.com/en/indicator/vietnam/crude-oil-exports.

5 Government Portal, "PVN contributes VND108 trillion to State budget" (8 January 2020), http://baochinhphu.vn/Thi-truong/Tap-doan-Dau-khi-nop-ngan-sach-108-nghin-ty-dong/384544.vgp.

6 VT Nguyen, SO Ogunlana and PK Dey, "Risk management in oil and gas construction projects in Vietnam" (2007) 1 *International Journal of Energy Sector Management* 175, p176, www.emerald.com/insight/content/doi/10.1108/17506220710761582/full/html.

Canada and Australia – engaged in the Vietnamese petroleum value chain. Their activities accounted for about 4.6% of all foreign investment projects, with FDI from such investors accounting for more than $45 billion in terms of investment value.[7] Many large projects involving gas, electricity, refining and petrochemicals, and technical services have been brought on stream to fuel the development of the national economy and the industrialisation and modernisation of Vietnam.[8] In addition to acting as the host for petroleum contracts, PVN has contributed a stake of between 25% and 30% to various energy-related projects. This has enabled it to familiarise itself with advanced technologies and good governance practices in energy projects.[9]

Oil and gas projects can be classified into various categories based on their position in the value chain and the nature of their activities. The value chain starts with the identification of suitable areas for exploration activities. If the outcome of the initial exploration activities is positive, petroleum fields are then appraised, developed and produced. These are generally known as 'exploration and production (E&P) activities' or 'upstream' oil and gas activities. A number of auxiliary services are also involved in the E&P process, such as geological and geophysical surveys and analysis, drilling, equipment supply and engineering consultancy.[10] Upstream activities are PVN's core business, in accordance with the Strategic Plan for Vietnam Oil and Gas Sector Development to 2025, with a Vision to 2035.[11] Accordingly, the company has endeavoured to increase reserves for future exploitation, incentivise deepwater development projects and increase investment opportunities globally.

Since the 1980s, when the first E&P project commenced in the form of a joint venture with a Russian partner, Vietsovpetro, 105 petroleum contracts have been signed with IOCs (66 are still in force, while 39 have expired), and around 25 oil and gas fields have been developed. New facilities have been successfully interconnected with existing ones, to speed up their progress, improve project efficiency and ensure stable production.[12]

This chapter outlines the current state of petroleum contracts in Vietnam, which primarily take the form of product sharing agreements (PSAs) between the NOC and investors, and provides a critical analysis of some of the main challenges facing investors under this regime. It further makes a number of recommendations for mitigating the risks in petroleum contracts.

7 Vietnam Ministry of Planning and Investment, "FDI lays foundation for acceleration of oil and gas sector" (6 October 2018), www.mpi.gov.vn/en/Pages/tinbai.aspx?idTin=41124&idcm=92.
8 VT Le et al (n 4), p66.
9 *Ibid.*
10 S Tordo, BS Tracy and N Arfaa, "National Oil Companies and Value Creation", World Bank Working Paper No 218 (2011), pp1–2, https://elibrary.worldbank.org/doi/abs/10.1596/978-0-8213-8831-0.
11 Prime Minister's Decision 1749/QD-TTg dated 14 October 2015.
12 PVN, "Oil and gas exploitation", www.pvn.vn/Pages/detailv4.aspx?NewsID=5e1ae9ea-1ec3-4704-83e4-9b7614d04cee.

2. Overview of the Vietnamese PSA regime

First and foremost, the Petroleum Law provides that all petroleum within its jurisdiction, both onshore and offshore – including in the exclusive economic zone (EEZ), where the state exercises economic interests over such resources – is the exclusive property of the state.[13] Any provisions to the contrary in other legal instruments or rights granted or vested thereunder in derogation thereof are expressly superseded by this provision.[14] This approach is consistent with applicable international standards, whereby all petroleum resources and activities are subject to state control, management and decision.

Under the Petroleum Law, the responsibility for managing petroleum activities rests with the government, under the Ministry of Industry and Trade (MOIT).[15] The MOIT's tasks in this regard include:

- drafting regulations or delegating the drafting of regulations to authorised persons;
- developing strategy;
- submitting petroleum contracts and investment projects for approval by the prime minister;
- monitoring petroleum operations; and
- resolving claims and disputes arising from and relating to petroleum activities.[16]

The authority to implement government policy relating to petroleum development is also shared with other state departments,[17] such as:

- the Ministry of Finance, with regard to fiscal regimes;[18] and
- the Ministry of Planning and Investment, with regard to the investment registration procedure.[19]

Provincial bodies also exercise such powers within their administrative

---

13 Article 53 of the Vietnam Constitution 2013: "Land, water resources, mineral resources, resources in the sea and airspace, other natural resources, and property managed or invested in by the State are public property, owned by all the people, and represented and uniformly managed by the State."

14 Petroleum Law 18-L/CTN dated 6 July 1993 (amended by Law 19/2000/QH10 dated 9 June 2000 and Law 10/2008/QH12 dated 3 June 2008), Article 1: "All petroleum contained within the subsoil of the land, islands, internal waters, sea territory, exclusive economic zone and continental shelf of the Socialist Republic of Vietnam is the property of the Vietnamese people and is subject to uniform management by the State of Vietnam."

15 *Ibid*, Articles 38(1) and 38(2); further regulated by Government Decree 98/2017/ND-CP dated 18 August 2017 with the new Department of Petroleum and Coal within the MOIT. See also www.moit.gov.vn/web/web-portal-ministry-of-industry-and-trade/home.

16 *Ibid*, Article 38(2).

17 *Ibid*, Article 38(3).

18 Ministry of Finance Circular 36/2016/TT-BTC dated 26 February 2016, which provides guidance on taxes on petroleum exploitation and production in accordance with the Petroleum Law. See also https://mof.gov.vn/webcenter/portal/btc?_afrLoop=25977011650400O.

19 Government Decree 121/2007/ND-CP, Articles 8 and 9, amended by Decree 17/2009/ND-CP, Article 1(4)): "Petroleum projects are approved under the form of Investment Certificate issued by Ministry of Planning and Investment". See also www.mpi.gov.vn/en/Pages/default.aspx.

areas.[20] In Vietnam, there are 63 provinces (and cities directly governed by the central government), which are subdivided into districts (and cities directly governed by provincial governments).[21]

PVN has been involved in petroleum activities since the mid-1990s in accordance with Decision 330/TTg.[22] PVN was then transformed into a national group of companies under the form of a parent company and its subsidiaries,[23] and subsequently became a limited liability company totally owned by the state.[24] The core functions of PVN include:

- conducting petroleum operations;
- entering into petroleum contracts with other entities; and
- managing/supervising the exploitation of oil and gas resources with its partners.[25]

In particular, PVN is mandated to:

- allocate acreage by tender or direct negotiation with prospective investors, while retaining or competing for such acreage itself;[26]
- enter into contracts for and on behalf of the state with selected licensees, and participate in joint ventures with foreign parties; and
- administer petroleum contracts and act as a technical liaison for the state with the licensee.[27]

Petroleum contracts in Vietnam primarily take the form of PSAs and joint

20 Petroleum Law, Article 38(4); Construction Law 50/2014/QH13, Article 103(2): competence of provincial authorities to issue, revise, renew and withdraw construction licences.

21 Under Vietnamese law, there are two types of cities: those directly governed by the central government and those governed by provincial governments. There is also a lower level of local government – communes – but these play an insignificant role in promulgating and invalidating legal documents, so that they are not considered in the context of this chapter. Each province has its own local government consisting of a representative organ elected by its people every five years, called the People's Council; and an administrative organ elected by the People's Council, called the People Committee. The People's Committee is the People's Council's executive organ and is in charge of local state administration. The People's Committee is responsible for implementing the Constitution, national laws, legal instruments issued by higher state organs and resolutions of the People's Council. The People's Committee can also, within the scope of its duties and powers, issue decisions and directives and supervise their implementation. Vietnamese National Assembly, Law 11/2003/QH11 (2003) on Organisation of People's Councils and People's Committees, Article 2.

22 Prime Minister's Decision 330/TTg dated 29 May 1995 on the establishment of Vietnam National Oil Company.

23 Prime Minister's Decision 198/2006/QD-TTg dated 29 August 2006 approving the Establishment Plan of the National Oil and Gas Group.

24 Prime Minister's Decision 924/QD-TTg dated 18 June 2010 on the transfer of PVN from its parent company to a one-member limited liability company owned by the state.

25 Government Decree 149/2013/ND-CP dated 31 October 2013, Article 3(3).

26 TD Ha, "Upstream Regulations in Vietnam – Conflict of Interests", *Vietnam Business Law Blog* (25 November 2018), https://vietnam-business-law.info/blog/2018/11/25/upstream-regulations-in-vietnam-conflict-of-interests.

27 Petroleum Law, Article 3; Government Decree 95/2015/ND-CP dated 16 October 2015 detailing provisions of the Petroleum Law.

28 Petroleum Law, Article 15: "A Petroleum Contract may be entered into in the form of a production sharing contract, joint venture agreement or other forms of contract... A Petroleum Contract shall conform to the Model Contract issued by the Government of Vietnam..."

venture agreements, although other forms can be approved by the prime minister.[28] Since the first PSA was signed with oil companies Deminex (Block 15), AGIP (Blocks 04, 12) and Bow Valley (Blocks 28, 29) between 1978 and 1979, the PSA regulations have been continually revised in order to encourage foreign investment and ensure equity between the revenue of the state and the profits of IOCs, while enhancing the role of the state in managing the operation of oil and gas activities. The key advantage of the PSA is that it enables the government to reach agreement with investors on a wide range of issues – in particular, the financial arrangements (obligations and responsibilities), which will depend on the different geographical and economic conditions of oil fields.[29]

Almost all PSAs must comply with the model PSA promulgated by the government. The model PSA was first introduced through Decree 139/2005/ND-CP. Almost eight years later, the government issued a revised model PSA through Decree 33/2013/ND-CP, which became effective on 8 June 2013. This applies to all PSAs signed after that date, except for blocks for which the prime minister has approved basic technical and commercial terms.[30]

Under the model PSA, the basic terms for E&P activities are as follows. The first is the ratio participation of PVN, which is negotiable depending on each project's characteristics. PVN frequently opts for a stake of around 10% to 20% in PSAs or a higher proportion in joint operating agreements (JOAs).[31] The JOA is an extended type of conventional PSA, which has been utilised for most prospective projects since 1998, on the basis that foreign parties will bear all costs and risks during the exploration phase of the project. The cooperation is represented by the joint operating company (JOC), a Vietnamese legal entity which acts as agent on behalf of the contracting parties. The major differences between conventional PSAs and JOAs are that in the latter, PVN has a higher participating interest – normally a stake of 30% to 50% – and the right to assign its own staff to the JOC from the start of a given project.[32]

Second, the term of the PSA is limited according to the provisions of law. In particular, the exploration phase is:

- five years for oil projects with a duration of up to 25 years; and
- seven years for gas and incentivised projects (ie, deepwater or remote offshore areas) with a duration of up to 30 years.[33]

---

29 Coordinating Committee for Geoscience Programmes in East and Southeast Asia, Vietnam, "Petroleum Agreements", Exploration Promotion Forum, www.ccop.or.th/epf/vietnam/vietnam_terms.html.

30 Petroleum Law, Article 15.

31 *Ibid*: "The Contracting Parties may agree to appoint a Party to act as an Operator or hire an Operator or establish a Joint Operating Company according to the regulations of the Government of Vietnam."

32 For example, Hoang Long Joint Operating Company was established by PetroVietnam Supervision Company, SOCO Vietnam Ltd, Amerada Hess Vietnam Ltd and OPECO Vietnam Ltd. The petroleum contract was signed on 8 November 1999 and was effective from 8 December 1999; www.hlhvjoc.com.vn/hoanglong/en/news.html.

33 Petroleum Law, Article 17(1).

The term can be extended for up to two years during the exploration phase and five years during the production phase.[34] In the case of gas projects, due to the lack of a local consuming market and the necessary infrastructure (eg, pipelines, gas processing plants, gas-fired power plants), investors can reserve their rights over the block in the event of a commercial discovery of natural gas for a maximum seven-year period, while other obligations under the PSA must be honoured.[35]

Third, the contractual area for exploration activities may not be larger than two blocks, except in specific cases permitted by the Vietnamese government.[36] For example, Spanish oil company Repsol was allowed to commence exploration activities in five blocks (Blocks 133–134, 135–136, 146 and 147) and production activities in four blocks (Blocks 07/03 CRD, 46-CN, 16-1 (TGT Unit) and 15-2/01).[37] However, due to pressure exerted by China, which has made territorial claims over the relevant area, Repsol has since transferred its stakes in three blocks to PVN (07/03 CRD and 135-136/03 PSC).[38]

Fourth, financial obligations and incentives granted by the Vietnamese government during the term of the PSA are the most crucial considerations for investors when deciding whether to conduct E&P activities. In addition to royalty tax, which is subject to the rate of production output,[39] and after allowing the maximum ratio of annual oil/gas production for cost recovery,[40] the remaining production is shared between the investors and PVN on a quarterly basis.[41]

In addition, the royalty tax, corporate income tax and export tax rates are now specified in the model PSA,[42] in conjunction with a stabilisation clause, which provides that investors will be unaffected by fluctuations in these tax rates.[43] However, the stabilisation clause has been narrowed significantly under the current regime. Under the previous model PSA (Decree 139/2005/ND-CP), investors enjoyed protection against any adverse effects on their 'economic

34 *Ibid*, Article 17(2).

35 *Ibid*, Article 17(3).

36 *Ibid*, Article 18.

37 Repsol, "Our operations in Vietnam" (31 December 2019), www.repsol.com/en/repsol-worldwide/asia/vietnam/index.cshtml.

38 BBC, "Repsol to sell shares of oil backpack: China threatens Vietnam's success in the East Sea?" (20 June 2020), www.bbc.com/vietnamese/vietnam-53103677; Repsol Group, "Annual Financial Report 2020", p41, www.repsol.com/content/dam/repsol-corporate/en_gb/accionistas-e-inversores/pdfs/2020-consolidated-annual-financial-report_tcm14-209133.pdf.

39 Model PSA (under Government Decree 33/2013/ND-CP), Article 1(1)(17) – Definition of Oil Royalty Tax; Article 6(1)(1) – Contribution of Oil Royalty Tax; Article 1(1)(45) – Definition of Gas Royalty Tax; and Article 6(2)(1) – Contribution of Gas Royalty Tax. This tax rate ranges from 6% to 25% in typical oil projects, and 4% to 20% in gas and incentivised projects.

40 *Ibid*, Article 1(1)(16) – Definition of Cost Oil/Gas; Article 6(1)(2) – Contribution of Cost Oil; and Article 6(2)(2) – Contribution of Cost Gas.

41 *Ibid*, Article 6(1)(3) – Distribution of Profit Oil; Article 6(2)(3) – Distribution of Profit Gas; and Article 6(2)(4) – Distribution Principles.

42 *Ibid*, Articles 7(3) and 7(4).

43 *Ibid*, Article 18(1)(3). The stabilisation clause in the model PSA is invoked when there are changes to the law that "adversely affect the economic benefits of the contractor".

benefits'; however, this clause in the new model PSA now covers only these specific types of taxes. Thus, investors will still be exposed to changes to environmental protection fees, profit surcharge, value added tax and any new taxes or fees which the government may impose during the lifetime of the PSA. This will be of particular concern to investors, given the importance of the stabilisation clause in general and the quick pace of change in Vietnam's legal framework in particular.[44]

In addition to applicable taxes, investors must pay environmental protection fees and a surcharge imposed on profits from oil or gas, which may vary from time to time.[45] Investors are also subject to new compulsory payments of:

- a signing bonus;[46]
- incremental production bonuses once the average daily production volume is reached;[47]
- a documentation fee;[48] and
- a fee to the Fund for Scientific Research and Development of Oil and Gas Technology.[49]

These bonuses and fees are not cost recoverable and are not deductible for corporate income tax purposes.[50]

Finally, investors must agree to PVN's participation if PVN decides to participate in their commercial discovery projects.[51] These carried costs are deductible from the investors' cost recovery from oil or gas, although the rate of deduction is negotiable among the parties.[52] The model PSA also sets out the procedure for PVN to exercise its pre-emptive rights if an investor assigns all or part of its participating interest to a third party, including a change of control or ownership of an investor; and requires PVN to confirm whether it wishes to exercise such rights within 120 days.[53] However, reorganisations, internal financial arrangements and mergers of investors' parent companies are exempt if the model agreement fails to clarify particular issues, such as a transfer from investors to its affiliates.[54]

---

44 QA Lam and VH Nguyen, "Vietnam's oil and gas sector: the new model production sharing contract", Mayer Brown (3 June 2013), www.lexology.com/library/detail.aspx?g=97a9c824-e831-4a5f-b180-ae00550d3443#:~:text=In%20Vietnam%2C%20oil%20and%20gas,%22Old%20Model%20PSC%22.

45 Model PSA (under Government Decree 33/2013/ND-CP), Article 7(7).

46 *Ibid*, Article 9(1).

47 *Ibid*, Articles 9(2), 9(3) and 9(4).

48 *Ibid*, Article 9(5).

49 *Ibid*, Article 10(1)(3).

50 *Ibid*, Articles 9(6) and 10(1)(4).

51 *Ibid*, Article 12(1)(1).

52 *Ibid*, Article 12(1)(2)(b).

53 *Ibid*, Article 12(2)(2). However, sometimes all or part of the investors' interests in a PSA are transferred outside the Vietnamese territory, which can cause difficulties in enforcing Vietnam laws and PSA provisions. This is analysed in the following section – in particular, in relation to *ConocoPhillips v Viet Nam*.

54 *Ibid*, Article 12(2)(4).

In summary, the new model PSA has tightened the rights of parties and introduced new obligations for investors that may affect the decision-making process when considering whether to invest in Vietnam's oil and gas sector. The PSA regime in Vietnam faces significant challenges, which are considered in the following section.

3. Critical analysis of PSA-related risks for investors

3.1 Pressures on increasing exploitable volume in a challenging period

The Vietnam oil and gas upstream market is forecast to grow at a low compound annual growth rate of less than 2% from 2020 to 2024. Despite the advantage of a 40% reduction in the cost of offshore drilling,[55] certain factors have had a major negative impact on E&P activities.

First, given that crude oil is an essential commodity and one of the most highly traded commodities in the global market, depressed oil prices may threaten not only the stability of the oil industry, but also the entire global economy.[56] As a result, PVN issued a directive on 11 March 2020 to request that its units plan for both short-term shocks and sustained low prices.[57] In a worst-case scenario, with a price of $30 to $35 per barrel, $3 billion of the group's expected revenues would be wiped out.[58]

Second, the volume of exploited petroleum did not increase significantly between 2011 and 2019. Notably, restrictions on energy supplies, combined with a significant increase in energy consumption,[59] led to increased reliance on imported fuels: Vietnam became a net importer of energy in 2015 and the share of imported energy in the total supply has also increased.[60] In recognition of the importance of energy security and security of supply, Report 12005/ TTr-BCT of 21 December 2017 of the MOIT to the prime minister emphasised the conditions that will ensure sufficient domestic energy sources to meet national socio-economic development objectives (with an average gross domestic product growth rate of around 7% per annum).[61]

---

55 Mordor Intelligence, "Vietnam Oil and Gas Upstream Market – Growth, Trends, and Forecasts (2020–2025)', www.mordorintelligence.com/industry-reports/vietnam-oil-and-gas-upstream-market.

56 RO Rechtsteiner "Oil prices could remain depressed for at least a year. Here's why", *World Economic Forum*, 1 April 2020, www.weforum.org/agenda/2020/04/oil-prices-could-remain-depressed-for-at-least-a-year-heres-why/.

57 PVN Directive 1151/CT-DKVN dated 11 March 2020.

58 Vietnam National Union of Oil and Gas Workers, "Loss of billions US dollar due to the double impacts of the COVID-19 pandemic and the decline in oil prices" (17 March 2020), https://congdoandaukhi.vn/pvn-se-thiet-hai-hang-ty-usd-do-dich-covid-19-va-gia-dau-giam-sau/.

59 From 2007 to 2017, Vietnam's total primary energy supply grew at a rate of 4.7% per annum, increasing from 1,900 petajoules (PJ) in 2007 to 3,000 PJ in 2017, with the highest growth rate in hydropower (14.5%), following by coal (11.3%), oil and gas (4.3%) and renewables. The Vietnam Electricity and Renewable Energy Authority, in collaboration with the Danish Energy Agency and the Danish Embassy in Hanoi, "Vietnam Energy Outlook Report 2019", p32, https://ens.dk/sites/ens.dk/files/Globalcooperation/vietnam_energy_outlook_report_2019.pdf.

60 Customs News, "Challenges to ensure energy security" (12 August 2018) https://customsnews.vn/challenges-to-ensure-energy-security-8005.html.

Third, China's constant interference in Vietnam's claims to its EEZ has negatively affected the prospects of projects in this area,[62] with financial implications for all parties concerned. For instance, in 2018 Repsol was instructed by PVN to refrain, for the time being, from performing the programmed activities relating to the Ca Rong Do (Block 07/03) development project. Furthermore, in July 2017, PVN instructed Repsol to stop CKN-1X drilling activities in Exploratory Blocks 135–136/03. Repsol has since initiated a compensation claim for the damages resulting from this situation.[63]

Given these pressures, the Vietnamese government has been seeking to increase extraction in existing facilities and to promote the conduct of further surveys and E&P activities in deepwater blocks where there are vast potential reserves.[64] There has also been some positive progress in the upstream oil and gas market. For example, from 2011 to 2019, PVN entered into 24 new petroleum agreements and 31 of its exploration wells indicated prospects for petroleum production.[65]

However, despite these promising developments, investors have been deterred by factors such as:

- geographical and geological constraints (eg, deepwater zones, the complex structure of the seabed and small and non-commercial reserves);
- territorial disputes;
- PVN's limited budget and autonomy;
- non-bankable PSAs under the current form contract;
- insufficient financial incentives; and
- legal risks.

In turn, this has led major IOCs to disinvest from the Vietnam market.[66]

3.2 Major legal risks

Given the challenges presented by current geopolitical and economic realities,

---

61 MOIT Report 12005/ TTr-BCT dated 21 December 2017 submitted to the prime minister for approval of Master Plan for National Energy Development from 2016 to 2025, with a vision towards 2035, "Specific Targets", Sub-section 1–2. The total primary energy supply will be 137 million to 147 million tons of oil equivalent (MTOE) in 2025; and 218–238 MTOE in 2035. Total final energy consumption will be 83–89 MTOE in 2025; and 121–135 MTOE in 2035.

62 Mordor Intelligence (n 55).

63 Repsol SA and investees comprising the Repsol Group, "Consolidated Financial Statements and Consolidated Management Report as at 31 December 2019" (Audited Report), pp57–58 www.repsol.com/imagenes/global/en/ORI20022020_2019_annual_financial_report_tcm14-174953.pdf.

64 Politburo of Vietnam Communist Party Resolution 41-NQ/TW dated 23 July 2015 on the Strategic Plan for Vietnam Oil and Gas Sector Development to 2025, with a Vision to 2035.

65 PVN, "Reviewing exploration and production strategic plan up to 2035" (6 March 2020) www.pvn.vn/Pages/detail.aspx?NewsID=e2d019b7-1b4f-441b-b17f-057c7e63b734.

66 Editing Board Opinion, "PVN has not had sufficient autonomy", *Journal of Vietnam Energy* (1 June 2020) http://nangluongvietnam.vn/news/vn/nhan-dinh-phan-bien-kien-nghi/neu-tap-doan-dau-khi-viet-nam-khong-co-quyen-tu-chu-can-thiet.html.

as well as the dire impact of the COVID-19 pandemic on many key sectors, there are numerous inherent legal risks pertaining to the Vietnamese legal ecosystem, especially in relation to the PSA. The most significant are outlined below.

(a) *Relationship of the PSA with the petroleum law/regulatory framework*

Vietnam has established a system of specialised legal instruments and regulations that plays an important role in attracting foreign investment to the oil and gas industry. The first Petroleum Law was enacted in July 1993;[67] this was subsequently amended in 2000[68] and 2008,[69] as the government made efforts to modernise the legal provisions governing this sector. The Petroleum Law has two key aims:

- to ensure that petroleum operations are conducted exclusively under the control and supervision of the competent state authority; and
- to give the state the maximum possible flexibility in conducting petroleum operations, whether through state authorities, the NOC or in any other manner that it may deem appropriate – all within the bounds of established international norms and standards, to attract foreign investment.[70]

The Petroleum Law also proposed the issuance of regulations (referred to as 'decrees')[71] and model contracts[72] by the competent authority from time to time. These are subsidiary and/or complementary instruments of the Petroleum Law, and are not themselves enacted as laws *per se*. These regulations afford a great deal of flexibility, allowing for changes to be made quickly in response to developments, without the need for protracted and often non-expert legislative processes. However, these regulatory instruments and any guiding amendments thereto must always be consistent with the Petroleum Law.[73] Such swift and responsive developments may result in pragmatic solutions to pressing and/or unexpected problems; yet at the same time, they can be perceived as unpredictable elements by parties (especially new potential investors) which are unfamiliar with the Vietnamese energy ecosystem and legal regime.

The core rationale for having a brief but thorough Petroleum Law is that it

---

67 Law 18-L/CTN dated 6 July 1993 of the National Assembly on Petroleum.

68 Law 19/2000/QH10 dated 9 June 2000 amending several provisions of the Petroleum Law.

69 Law 10/2008/QH12 dated 3 June 2008 amending several provisions of the Petroleum Law.

70 Joint United Nations Development Programme/World Bank Energy Sector Management Assistance Programme (ESMAP), "Vietnam's Petroleum Sector: Technical Assistance for the Revision of the Existing Legal and Regulatory Framework" (2004), p5, https://esmap.org/sites/default/files/esmap-files/FR05304VietamFinal.pdf.

71 Petroleum Law, Article 39 – Regulations: "Vietnam Government shall govern petroleum activities nationwide."

72 *Ibid*, Article 15 – Petroleum Contracts: "Petroleum Contracts shall follow the sample contract issued by the Government in which there includes the main contents as follows..."; Government Decree 33/2013/ND-CP dated 22 April 2013 providing the Model PSA.

73 ESMAP (n 77), pp6–7.

is supposed to cover all essential concepts while not setting them in stone through the inclusion of unnecessary detail.[74] This legislative scheme provides both the government and foreign investors with a clear legal and contractual context for the negotiation of E&P arrangements that are mutually advantageous and facilitate the development of Vietnam's oil and gas resources.[75]

However, there are certain inadequacies in the legal framework governing petroleum activities in Vietnam. First, the incentives provided by the Petroleum Law and other relevant legal instruments are no longer attractive to foreign investors, as the crude oil price has plunged since 2014, near-shore fields have been exhausted and the volumes available in marginal and deepwater fields remain uncertain. It is thus suggested that the Petroleum Law and other relevant legal instruments should be revised to afford sufficient rewards for investors which are willing to take the risks and collaborate with the PVN in the project execution stages.[76]

In the meantime, the Law on Investment[77] and the Law on State Capital Management and Usage in Enterprises[78] have proved to be inappropriate for the highly specialised petroleum sector. According to these laws, regardless of the size of the investment in a project or the proportion of foreign-owned capital, all parties must comply with the registration procedure, including obtaining the approval of the National Assembly[79] or the prime minister.[80] This protracted procedure discourages engagement by foreign partners in Vietnam oil and gas development.[81]

Another noteworthy legal instrument which applies to the construction of petroleum facilities is the Law on Construction 2014[82] and supplementary regulations. Accordingly, offshore production facilities must undergo mandatory appraisal procedures.[83] Given the special features of refineries and petrochemical plants, which involve highly technical expertise and technology – for example, technology licensing and complex engineering methodologies, from conceptual selection to front-end design and detail verification – these

74 *Ibid*, pp8–9.
75 *Ibid.*
76 HM Nguyen, "Enhance the legal framework for the sustainable development of Vietnam's petroleum industry", *Journal of Industry and Trade* (5 July 2018), https://congthuong.vn/hoan-thien-hanh-lang-phap-ly-giai-phap-cot-loi-phat-trien-ben-vung-nganh-dau-khi.html.
77 Law on Foreign Investment in Vietnam (1987, amended in 1990 and 1992); Law on Foreign Investment in Vietnam 1996 (amended in 2000); Law on Investment 2005 (59/2005/QH11); Law on Investment 2014 (67/2014/QH13) and Law on Investment 2020 (61/2020/QH14, effective since January 2021).
78 The Law on State Capital Management and Usage in Enterprises 69/2014/QH13 dated 26 November 2014.
79 Law on Investment 67/2014/QH13, Article 30.
80 *Ibid*, Article 31(1)(d).
81 HM Nguyen (n 76).
82 Law on Construction 50/2014/QH13 dated 18 June 2014.
83 Government Decree 59/2015/ND-CP, Article 24 (applicable to state budget-funded projects) and Article 25 (applicable to other economic sector financed projects).

protracted assessment and approval procedures not only delay project schedules, but also reduce business opportunities for foreign investors.[84]

(b) *PSA and fiscal regime*

In addition to the requirement to comply with the petroleum legislation, the most significant concerns among petroleum investors relate to the collection of resource rent by the Vietnamese government. The main objective of the petroleum fiscal regime is to enable the state to collect revenues from petroleum extraction, while encouraging investors to ensure optimal economic benefits. However, achieving an equitable balance between these objectives remains a challenge.[85] The fiscal regime should establish the essential elements of the applicable Petroleum Law in a way that enables potential investors to easily understand the relevant tax provisions and estimate, with reasonable certainty, the tax amounts payable under this fiscal package. The contractual arrangements should further be reasonably competitive with similar investment opportunities around the world.[86]

In this context, the Vietnamese fiscal regime for petroleum activities is not set out in either the Petroleum Law itself or a companion petroleum revenue law. Instead, it is governed by various individual tax statutes – such as those on royalty tax, export/import tax, incorporate/personal income tax and value added tax – which are uniformly enforced under the Petroleum Law;[87] as well as by secondary legal instruments such as Circular 36/2016/TT-BTC of the Ministry of Finance. There are major limitations to this system. First, the stability of the petroleum tax regime is directly affected when the Ministry of Finance issues guidelines on the fiscal aspects of E&P activities.[88] However, ministerial circulars in Vietnam are frequently amended and can easily conflict with (or be nullified by) revised fiscal laws and regulations.

Second, Circular 36/2016/TT-BTC provides that the taxation obligations of investors will be calculated on a 'ring-fenced' basis – that is, separately for each PSA – even where the investor has entered into several agreements.[89] This ring-fenced calculation is criticised as a disincentive to exploration, because the

---

84 HM Nguyen (n 76).

85 C Nakhle, "Petroleum fiscal regimes – evolution and challenges", in P Daniel, M Keen and C McPherson (eds), *The Taxation of Petroleum and Minerals: Principles, Problems and Practice* (Taylor & Francis, 2010), p89, www.international-arbitration-attorney.com/wp-content/uploads/arbitrationlaw1394930.pdf.

86 ESMAP (n 77), p10.

87 Law on Petroleum, Article 32(1): "Organizations, individuals executing the petroleum operations, foreign expats, Vietnamese working for Petroleum contractors, Joint Ventures and subcontractors shall perform their tax duties in accordance with tax regime"; Article 7(1) of the Model PSA (Decree 33/2013/ND-CP dated 22 Apr 2013): "Contractors shall be subject to applicable taxes in accordance with this Contract and comply with regulations of fiscal regime in regards of petroleum exploration, production in Vietnam."

88 Ministry of Finance Circular 36/2016/TT-BTC, Preamble: "The Minister of Finance issues this Circular guiding the implementation of regulations on tax to the organizations and individuals conducting the search, exploration and extraction of oil and gas according to regulation of Law on Petroleum."

89 Ministry of Finance Circular 36/2016/TT-BTC, Article 6(1).

related expenditures cannot be deducted from the consolidated corporate income tax if exploration is unsuccessful in a contractual area.[90]

In fact, the inconsistencies between the various legal instruments are the primary cause of tax-related disputes. PVN, on behalf of the government, has faced several claims by investors which argued that they were not liable to pay corporate income tax on profits derived from the production of oil and gas in Block 12W, in accordance with the applicable provisions of Vietnamese law and the terms of the PSA.[91] In the signed PSA, as an additional element of the total fiscal package, a stabilisation clause provided that the investors would be protected where possible from any adverse economic effects of certain new statutes and regulations. This meant that the investors were entitled to apply more favourable commercial terms, subject to the government's approval, and that PVN was obliged to assist its partners in obtaining such approval.

In response to these claims by various investors, PVN stated that there was no provision in the PSA that conferred tax exemptions or reductions. With regard to the Block 12W PSA, there was also no mention of such tax benefits. PVN further explained that if a tax exemption or reduction is granted under a particular PSA, this will be expressly stated in the contract or the applicable investment certificate.

Based on the facts presented by the parties, the tribunal found that "the claimants could not benefit from the tax incentives since they had not been negotiated for and had not been specifically approved by the competent Vietnamese authorities".[92]

Given current global economic realities, it is likely that oil prices will continue to fluctuate; thus, the applicable fiscal terms should be competitive across a broad price range, to ensure that offshore activities do not become uneconomical. Accordingly, it is recommended that cost recovery be fixed at a higher level. This is essential to make Vietnam competitive with its neighbours. For example, the typical cost limits elsewhere are:

- 70% in Cambodia and the Philippines;
- between 50% and 75% in Malaysia; and
- 85% in Indonesia.[93]

Second, a high cost limit need not necessarily result in a low government take, as the profit oil and profit gas rates could also be increased. If a higher cost

90 ESMAP (n 77), p26.
91 Due to the confidentiality of this dispute, the details of each relevant party and the precise wording of their documentation cannot be provided.
92 PVGas, "Petrovietnam press release: International arbitral tribunal sides with Petrovietnam in Production-Sharing Contract tax incentive dispute" (6 January 2015), www.pvgas.com.vn/news/petrovietnam-press-release-international-arbitral-tribunal-sides-with-petrovietnam-in-production-sharing-contract-tax-incentive-dispute.
93 ESMAP (n 77) pp16–17.

limit were introduced, investors would recover their investments faster, which would encourage E&P activities.[94]

(c) Dispute settlement mechanism

As a complex, valuable and long-term arrangement which is often subject to shifting political and sovereign concerns, the PSA is frequently the subject of disputes,[95] both in Vietnam and further afield. Such disputes trigger a number of key questions.

First, an 'international investment dispute' is defined under Vietnamese law as a dispute in which a foreign investor sues the Vietnamese government or other state bodies or organisations under an international treaty signed by Vietnam or a contract between the state and foreign partners.[96]

Second, a dispute settlement mechanism is typically:

- set forth in the inter-governmental investment and trade agreements to which Vietnam is a signatory;
- prescribed in petroleum contracts or other arrangements between government bodies and foreign partners;[97] or
- specified in specific Vietnamese laws, where applicable.[98]

Vietnam is also a member of the World Trade Organization[99] and has entered into numerous free trade agreements (FTAs), such as:

- the Comprehensive and Progressive Agreement for Trans-Pacific Partnership, signed in March 2018;
- the EU-Vietnam FTA, signed in 2016; and
- approximately 60 other bilateral treaties with other countries.

Such treaties include provisions on investor-state investment dispute settlement.[100] The typical mechanism is usually good-faith and amicable negotiation between the parties within a certain timeframe once a dispute has arisen. If this is not possible, foreign investors have the right to bring an action before the International Centre for Settlement of Investment Disputes (ICSID) or an *ad hoc* arbitration tribunal established under the rules of the United Nations Commission on International Trade Law (UNCITRAL) where both

---

94 *Ibid*, p18.

95 JL Loftis, RR Landicho and F Fraser, "Chapter 14 – Complexity and commercial disputes in product sharing contracts", in JM Gaitis (ed), *The Leading Practitioners' Guide to International Oil & Gas Arbitration* (JurisNet, 2015), p585.

96 Prime Minister's Decision 14/2020/QD-TTg dated 8 April 2020 issuing the Rules of Coordination in International Investment Dispute Settlement, Article 2(1).

97 Government Decree 33/2013/ND-CP.

98 Law on Investment 67/2014/QH13, Article 14(4).

99 Vietnam became the 150th Member of the WTO on 11 January 2007.

100 U Turksen and Q Chau (2019) "To sign or not to sign? A conundrum of Vietnam's accession to the ICSID", 24 *Coventry Law Journal* 1, p4.

states are members of that organisation. The arbitration award will be final and binding on the parties.[101]

In another tax-related case in 2017, two Vietnamese oil fields were sold by two UK subsidiaries of ConocoPhillips to Perenco, with a value of $1.29 billion, yielding a profit of $896 million.[102] The Vietnamese government believed that it had the right to tax this previously untaxed gain, as it was generated through exploitation of the country's oil resources under the UK-Vietnam double taxation treaty. The multinational oil companies launched a pre-emptive legal strike, seeking to stop Vietnam from levying an estimated $179 million (£140 million) in taxes on the profits from the sale of the oil fields.[103] The dispute was submitted to the UNCITRAL Court of Arbitration under the terms of the UK-Vietnam bilateral investment treaty. In January 2020 ConocoPhillips agreed to settle the dispute with Vietnam; further information in this regard has not been disclosed.[104]

Investors can also use alternative dispute resolution (ADR) mechanisms – such as consultancy, reconciliation, mediation or private judge and summary jury trials – which are often included in international treaties or agreements between parties. Indeed, according to the ICSID Convention and Rules, disputing parties may select other ADR mechanisms, but these are generally non-binding and aim to assist the parties in reaching an amicable settlement through voluntary agreement.[105]

Third, the question of law in the case discussed above is whether foreign investors have a right to the corporate income tax incentives connected with oil and gas projects. In other cases with similar subject matter, the defendant is usually the host state, rather than a business entity.[106] However, in this dispute, the respondent is PVN, based on the PSA signed between the parties – in particular, with regard to tax obligations and the warranty of stability to foreign partners in case of any modification of applicable laws. The case illustrates that the dividing line between the regulatory functions of the state and the business activities of the NOC is blurred.

Fourth, a dispute could arise due to the amendment of applicable rules. In principle, if various legislative instruments promulgated by the same agency contain different provisions on the same issue, those promulgated most recently will apply.[107] However, if the investors deem that their interests or

101 *Ibid*, p13.

102 United Nations Conference on Trade and Development, *ConocoPhillips and Perenco v Viet Nam*, Investment Policy Hub, https://investmentpolicy.unctad.org/investment-dispute-settlement/cases/906/conocophillips-and-perenco-v-viet-nam.

103 *Ibid*.

104 S Perry, "Conoco settles tax dispute with Vietnam", *Global Arbitration Review* (22 January 2020), https://globalarbitrationreview.com/article/1213273/conoco-settles-tax-dispute-with-vietnam.

105 ICSID, "Other Alternative Dispute Resolution Mechanisms", https://icsid.worldbank.org/en/Pages/process/Other-ADR-Mechanisms.aspx.

106 For example, in *Shell Philippines Exploration BV v Republic of the Philippines* (ICSID Case ARB/16/22), https://icsid.worldbank.org/en/Pages/cases/casedetail.aspx?CaseNo=ARB/16/22, the defendant is a state –the Philippines.

107 Law on Promulgation of Legal Documents 80/2015/QH13, Article 156(3).

benefits have been adversely affected by new regulations, they can bring an action against the government or governmental bodies under petroleum contracts or invoke the dispute settlement provisions in investment treaties. This is a source of risk, which requires diligent review by the legislature when enacting or amending the applicable rules.

Fifth, the application of Vietnam's legislative instruments should not obstruct the implementation of the international agreements to which Vietnam is a signatory. This means that in case of differences and/or incompatibilities between domestic law and international treaties, the latter will apply.[108] However, many secondary legislative instruments at the provincial[109] and ministerial levels (including guidance documents) are not assessed regularly or swiftly with regard to their compatibility and consistency with Vietnam's international treaty obligations. This in turn creates the inevitable problem of legal uncertainty.

In addition, although the New York Convention on the Recognition and Enforcement of Foreign Arbitral Awards 1958 came into force in Vietnam in 1995, there are still significant concerns as to the extent to which foreign arbitration awards can be enforced in Vietnam. Many applications for the enforcement of foreign arbitral awards have been annulled by the Vietnamese courts: according to statistics from the Vietnam Supreme People's Court, 46% of applications for the enforcement of foreign arbitral awards (24 out of 52) were annulled between 2005 and 2014.[110]

Key considerations of the Vietnamese courts in deciding whether to enforce foreign arbitral awards include:

- the validity of the arbitration agreement;
- the capacity to execute the arbitration agreement;
- the notifications rendered to the award debtor during the proceedings;
- the jurisdiction of the arbitral tribunal;
- the composition of the arbitral tribunal or the arbitral procedure;
- the enforceability of the arbitral award; and
- whether the award is contrary to fundamental principles of Vietnamese law.

Despite the efforts of Vietnam to provide and interpret the limited grounds for refusal of foreign arbitral awards, decisions to annul remain too abstract and vague.[111]

108 *Ibid.*

109 The local authorities in Vietnam can decide on WTO and/or other trade and investment-related matters with autonomy and considerable discretion. Vietnamese National Assembly, Law 11/2003/QH11 (2003) on Organization of People's Councils and People's Committee's, Article 2.

110 S Burkill, "Enforcement of foreign arbitral awards in Vietnam", Watson Farley & Williams (27 April 2020), www.wfw.com/articles/enforcement-of-foreign-arbitral-awards-in-vietnam/.

111 MD Nguyen, "Enforcement of arbitral awards and other aspects of international arbitration in Vietnam" (6 December 2018), https://adr.com.vn/upload/files/1130enforcementSeoul2018%20%5Bfor%20 audiences%5D.pdf.

4. Recommendations and conclusions

Independence, sustainability and ongoing investment in the energy sector will continue to play a major role in Vietnam's economic development. It is further clear that the energy market and projected growth present numerous opportunities for investors. This chapter has critically assessed the PSA regime in Vietnam in order to identify the key risks for various stakeholders, including the Vietnamese government and foreign investors. One key concern is the overlapping regulations and inconsistencies within the legislative framework, which is exacerbated by multi-agency competences. These features of the Vietnamese legal framework create uncertainties and reduce opportunities for investors.

Accordingly, there is an urgent need to strengthen Vietnam's legal framework and enhance the implementation capacity of the various agencies that govern the energy sector. The governance capacity of state bodies and the NOC should also be enhanced by separating governance and business activities, in order to avoid conflicts of interest and operate in line with internationally accepted principles of competition law.[112] In short, if the rule of law were strengthened, the remaining elements that are necessary for investment to the benefit of society should fall into place and the inherent risks in this sector would be significantly mitigated. Such reforms would also optimise Vietnam's ambitions towards regional and international integration and competition in energy trade.

For investors, especially during the project phase, there are two important aspects to consider: legal certainty and the efficiency of the dispute settlement regime. In addition to the particularities and complexities of the national legal regimes that govern energy investment, PSAs are often complicated and disputes are not uncommon in relation to issues such as cost and profit oil. As in most commercial disputes, it is expected that any claim, discrepancy or difference between the parties will be settled through ADR, including mediation[113] or arbitration. Thus, a transparent process for the recognition and enforcement of foreign judgments and arbitral awards should be ensured by formally signing up to international legal instruments and transposing such commitments into national law. Once these elements have been embedded in the Vietnamese investment ecosystem in general, and the energy industry in particular, Vietnam is likely to become an important player in the energy investment and trade sector in Southeast Asia.

---

112 Separate and detailed recommendations in relation to improving competition and integrity in the procurement of energy projects have been provided by the authors elsewhere. See TH Nguyen and U Turksen (2018) "Competition and Procurement in Energy Projects in Vietnam: Risks, Opportunities and Future Prospects", *International Energy Law Review*, Issue 4, pp116–135.

113 TH Nguyen, "Commercial mediation in Vietnam", Vietnam International Arbitration Centre (29 October 2019), www.viac.vn/tin-tuc-su-kien/hoa-giai-thuong-mai-tai-viet-nam-n694.html; TH Nguyen and U Turksen (2019), "The External Effects of the Energy Union Strategy on Trade and Investment in Renewable Energy from the EU to Vietnam: An Initial Assessment", *Oil, Gas and Energy Law Intelligence* (Special Issue on The Energy Union in the Next Decade) No 3, www.ogel.org/article.asp?key=3834; and Turksen and Chau (n 100).

About the authors

Adam Abukari
Research fellow, Coventry University
adam.abukari@coventry.ac.uk

Adam Abukari is a research fellow (EU PROTAX H2020 project) at Coventry University, United Kingdom. His current work involves finding innovative solutions for tax crime, money laundering, corruption and related financial crime, primarily in the context of the European Union. Adam previously worked in project management, research and consultancy roles at a number of companies in Ghana. He has more than 12 years of experience in consultancy, advocacy, counselling, management, publishing and research. Adam's PhD concerned the rule of law and justice in petroleum law in sub-Saharan Africa.

His research interests include the codification of petroleum law; the rule of law in petroleum legal arrangements; human rights; environmental justice and sustainability; tax crime and related financial crime; and developments in EU and UN law. Generally, Adam's research is based on interdisciplinary and transdisciplinary relations between law, business and development.

Terrance Ali
Petroleum engineer, Ministry of Energy and Energy Industries
tali@energy.gov.tt

Terrance Ali is a petroleum engineer at the Ministry of Energy and Energy Industries in Trinidad and Tobago. He has more than eight years' experience regulating the energy industry in Trinidad and Tobago. His main focus is the management of the technical components of production sharing contracts (PSCs) and exploration and production licences which are executed with upstream entities.

He has also been heavily involved in the deepwater exploration campaigns conducted over the last decade in Trinidad and Tobago, and regularly liaises with the legal department to resolve contractual issues pertaining to PSCs. Terrance has also served on the CO_2 Enhanced Oil Recovery Road Map Project, which aims to promote the implementation of carbon dioxide enhanced oil recovery in Trinidad and Tobago.

Terrance has a BSc in chemical and process engineering (first-class honours, 2012) and an MSc in petroleum engineering (distinction, 2016), both from the University of the West Indies (UWI).

Sanzhar Amangeldy
Senior associate, Unicase Law Firm
sanzhar.a@unicaselaw.com

Sanzhar Amangeldy is a senior associate at Unicase Law Firm. Sanzhar has previously worked for oil company Agip KCO (a subsidiary of ENI SpA). He mainly concentrates his practice on commercial and business law, M&A, antitrust, construction, energy and IT law. He represents a diverse variety of clients throughout Kazakhstan. Sanzhar joined Unicase right after his graduation from law school. His clients are international corporations in the spheres of IT, construction, renewable energy, mining, oil and gas, development banks, state-owned enterprises and participants of the Global Fortune 500.

He has extensive knowledge connected to the construction of power stations and roads, and the transmission and distribution of renewable energy in Kazakhstan. His legal drafting and negotiating skills are highly appreciated by clients, who especially highlight his flexible attitude and innovative assessment of any situation. He excels at the structuring of cross-border transactions.

Julian Cardenas
Research professor, University of Houston Law Center
jcardenasgarcia@uh.edu

Julian Cardenas is a professor of transnational petroleum law (*lex petrolea*), investment arbitration and diplomacy of oil and gas at the Law Center of the University of Houston (UH). He is a researcher affiliated with the Environment, Energy and Natural Resources Center of UH and coordinator of the programme "Inter-American Hydrocarbon Regulators Dialogue" – an initiative that seeks to create a forum for research and knowledge between oil companies, regulatory agencies and academia. Julian works with companies and government agencies in various areas of regulation and public policy in the hydrocarbons sector in the United States, Latin America and Africa. Since June 2019, he has served as a member of the *ad hoc* administrative board of Petróleos de Venezuela SA. Before joining UH, he practised international arbitration in the energy and construction sector and was a career diplomat at the Ministry of Foreign Affairs of Venezuela.

Aaron M Cooper
Lecturer, Coventry University
a.cooper8640@gmail.com

Aaron M Cooper is a lecturer in law at Coventry University. His research explores the link between the development and regulation of geoengineering and the consequences for Arctic indigenous peoples. Over the years he has published on issues such as climate change; oil, gas and energy law; sustainable development; and energy transitions. Together with Dr Flavio Inocencio, he has also published a book chapter on oil and gas contracts and joint operating agreements. As well as lecturing to undergraduate and postgraduate students on public international law, human rights and international environmental law, Aaron holds a visiting lecturer post at the Siberian Federal University in Krasnoyarsk, Russia, teaching environmental law and sustainable development. He also teaches at institutions in China, Germany and Belgium. He is currently advising the Low Carbon Vehicle Partnership's legal affairs committee on how the group can increase its compliance with environmental law; and previously provided consultancy services to the International Energy Law Advisory Group in Brazil.

Alicia Elias-Roberts
Deputy dean and lecturer, University of the West Indies
alicia.elias-roberts@sta.uwi.edu

Alicia Elias-Roberts is an academic who teaches oil and gas law and international environmental law at the UWI. She is a graduate of the University of Oxford and the University of Houston. She is the deputy dean in the Faculty of Law at the UWI St Augustine Campus in Trinidad and Tobago. Alicia has over 20 years' experience as an energy and environmental law legal consultant. She has provided expert legal advice to several governments in the Caribbean region and internationally in the areas of conservation and biodiversity law, multilateral environmental agreements, maritime law, oil and gas law, treaty law and procurement law, to name a few. She is an attorney at law admitted to practise in New York, United States, Trinidad and Tobago and Guyana.

Ebtissam El Kailani
Senior legal counsel, Vestas
eieli@vestas.com

Ebtissam El Kailani is a French/Libyan lawyer with a PhD in comparative contract law from civil law, common law and Arabic jurisdictions from *Université Paris 1 Panthéon-Sorbonne*. Her practice over more than 18 years has encompassed inter-jurisdictional energy, investment and commercial arbitration, foreign direct investment (FDI), contract negotiations and public-private partnerships (PPPs). She has previously worked with the United Nations, Al Kilani Law Firm, August & Debouzy, Curtis, Mallet, Colt & Mosle LLP and Groupe Engie.

She recently joined Vestas as senior legal adviser covering the Middle East and North Africa with regard to corporate and transactional matters in the renewable energy sector.

Nuno Frota
Of counsel, Clyde & Co LLP
nuno.frota@clydeco.com

Nuno Frota is of counsel at the London office of Clyde & Co LLP, focusing on international trade and commodities. He is a member of the firm's Africa strategy team.

Seconded to a major Sino-Angolan international oil company (IOC) in 2011, Nuno assisted management with PSCs. He joined the third-largest global commodities trader in 2012. He was also senior legal counsel for Africa in Mozambique and Angola for a major commodity trader, and an adviser to Johannesburg-based metal traders active in the Democratic Republic of Congo.

Nuno holds an LLM from the University of Manchester School of Law (United Kingdom) and a PGDip in international commercial law from the University of Lisbon School of Law (Portugal). He is treble qualified as a solicitor of the senior courts of England and Wales and a member of the Angolan Bar Association and the Portuguese Bar Association (non-practising).

Banuchichak Hilalqizi
International lawyer
banuchichak.hilalqizi35@law.ac.uk

Banuchichak Hilalqizi is a qualified lawyer in Baku, Azerbaijan and an aspiring solicitor in the United Kingdom. She has an LLB (first-class honours) (Baku, Azerbaijan), an LLM in international business law (United Kingdom) and an MA in law (United Kingdom). She has also completed strategic management and consulting courses at the Chartered Management Institute (United Kingdom).

Banuchichak has worked at several different law firms and companies. Initially focused on international law, she took an internship and worked at different embassies, and participated in international law conferences at the European Court of Human Rights and the European Commission, among others. She went on to specialise in international business law and has since worked as a corporate lawyer in Baku, Azerbaijan. She is now an aspiring solicitor currently practising law at Norton Rose Fulbright LLP in London. She speaks Azerbaijani, Turkish, Russian and English.

Flavio GI Inocencio
Director, Helios Advisory
flavio@heliosadvisory.net

Flavio GI Inocencio is a director at Helios Advisory and a lecturer in law. He holds a law degree from NOVA School of Law (Portugal, 2005) and a PhD in law from Nottingham Trent University (United Kingdom, 2011). He has worked for several public and private institutions in the United Kingdom, Austria, Portugal and Angola. Flavio has also worked on several FDI projects, both as a lawyer at the Investment Promotion Agency and at various different law firms.

Flavio was director on the LLM in oil and gas law at Coventry University from 2016 to 2018. He has published several works, including three books – one on the Organization of the Petroleum Exporting Countries (OPEC). Flavio also teaches oil and gas law and mining law at Agostinho Neto University Law School and is affiliated with the Research Centre at NOVA School of Law in Lisbon.

Ngutor S Jato
Associate, Serenity Legal Union and Partners
njato@nigerianbar.ng

Ngutor S Jato is an oil, gas and energy law specialist. He has been instructed in both litigable and non-litigable cases that involve the recovery of debts and the interpretation of legal instruments including concessions, employment contracts and statutes.

Ngutor is an enthusiastic legal practitioner with a strong work ethic and career competencies which he continues to build in his practice with Serenity Legal Union and Partners.

Ngutor is qualified and licensed to practise in Nigeria, with a focus on the regulation, taxation and sustainable use of the environment and natural resources. His legal expertise extends to legal risk management, contract negotiations and drafting.

Carlos Manosalvas Silva
Partner, Manosalvas & Partners Abogados
cmanosalvas@lawmpa.com

Carlos Manosalvas Silva is a partner at Manosalvas & Partners Abogados, which has offices in Spain, Ecuador, Peru and Portugal. He is a representative of the Faculty of Law to the University Council (2005) and an attorney of the Courts of Ecuador. He has a master's degree in negotiation and foreign trade and a master's degree in international environmental law, both from the School of International Sciences of the Central University of Ecuador. He is a criminal law specialist and holds a PhD in law, with a focus on criminal law, from the National University of Rosario Argentina. Carlos is a member of LES (Licensing Executives Society) Andean Community, having previously held the position of secretary (2012–2013), and is a member of the Bar Association in Quito. In addition, he is an integrated internal auditor of ISOS 9001, 14001 and OSHAS 18001 (2010); and in 2016 he co-authored a book called *Judicial Rulings that Violate Human Rights in Ecuador*, published by the Editorial Fund of the Interamerican Institute for Democracy.

Risa J Mark
Legal Officer I, Ministry of Energy and Energy Industries
rmark@energy.gov.tt
risajmark.law@gmail.com

Risa J Mark is an attorney at law based in Trinidad and Tobago. She was called to the bar of Trinidad and Tobago in November 2019 and has worked as a legal officer with the Ministry of Energy and Energy Industries since December 2019. She obtained a BSc in international tourism management (2013) and an LLB (2017) from the UWI, and a legal education certificate from Hugh Wooding Law School (2019)

Risa's specialisms include energy and tourism development.

Asma Muttawa
International energy lawyer
asmamuttawa@gmail.com

Asma Muttawa is an international energy lawyer and an honorary lecturer at the Centre for Energy, Petroleum and Mineral Law and Policy (CEPMLP), University of Dundee.

Recently, Asma was general legal counsel at OPEC and special adviser to the secretary general on the OPEC+ Cooperation, which began with the Declaration of Cooperation concluded during her tenure as general legal counsel in 2016 and culminated with the Alliance of Cooperation.

Previously, Asma worked for Schlumberger covering Libya and Europe, Central and Eastern Europe and Africa in relation to legal operations, corporate governance and compliance. She also worked for various UN organisations leading programmes on various legal and governance issues.

Asma has an LLB (Hons) and an LLM in international and comparative business law. She is experienced in litigation in both common and civil law jurisdictions, as well in arbitration and negotiation. She is a longstanding member of the Association of International Petroleum Negotiators, the Chartered Institute of Arbitrators and was an officer and vice chair of the International Bar Association Corporate Counsel Forum for four years.

Ali Nasir
Vice president of legal, commercial and planning, Premier Oil Indonesia
anasir@premier-oil.com

Ali Nasir is a senior member of the Premier Oil Indonesia management team, responsible for managing all legal, commercial and planning aspects of the company. He is also chairman of the Regulatory Affairs Committee of the Indonesian Petroleum Association. Ali has extensive experience in the oil and gas industry and has worked for various IOCs and government institutions. He was an expert staff member for the minister of energy and mineral resources and a member of the National Exploration Committee (2015–2016). Prior to this, he worked for the OPEC Secretariat in Vienna as a legal adviser for international matters (2006–2014). Earlier in his career he worked for VICO Indonesia (2004–2006), Total E&P Indonesie (1998–2003) and Unocal Indonesia Company (1996–1997).

Ali graduated from the University of North Sumatra Law School in 1996 and obtained his LLM in petroleum law and policy from the CEPMLP, University of Dundee (United Kingdom) in 2004.

Ha T Nguyen
Legal executive, Airports Corporation of Vietnam
theha2911@gmail.com

Ha T Nguyen is interested in cross-border trade and investment, energy, infrastructure construction, competition and state-owned enterprises. He has published several articles on the Vietnam oil and gas sector, renewable energy, the privatisation of state-owned enterprises and competition. He has participated in energy megastructure projects in Vietnam and other Association of South East Asian Nation countries (eg, Nghi Son Refinery & Petrochemicals Plant; Song Hau 1 coal-fired power plant; offshore petroleum production platforms in Vietnam; and the Petronas RAPID project, Malaysia); and in airport projects in Vietnam (eg, T3 Terminal – Tan Son Nhat Airport, Long Thanh International Airport (phase 1)). He is also counsel at Huy & Partners LLC.

Paulo Henrique Reis de Oliveira
Lawyer, KINCAID | Mendes Vianna Advogados
oliveira.phro@usp.br

Paulo Henrique Reis de Oliveira is a master's student in international and comparative law at University of São Paulo (USP). He is a specialist in maritime law; editorial coordinator of the *Bulletin of the Brazilian Society of International Law*; a researcher at *Centro de Estudos de Direito do Mar Vicente Marotta Rangel* (CEDMAR) USP and the Centre for the Study of International Courts (USP); a member of the New-Gen Committee of the Centre for Arbitration and Mediation of the Chamber of Commerce Brazil-Canada; a member of the Brazilian Association of Maritime Law; and a lawyer at KINCAID | Mendes Vianna Advogados. As a professor, he has experience in international law, maritime law, insurance law and research methodology. As a lawyer, he works in the fields of maritime law, art law, insurance law, petroleum law and international cooperation.

Saniya Perzadayeva
Managing partner, Unicase Law Firm
saniya.p@unicaselaw.com

Saniya Perzadayeva is managing partner at Unicase Law Firm. She is a recognised expert in areas such as infrastructure and PPPs, project finance and construction, energy and renewables. She advises on various legal issues, in particular on corporate and commercial matters, energy, real estate, infrastructure and PPPs.

Saniya has over 18 years' experience advising clients on a broad range of legal issues, with a particular emphasis on corporate and commercial law. She is experienced in banking and finance, debt and deposit operations, cross-border finance transactions, syndicated loans and securities transactions. She is an expert in corporate law and M&A law, both in Kazakhstan and in other Commonwealth of Independent States countries.

Saniya provides consulting services to investment banks on the syndication of commercial tranches for the financing of various social and commercial projects; drafts Kazakhstan security documents for project financings; and advises international companies on the investment regime and guarantees provided to investors under Kazakhstan laws.

Indira Rampaul-Cheddie
Senior state counsel, Ministry of Energy and Energy Industries
irampaul@energy.gov.tt

Indira Rampaul-Cheddie is a senior state counsel at the Ministry of Energy and Energy Industries. She has spent over 20 years in the petroleum industry in legal, commercial and leadership roles. She specialises in negotiation, the drafting of petroleum contracts, policy and regulatory issues.

She has presented and/or published for the Regional Association of Oil, Gas and Biofuels

Sector Companies in Latin America and the Caribbean; the Society for Petroleum Engineers; the Association of International Petroleum Negotiators; the *Oil, Gas and Energy Law Intelligence Journal*; the *Journal of Energy and Natural Resources Law*; CEPMLP; and the *Centre Annual Review*, UWI and University of Trinidad and Tobago.

Indira has done work for the Guyanese Bar Association; the Energy Chamber of Trinidad and Tobago; the Earth Institute of Columbia University; the Government of the Democratic Republic of Timor-Leste; the Inter-American Development Bank; the American University in Egypt; and Seton Hall Law School.

Barbara Mourão Sachett
PhD student, São Paulo University
barbara.sachett@usp.br

Barbara Mourão Sachett has a master's in international law from the University Estadual Paulista – Júlio de Mesquita Filho (UNESPFranca). She is a PhD candidate (international and comparative law) at the Faculty of Law of São Paulo University, Brazil.

In addition, she is a lecturer at the Methodist University of São Paulo and a researcher at Centro de Estudos em Direito do Mar-Vicente Marotta Rangel (CEDMAR-USP) at the Faculty of Law of São Paulo University and at the Núcleo de Estudos em Tribunais Internacionais (NETIUSP) at the Faculty of Law of São Paulo University. She is a member of the Associação Brasileira de Direito Internacional (ABDI).

Júlia Schütz Veiga
PhD student, NOVA School of Law
julia.schutz@gmail.com

Júlia Schütz Veiga is a PhD candidate at NOVA School of Law, UNL, on the law studies programme, and a postgraduate student in biotechnology at UniCesumar, Petropólis, Brazil. She holds a master's degree in law and economics of the sea from NOVA School of Law. She has spent the last four years researching on the law of the sea, and has leveraged her academic knowledge to strengthen Brazilian government policies relating to the conservation and sustainable use of marine biological biodiversity. Júlia also has a specialisation in international law at the Federal University of Rio Grande do Sul, Brazil, and is a researcher at NOVA Ocean Knowledge Centre and CEDIS, NOVA School of Law, and CEDMAR, University of São Paulo (USP), Brazil.

Marlina Tambunan
Legal manager, Premier Oil Indonesia
mtambunan@premier-oil.com

Marlina Tambunan is responsible for managing all legal and compliance aspects of the Indonesia business unit. She currently lectures at *Sekolah Tinggi Hukum Indonesia* and *Sekolah Pascasarjana Universitas Padjajaran* in Jakarta. Marlina has extensive experience in the oil and gas industry and has worked for various IOCs, national oil companies and government institutions.

Marlina graduated from the Faculty of Law of *Universitas Katolik Parahyangan*, Bandung (Indonesia) in 2001; and obtained her LLM in international law and the laws of international organisation from the Faculty of Law of the *De Rijksuniversiteit Groningen* (Netherlands) in 2002.

Philip Teoh
Partner, Azmi & Associates
philipteoh@yahoo.com

Philip Teoh is a dual-qualified Singapore and Malaysian lawyer with more than 31 years of experience. He is a partner and practice head of shipping, international trade, insurance, oil and gas and arbitration at Azmi & Associates, a full-service Malaysian law firm.

He is an accredited arbitrator with the key maritime arbitration and international arbitration centres around the world. Philip is also an adjunct lecturer with Brickfields Asia College, Malaysia's largest law school. He has authored key practitioner texts on the sale of goods, equity, conflict of laws, bailment, lien, shipping, carriers (land, air and sea), forms and precedents on shipping, insurance claims, wills and will trusts, annotated merchant shipping laws and annotated sale of goods.

In *Chambers 2021*'s ranking of maritime lawyers, he was described as "very knowledgeable and approachable, quickly grasping the situation and always quick to offer the correct advice. He is able to quickly resolve matters to our satisfaction without the need of progressing to court".

Umut Turksen
Professor in law, Centre for Financial and Corporate Integrity, Coventry University
umut.turksen@coventry.ac.uk

Umut Turksen leads the EU-funded TRACE Project and the Law, Risk and Compliance Cluster at the Centre for Financial and Corporate Integrity, Coventry University. He is interested in the practical application of the law in innovation, societal security and development. He has published several books and articles on energy, financial crime and international trade and economic law. He has provided consultancy and training to prestigious international businesses and government projects, including technical assistance programmes for multinational corporations (eg, France Telecom, Equas Ltd, Wilmington Plc) and international organisations (eg, Commonwealth, NATO, EUROPOL); and professional development training for practitioners and EU-funded projects (eg, CEPOL, SecuCities, MUTRAP III, COFFERS, PROTAX, VIRTEU). Umut is also a member of the Innovation Caucus and of counsel to Rajah & Tann LCT Lawyers, Vietnam.

About Globe Law and Business

Globe Law and Business was established in 2005. From the very beginning, we set out to create law books which are sufficiently high level to be of real use to the experienced professional, yet still accessible and easy to navigate. Most of our authors are drawn from Magic Circle and other top commercial firms, both in the UK and internationally.

Our titles are carefully produced, with the utmost attention paid to editorial, design and production processes. We hope this results in high-quality publications that are easy to read, and a pleasure to own. Our titles are also available as ebooks, which are compatible with most desktop, laptop and tablet devices. In 2018 we expanded our portfolio to include journals and Special Reports, available both digitally and in hard copy format, and produced to the same high standards as our books.

In the spring of 2021, we were very pleased to announce the start of a new chapter for Globe Law and Business following the acquisition of law books under the imprint Ark Publishing. We are very much looking forward to working with our new Ark authors, many of whom are well known to us, and to further developing the law firm management list, among other areas.

We'd very much like to hear from you with your thoughts and ideas for improving what we offer. Please do feel free to email me at sian@globelawandbusiness.com with your views.

Sian O'Neill
Managing director
Globe Law and Business
www.globelawandbusiness.com

www.ingramcontent.com/pod-product-compliance
Ingram Content Group UK Ltd.
Pitfield, Milton Keynes, MK11 3LW, UK
UKHW050306190226
468143UK00009B/6

9 781787 426870